Temperature Conversion Table

Y0-ASX-819

American Oven Temperature Terms	Degrees Fahrenheit	Degrees Centigrade (Celsius)
	160 170	71 77
	200 212	93 100
Very Slow	225 230 250	107 110 121
Slow	275 300 302	135 149 150
Moderately Slow.	320 325	160 163
Moderate	350 356 375	177 180 190
Hot	390 400	200 205
	425 428	218 220
	437 450	225 232
Very Hot	475 500	246 260
Broil.	525 550	274 288

Volume 18

Que-Sau

WOMAN'S DAY ENCYCLOPEDIA OF COOKERY

**1979 Edition
For WOMAN'S DAY**

JEANNE VOLTZ, *Food Editor*

For FUNK & WAGNALLS, INC.

Supervising Editor—**NORMA H. DICKEY**
Production Editor—**KATHIE L. ATTLEE**
Production Executive—**EDWARD HAAS**
Editorial Staff—**DONNA L. AMOS, JUNE V. ROOK**
Art Director—**MURRAY KESHNER**
Layout Artists—**MARTIN GORDON, HERBERT ASCHER**

Special Project Staff:

Contributing Editors—**INEZ M. KRECH, JAMES W. TRAGER**

Original Edition

Prepared and edited by the Editors of WOMAN'S DAY
GLENNA MCGINNIS, *Food Editor*

Special Project Staff:

Editor—**NIKA STANDEN HAZELTON**
Associates—**L. GERALDINE MARSTELLER, HELEN FEINGOLD, SUSAN J. KNOX**

First Revised Edition
Special Project Staff:
Editor—**MARIE ROBERSON HAMM**
Associate Editor—**ISABEL CORNELL**

*Copyright © 1966, 1973, 1979 by CBS Publications,
the Consumer Publishing Division of CBS, Inc.,
All Rights Reserved.
Distributed by Funk & Wagnalls, Inc.*

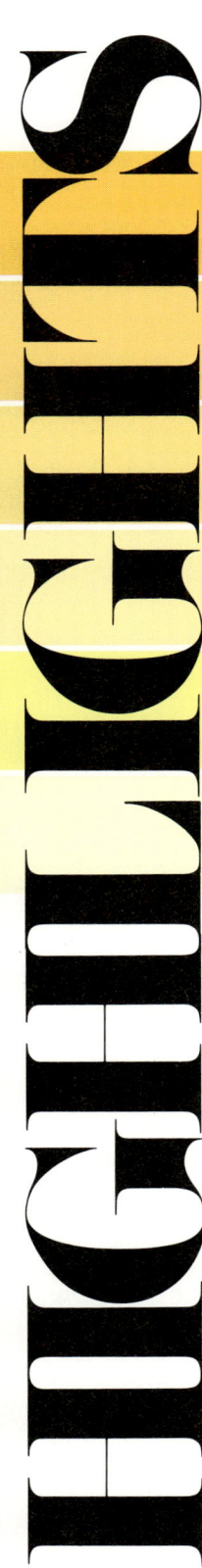

HIGHLIGHTS

Volume 18

Quenelle–Sauce

Arranged alphabetically, the articles in this volume fall between the two words listed above. Among the interesting and informative entries found in this volume, several sections are worthy of special attention. We have listed these below for your convenience.

HOW TO COOK SUPERBLY:	
RICE by Helen Evans Brown	33
RICE COOKBOOK	34
RUSSIAN COOKERY by Princess Alexandra Kropotkin	53
RUSSIAN COOKBOOK	55
SALAD COOKBOOK	68
SALMON by James A. Beard	85
SALMON COOKBOOK	88
SANDWICH COOKBOOK	96
HOW TO COOK SUPERBLY: THE BASIC SAUCES,	
BROWN AND WHITE by Helen Evans Brown	109
SAUCE COOKBOOK	111
50 MENUS	124

How to use the Woman's Day Encyclopedia of Cookery

The twenty-two volumes of the Woman's Day Encyclopedia contain a wealth of alphabetically arranged information. If you wish to prepare Apple Pie, look under Apple in volume 1. But to find all of the information in all of the volumes, you should use the twenty-third volume, the Index. Composed of five separate indexes, volume 23 includes: meal and menu planning; information on nutrition and diet; techniques of cookery and equipment use; a listing by author; and an alphabetical listing by ingredients.

This Encyclopedia contains many individual entries that supplement one another. Meal and Menu Planning, for instance, is treated throughout the Encyclopedia in many different entries. The first index in volume 23 collects these entries and lists volume and page numbers for such diverse items as Busy Day Dinners and Low Cost Meals. How to entertain or cook in different national styles will be simplified by consulting such items as Parties or Mexican Cookery. If you want to cook for a crowd or make up a Christmas menu, this index shows you where to find Quantity Cooking and three separate styles of Christmas meals.

If you are learning to cook or beginning to plan diets for a family, two other indexes offer assistance. The Encyclopedia entries that contain information on nutrition and diet are listed in one index, and techniques of cookery and equipment are listed in the other. If you want to know which foods are necessary in your child's diet or how to cut down on cholesterol, see the second index. If you want to find out which pan is appropriate for a layer cake, see Bake in the third index.

The fourth index in volume 23 is a listing by author of all the special articles in the Encyclopedia. Here you will find titles and location of articles by noted cookbook authors and food and health authorities.

A major part of volume 23 is the listing of all the recipes contained in the Encyclopedia, arranged alphabetically by main ingredient and by one or more menu categories. Thus, an Abalone Chowder recipe in volume 1 is listed in this Index under ABALONE and under SOUPS. A Crabmeat Dip recipe appears under CRABS, under DIPS, APPETIZER, and under APPETIZERS.

These volumes offer helpful advice on cooking, meal planning, food budgeting, and entertaining. Brimming with tempting recipes, mouthwatering photos, and interesting tid-bits about the origin and history of some of the ingredients, the Woman's Day Encyclopedia of Cookery is indeed a browsing library for food lovers.

QUENELLE—A dumpling made of fish or meat forcemeat, bound with eggs, and generally poached in boiling salted water or stock. The word "quenelle" is thought to have come from the German *knödel,* "dumpling."

Small quenelles are used as a garnish; larger ones are served as a separate dish.

PIKE QUENELLES

- ½ cup water
- ¾ cup butter or margarine
- ½ cup all-purpose flour
- ¼ teaspoon salt
- 2 eggs
- 1 pound pike
  Salt, pepper, and grated nutmeg
- 2 egg whites
- ½ cup heavy cream

Heat water and ¼ cup butter in saucepan until butter is melted and water boils. Add flour and salt, and stir briskly until mixture leaves the sides of the pan, forming a ball. Remove from heat and beat in eggs, one at a time. Continue beating until mixture is smooth; cool. Remove bones and force fish through finest blade of food chopper 3 or 4 times. Work ground fish with wooden spoon until smooth. Beat in cooled pastry mixture. Add salt, pepper, and nutmeg to taste. Beat in gradually, one at a time, egg whites, remaining ½ cup butter, softened, and cream. Chill overnight. Next day, shape quenelles with a pastry tube, in a dessert spoon by leveling pastry and sliding it into a buttered skillet, or by rolling paste into cylinders. Cover with boiling salted water and simmer for 10 minutes, or until done. Remove and drain. Serve plain or with a lobster or shrimp sauce. Makes 4 to 6 servings.

CHICKEN QUENELLES

- ½ cup water
- ¾ cup butter or margarine
- ½ cup all-purpose flour
- ¼ teaspoon salt
- 2 eggs
- 2 cups finely ground cooked chicken
  Salt, pepper, and grated nutmeg
- 2 egg whites
- ½ cup heavy cream
  Melted butter or margarine

Heat water and ¼ cup butter in saucepan until butter is melted and water boils. Add flour and salt, and stir briskly until mixture leaves the sides of the pan, forming a ball. Remove from heat and beat in whole eggs, one at a time. Continue beating until smooth. Cool. Work chicken with wooden spoon until smooth. Beat in cooled pastry mixture. Add salt, pepper, and nutmeg to taste. Gradually beat in egg whites, one at a time, remaining ½ cup butter, softened, and cream. Chill overnight. Next day, shape the quenelles with a pastry tube, or in a dessert spoon by leveling pastry and sliding it into a buttered skillet, or by rolling paste into cylinders. Cover with boiling salted water and simmer for 10 minutes, or until done. Remove and drain. Serve at once with melted butter. Makes 4 to 6 servings.

QUICHE—A savory baked custard tart thought to have originated in Lorraine, a province of eastern France bordering on Germany, although Alsace, the neighboring province, also lays claim to being the home of the true quiche. The word quiche is derived from the French-German dialect spoken in these regions and can be traced back to the German word *kuchen,* "cake."

The best-known quiche, Quiche Lorraine, is one made with eggs, bacon, cheese, and cream, baked in a pastry shell. It is always eaten as hot as possible. Any quiche makes an excellent luncheon or supper dish, or it can be served in the traditional way as a hot hors d'oeuvre.

QUICHE LORRAINE WITH CREAM CHEESE

- 8 ounces cream cheese
- ½ cup heavy cream
- 3 egg yolks
- 1 egg
- ¼ teaspoon freshly ground pepper
- ¼ teaspoon salt
- 6 slices of bacon
  Pastry for 1-crust 8-inch pie

Beat cream cheese with next 5 ingredients until smooth and blended. Cut bacon into 1-inch pieces and cook until lightly browned and almost crisp. Arrange in bottom of pastry-lined pie pan. Pour cheese mixture over bacon. Bake in preheated hot oven (400°F.) for 20 minutes. Reduce heat to moderate (350°F.) and bake for 10 minutes longer, or until puffed and golden-brown. Let stand for 2 or 3 minutes before cutting into wedges. Makes 4 to 6 servings.

LOBSTER QUICHE

- Pastry for 1-crust 9-inch pie
- 2 tablespoons finely chopped green onions
- 2 tablespoons butter
- 1¼ cups diced canned or fresh-cooked lobster
- 1 tablespoon freshly snipped dill
- 4 eggs, slightly beaten
- 2 tablespoons dry white wine
- ½ teaspoon salt
- ¼ teaspoon pepper
- 1¼ cups heavy cream, scalded

Line a 9-inch pie pan with pastry. Flute the edge, prick bottom with a fork, line with foil, and fill with beans or rice. Bake in preheated hot oven (400°F.) for 8 minutes. Remove foil and beans and bake about 3 minutes longer. Reduce oven heat to moderate (375°F.). Meanwhile, sauté onions in butter and spread in partly cooked shell; top with lobster and dill. Combine the eggs, wine, salt, pepper, and cream; pour into shell. Bake for 25 to 30 minutes, or until set.

Quiche Lorraine with Swiss Cheese

QUICHE LORRAINE WITH SWISS CHEESE

- 1½ cups (6 ounces) grated imported Swiss cheese
- 8 slices of crisp bacon, crumbled
- Pastry for 1-crust 9-inch pie
- 3 eggs
- 1 cup heavy cream
- ½ cup milk
- ½ teaspoon salt
- ¼ teaspoon pepper
- Dash of cayenne
- ½ teaspoon dry mustard

Sprinkle cheese and bacon into pastry-lined pie pan. Beat remaining ingredients together and pour over cheese. Bake in preheated moderate oven (375°F.) for 45 minutes, or until firm and browned. Cut into wedges and serve hot. Makes 6 servings.

QUINCE—The round to pear-shape fruit of a tree of the same name. When ripe the fruit is rich yellow or greenish-yellow with a strong odor, hard flesh. Its taste is so tart and astringent that it cannot be eaten raw.

QUINCE

Quinces are full of natural pectin and are used for making marmalade, jellies, jams, fruit paste, butters, preserves, and syrups.

Quince trees are usually small (fifteen to twenty feet high) and gnarled with many crooked branches. Sometimes the tree takes a bush form. The quince tree has been cultivated for over 4,000 years, and it still greatly resembles its ancient ancestor. Quinces are a native of western Asia and reached the Mediterranean countries quite early. The quince was given mythological significance by the Greeks and Romans, who considered it sacred to the Goddess of Love. If you gave a quince to someone of the opposite sex it was considered to be an engagement token.

The Romans used the quince in ways other than the ceremonial. The quince blossoms were made into perfume, and the fruit formed the base of a hair dye. But early Greeks and Romans also knew that the sacred fruit could be eaten in many ways. There is a 12th-century translation from the Greek which gives directions for quince honey: "Take quynces ripe and pare and heve hem smal,/And al for smal, but kest away the core,/In honey thene upboile hem, lese and more/De pepur (or ginger) with yt boiling." Translated into more modern English this means to peel and cut up the fruit, discarding the core, and boil in honey, adding pepper or ginger.

Roman recipes for quinces included a kind of reduced wine, fish sauces, sauces for minced meat, and quince purée. Apicius, the Roman who wrote the 1st century cook book that has come down to us as *The Art Of Cooking*, gives a recipe for keeping quinces fresh: "Choose faultless quinces with their twigs and leaves, and put them in a receptacle, and pour over honey and defrutum [a reduced wine]: you will keep them for a long time."

Many modern American uses of quinces are based on these early classical recipes, for quinces in jams and jellies are most popular. The English and Germans have sometimes been more inventive, serving roast quince, quince pie, and quince honey. Spaniards, Portuguese, and Latin Americans make quinces into a sweet paste. It is eaten with cream and other soft cheeses, an excellent flavor combination.

The early American colonists had developed a taste for quinces, and the settlers of Massachusetts wrote home for quince kernels almost immediately after arriving in this country. The fruit spread throughout the country. John Bartlett, a 19th century bibliographer and historian, saw quinces growing in Mexico and in a report of his experiences commented: "There are two varieties of the quince here, one hard and tart like our own, the other sweet and eatable in its raw state, yet preserving the rich flavor of the former. The Mexicans gathered and ate them like apples, but I found them too hard for my digestive organs." It is exactly this difficulty which makes it necessary to cook quinces. They are most often pared, cored, seeded, then stewed like apples or made into a preserve of some kind.

Availability—October to December. Quinces are easily bruised and must be handled carefully.

Purchasing Guide—Select quinces with a greenish-yellow or pale-yellow color. Avoid fruit with spots or bruises; punctures indicate worms.

Storage—Store in a cool, dark, dry place.

Caloric Value
4 ounces, raw = 65 calories

BAKED QUINCES

Wipe, quarter, core, and peel quinces. Put in a deep casserole and sprinkle with sugar, allowing 2 tablespoons for each quince. Add ½ inch water, and 1 sliced orange, if desired, for each 4 quinces. Bake in preheated slow oven (300°F.) for 2 hours, or until tender and deep red in color. Cool before serving.

QUINCE GINGER MARMALADE

- 6 pounds quinces
- 2 cups water
- Grated rind and juice of 4 lemons
- 2 tablespoons fresh gingerroot
- ¼ teaspoon salt
- Sugar

Pare quinces; cut into small pieces. Cook in water in large preserving kettle for 15 minutes. Add lemon rind and juice, gingerroot, and salt. Boil for 15 minutes. Measure and add an equal amount of sugar. Boil until quinces are translucent and deep red in color. Makes about 4 pints.
NOTE: If fresh gingerroot is unavailable, use preserved or crystallized gingerroot and ½ teaspoon ground ginger.

QUINCE JELLY WITHOUT PECTIN

- 3 pounds ripe quinces
- Water
- 3 cups sugar

Remove cores and blossom and stem ends from quinces. (Do not peel.) Slice quinces. Measure, and for each quart add 3 cups water. Put in kettle, bring to boil, and simmer for 45 minutes. Drain through damp cotton flannel, jelly bag, or 4 layers of cheesecloth. (For greater yield of juice, twist the two ends of the bag in opposite directions until most of the juice is extracted. Then strain through clean, damp cotton flannel or jelly bag. Do not squeeze or press.) Measure juice. There should be 4 cups. If not quite enough, add small amount of water to make up the amount. Put juice in large kettle and bring to boil. Add sugar and stir until dissolved. Boil rapidly until mixture sheets from a spoon. Pour into hot sterilized jars, and seal. Makes about four ½-pint jars.

RABBIT—A small furry mammal of the rodent family, the rabbit has large eyes, long ears, long strong hind legs and feet, and a short tail. It differs most significantly from its close relative the hare in its burrowing habits and in the fact that the young of rabbits are born naked, blind, and helpless whereas hares are born furred and able to see.

Rabbits have an average weight of three pounds and are sixteen to eighteen inches long. In addition to being hunted in their wild state they are bred for food, for their skins, and as pets.

Rabbit meat is practically all white, is fine-grained, and mild-flavored. It can be prepared in many of the ways in which chicken is prepared. Young animals can be panfried, broiled, and roasted. Older animals can be braised and fricasseed.

Availability and Purchasing Guide—Fresh rabbit, whole or cut into pieces, is available ready-to-cook in weights from 1½ to 3 pounds. Frozen rabbit is also available.

Look for firm, plump meat, light in color. Avoid any meat with stringy or tough appearance.

Storage—Refrigerate immediately.
Refrigerator shelf, raw: 2 days
Refrigerator shelf, cooked and covered: 1 to 2 days
Fresh, prepared for freezing; or frozen, refrigerator frozen-food compartment: 1 week
Fresh, prepared for freezing; or frozen, freezer: 2 to 3 months
Do not refreeze once thawed. Use within 2 days of thawing.

Nutritive Food Values
Domesticated, stewed, flesh only, 3½ ounces = 159 calories
Wild, ready to cook, 1 pound (bone in) = 490 calories

Basic Preparation—Wear rubber gloves when handling wild rabbits to avoid tularemia. They should be bled and eviscerated immediately. Skin as soon as possible after cleaning.

To Freeze—Wash thoroughly and wrap tightly, whole or cut into pieces, in moisture- vapor-proof material excluding as much air as possible. Seal.

WILD RABBITS

- 2 rabbits (1 to 1½ pounds each)
- 3 cups water
- 1 cup cider vinegar
- 2 tablespoons salt
- 1 teaspoon pepper
- 3 tablespoons mixed whole spice
- 1 Bermuda onion, sliced
- 1 carrot, diced
- 3 slices of bacon, diced
- 2 tablespoons butter or margarine
- 1 tablespoon sugar
- 3 tablespoons all-purpose flour
- 3 gingersnaps
- ½ cup dairy sour cream

Cut rabbits into 4 to 6 pieces. Wash in cold water several times. Remove excess skin and wash again. Dry on paper towels. Prepare a marinade of water, vinegar, seasonings, onion, and carrot; pour over rabbit in a glass or earthen jar. Refrigerate for 2 or 3 days. Remove rabbit from marinade and dry on paper towels. Strain marinade and reserve. Brown bacon with butter in a Dutch oven or skillet with a lid. Add rabbit and brown well. Cover and simmer for 1 hour. Sprinkle sugar over rabbit and allow to caramelize. Add flour, 2 cups marinade, and gingersnaps. Simmer for 20 minutes. Stir in sour cream and simmer 10 minutes longer. Taste for seasoning. Makes 4 to 6 servings.

JUGGED RABBIT

- 2 rabbits (about 3 pounds each) cut up
- 2 carrots, diced
- 1 onion, stuck with 3 cloves
- 6 garlic cloves, peeled
- 1 bay leaf
- 6 peppercorns
- 2 cups coarsely chopped celery
- 2 cups dry red wine
  Water
- 3 tablespoons shortening
- 1 tablespoon tomato purée
- 1 teaspoon salt
- ⅓ cup all-purpose flour
- 8 slices of crisp bacon
- 8 whole mushrooms, sautéed
- 2 tablespoons minced parsley

Put meat into a big bowl with carrots, onion, garlic, bay leaf, peppercorns, celery, and wine. Add water to cover and allow to marinate for 3 days. Remove pieces of meat from marinade and pat dry. Brown in shortening in a deep kettle. Add marinade, tomato purée, and salt. Simmer gently, covered, about 2 hours, or until meat is tender.

RACCOON

Remove meat and keep warm. Blend flour and ½ cup water. Stir into sauce. Bring just to a boil. Strain through a fine sieve. Add pieces of meat. Bring to a boil again. Serve garnished with bacon and mushrooms and sprinkled with parsley. Makes 6 to 8 servings.

RABBIT STEW

- 1 rabbit (about 3 pounds) cut up
- ½ cup all-purpose flour
- 3 tablespoons butter
- 1 cup diced celery
- 2 onions, sliced
- 1½ teaspoons seasoned salt
- 1 teaspoon salt
  Dash of pepper
- 1 bay leaf
- 4½ cups water
- 4 cups dry red wine
- 2 cups diced peeled carrots
- 4 potatoes, peeled and diced
- 1 can (4 ounces) sliced mushrooms, drained

Dredge meat with flour and brown on all sides in butter in kettle. Add next 6 ingredients, 4 cups water, and wine. Bring to boil, cover, and simmer for 2 hours, or until meat is almost tender. Add carrots and potatoes; simmer for about 30 minutes longer. Add mushrooms. Thicken with ¼ cup flour and remaining ½ cup water, blended. Makes 4 servings.

RACCOON or COON—A North American carnivorous mammal found throughout the United States and on the Pacific Coast from Alaska to South America. The common raccoon is a heavily built animal, about three feet long, blackish-gray in color with a pointed snout and a bushy tail striped black and white. It makes its home in trees, descending at night to feed, often on the banks of ponds and streams. Raccoons feed on a great variety of things, including fruits, green corn, fish, frogs, birds, small animals, and occasionally poultry. Raccoons are related to the South American kinkajou and the Asian panda.

Much used for food during America's pioneer days, they are still considered good game by many people. The meat is dark and the fat strong in flavor and odor. A dressed animal without head or feet weighs from five to fourteen pounds. Roasting is the preferred method of cooking young raccoons. Older ones should be braised or stewed. To improve the flavor of a dressed raccoon and to remove some of the gamy taste, the dressed carcass should be wrapped tightly in wax paper, plastic wrap or foil and refrigerated from four to seven days at a temperature as near 35°F. as possible.

Nutritive Food Value
4 ounces, roasted, meat only = 289 calories

RADISH

ROAST RACCOON WITH SWEET-POTATO STUFFING

   1 dressed raccoon (4 to 5 pounds)
   4 teaspoons salt
   3 cups mashed sweet potatoes
   ¾ cup seedless raisins
   2½ cups soft bread crumbs
   1¾ cups peeled diced apples
   ¼ cup corn syrup
   ¼ cup butter or margarine, melted
   ¼ teaspoon pepper

From the raccoon, remove the waxy nodules, commonly referred to as "kernels," from under each front leg and on either side of the spine in the small of the back. Wash meat thoroughly and dry. Remove part of the fat, leaving just enough to cover the carcass with a thin layer of fat. Sprinkle 1 teaspoon salt inside body. Fill with mixture of 2 teaspoons salt and remaining ingredients except pepper. Skewer the vent by inserting several toothpicks through the skin from side to side. Lace with string, tying the ends securely. Fasten both the forelegs and the hind legs with toothpicks and string. If there are any lean parts on the outside of the body, fasten a small piece of the surplus fat to this part with a toothpick. Sprinkle with remaining 1 teaspoon salt and pepper. Put on side on greased rack in shallow baking pan and roast in preheated slow oven (325°F.) for 45 minutes per pound. Turn when half done. Makes 6 to 8 servings.

RADISH—The pungent fleshy root of a hardy annual plant, *Raphanus sativus*, which is widely valued as a salad vegetable. Apparently it is native to the temperate regions of Asia, and it has been cultivated in China, Japan, and India for thousands of years. The name radish is derived from the Latin word for "root," *radix*.

Radishes come in many shapes and colors: round, long, or oblong, and white, pink, red, yellow, purple, or black. Their taste varies from mild to peppery. Depending on the variety, they can be from one inch to two or more feet long and weigh up to several pounds apiece. The oriental radishes are by far the largest, and since they are coarse in flavor and texture, are most often cooked or pickled.

Availability—Radishes are available year round. Peak season for red globe radishes, the most common variety, is May through July.

The long tapering varieties, both white- and red-skinned, are mild in flavor and at their peak from July through October.

The longer oval winter radishes, red, white, or black in color and about 6 inches long, are in season from December through February.

Purchasing Guide—Look for smooth, well-formed, firm radishes. The condition of the leaves is not always an indication of quality. Radishes are marketed in bunches or, with their tops removed, in small plastic bags.

Storage—Remove leaves and rootlets and wash thoroughly. Refrigerate.

Refrigerator shelf or vegetable compartment: about 1 week
Radishes cannot be frozen.

Nutritive Food Value
Common, raw, trimmed and sliced, ½ cup (2 ounces) = 10 calories
Oriental, 4 ounces, raw = 22 calories

Basic Preparation—Wash. Be sure all leaves and rootlets have been removed.

Radishes may be cut in attractive ways to use on a relish plate or to garnish salads.

RADISH SALAD

   2 cups sliced red or white radishes
      French dressing
      Salt and pepper
      Chopped parsley

Marinate radishes in French dressing. Add salt and pepper to taste Before serving, drain and sprinkle thickly with parsley. This radish salad can be added to any potato or green-vegetable tossed salad to give color and texture as well as flavor. Makes 4 servings.

RAGOUT—A French word for a stew made from meat, poultry, or fish, with or without vegetables. It is derived from *ragoûter,* "to stimulate the taste" The word has come directly into English, without the accent, and as an English word, ragout is most often used in reference to well-seasoned meat and vegetable stews cooked in thick rich sauces, usually brown.

VEAL AND PORK RAGOUT

   1½ pounds boneless stewing veal
   1½ pounds boneless pork shoulder
      All-purpose flour
   3 tablespoons butter or margarine
   1 onion, chopped
      Water
   ½ cup dry red wine
   1 tablespoon salt
   ½ teaspoon pepper
   2 parsley sprigs
   ½ bay leaf
   1 garlic clove, minced
      Veal bone, if desired
   4 to 6 raw small potatoes, peeled and quartered
   ½ pound mushrooms, halved
   1 can (1 pound) onions, drained
   1 can (1 pound) tiny carrots, drained
   ½ cup frozen peas

Cut meat into 1½-inch cubes. Dredge with flour and brown on all sides in butter. Add onion and brown a few minutes longer. Add 1 cup hot water and next 7 ingredients. Bake, covered, in preheated moderate oven (350°F.) for 1½ hours. Remove bone, and add potatoes, mushrooms, and enough water to almost cover. Return to oven; cook 40 minutes. Add onions, carrots, and and peas; cook for 20 minutes. Makes 6 to 8 servings.

LAMB RAGOUT IN CARROT-POTATO RING

- 2 cups cubed roast lamb
- 2 tablespoons lamb fat
- 8 small onions, quartered
- Water
- Salt and pepper
- All-purpose flour
- 4 medium potatoes
- 4 medium carrots
- 1 tablespoon margarine
- ⅓ cup hot milk
- Salt and pepper

Brown lamb in fat. Add onions and cook until lightly browned. Add 1½ cups water, ½ teaspoon salt, and dash of pepper. Bring to boil; cover and simmer for 30 minutes, or until onions are tender. Thicken gravy with a paste of a little flour blended with cold water. Cook potatoes and carrots together in boiling salted water until tender. Drain and mash. Add margarine, milk, and salt and pepper to taste. Beat until light and fluffy. Heap in ring around edge of deep 9-inch pie pan. Fill center with lamb mixture. Reheat, or keep warm in oven if necessary. Makes 4 servings.

RAISE, TO—The culinary process of making a food light and porous by the action of yeast. A yeast dough is placed in a warm spot, thus activating the yeast and producing a gas which expands, or raises, the dough. The dough literally rises in the bowl. When the dough rises until doubled in volume, it is ready to be shaped. After shaping, the dough is usually allowed to rise a second time until doubled in volume; then it is ready for baking.

RAISIN—The name given to several varieties of grapes when they are dried, either naturally in the sun, or by artificial heat. When grapes are dried, their skins wrinkle, they have a higher sugar content, and a flavor quite different from that of fresh grapes.

The word raisin comes from the Latin word *racemus* meaning "a cluster of grapes or berries." It is thought that the Egyptians were the first to notice that grapes left on the vine lost moisture and became sweeter. Thus dried, they kept better than when fresh.

Varieties of grapes dried to make raisins run from dark bluish-brown to golden. The two most popular varieties are muscats and sultanas. When the fruit is ripe it is picked and spread out on trays to dry in the sun. The golden sultanas are not dried in the sun, but dehydrated indoors and given a sulfur treatment. This preserves their golden color.

Raisins are good for snacks, eaten out-of-hand. They also mix well with nuts. In cooking they can be added to cereals, rice puddings, cookies, cakes, muffins, stuffing, salads, and rolls. They are an indispensable part of mince pie and fruitcake.

RAISIN

Availability and Purchasing Guide—Dark and golden (bluish- or reddish-brown) raisins are available year round seedless, seeded (the seed is removed after drying), and in clusters (grapes dried on the stem in large bunches to make fancy table raisins).

Storage—Store in a cool, dry place. In hot weather, refrigerate. If refrigerated, raisins will keep indefinitely.

Nutritive Food Values—Raisins contain a variety of vitamins and minerals, especially iron. Their natural sugar content makes them an excellent sweet for children.
Whole, ½ cup firmly packed (2.9 ounces) = 237 calories
Ground, ½ cup (4.7 ounces) = 387 calories

Basic Preparation—Add 1 cup water to every cup raisins. Cover and simmer for 10 minutes. Sugar is not necessary. Raisins combine better with other ingredients if they are first cooked or plumped in boiling water for 5 minutes, then drained.

RAISIN-NUT SANDWICHES

Put 1 cup seeded raisins and ¼ cup nuts through food chopper. Moisten with mayonnaise. Spread between slices of buttered bread.

RAISIN BREAD

- 1 cup water*
- 2 packages active dry yeast or 2 cakes compressed yeast
- 2 cups boiling water
- 2 cups seedless raisins
- ½ cup soft butter or margarine
- ¼ cup firmly packed brown sugar
- 2 eggs
- 2 tablespoons ground coriander
- 3 teaspoons salt
- ¼ cup wheat germ
- 1 cup nonfat dry milk powder
- 9½ cups sifted all-purpose flour

*Use very warm water (105°F. to 115°F.) for dry yeast; use lukewarm (80°F. to 90°F.) for compressed yeast. Sprinkle yeast or crumble cakes into water in large bowl. Let stand for a few minutes then stir until dissolved. Pour boiling water over raisins and let stand until lukewarm. Add yeast and remaining ingredients except 5 cups flour; mix well. Add remaining 5 cups flour; mix well and turn out on floured pastry cloth or board. Knead until smooth and satiny. Put in greased bowl; turn once, cover, and let rise until doubled, about 1 hour. Punch down and let rise for 30 minutes. Shape into 3 loaves and put in **greased loaf pans 9 x 5 x 3 inches. Let rise until doubled.** about 45 minutes. Bake in preheated moderate oven (350°F.) about 50 minutes. Makes 3 loaves.

RAISIN

RUMANIAN RAISIN COMPOTE

 2 cups golden raisins
 1 cup water
 1 cup honey
  Grated rind of 1 lemon
 ½ cup pine nuts

Soak raisins in water to cover for 1 hour; drain, reserving water. Combine water and honey and simmer for 2 to 3 minutes. Add raisins and lemon rind; simmer for 10 minutes longer over low heat. Skim with slotted spoon as needed. Add pine nuts to raisins. Chill thoroughly before serving. Makes 4 to 6 servings.

RAISIN-NUT PINWHEELS

 1 cup soft butter or margarine
 ½ cup sugar
 1 egg
 2 cups sifted all-purpose flour
 1 teaspoon baking powder
 1 cup dairy sour cream
  Raisin-Nut Filling

Cream butter and sugar until light. Beat in egg. Add sifted dry ingredients alternately with sour cream, beating until smooth. Chill overnight. Roll one fourth of dough at a time on well-floured board or pastry cloth to form a rectangle 10 x 6 inches. Dough will be soft. Keep in refrigerator until ready to use. Spread with one fourth of Raisin-Nut Filling and roll up from 10-inch side. Cut into 12 pieces and put 3 inches apart cut side down on greased cookie sheet. Bake in preheated moderate oven (350°F.) about 15 minutes. Repeat until all ingredients are used. Makes 4 dozen cookies.

Raisin-Nut Filling

Mix 1 cup chopped nuts, ¼ cup raisins, ¾ cup orange marmalade, ¼ cup sugar, and 1 teaspoon ground cinnamon.

RAISIN-FILLED COOKIES

 ½ cup sugar
 ½ cup shortening
 1 egg
 ½ cup milk
 2½ cups sifted all-purpose flour
 ¼ teaspoon salt
 2 teaspoons baking powder
 1 teaspoon vanilla extract
  Raisin Filling

Combine ingredients except Raisin Filling in order given; chill dough. Roll out thinly on floured board and cut as desired. Place a teaspoon full of filling between 2 cookies and press down edges with floured fork. Bake in preheated moderate oven (350°F.) for 15 minutes, or until browned. Makes 3 dozen.

Raisin Filling

Mix 1 teaspoon all-purpose flour and ½ cup sugar in small saucepan, add ½ cup water and 1 cup ground raisins, cook until thick; cool to room temperature.

RAISIN SPICE CAKE

 1 cup firmly packed brown sugar
 1 cup seeded raisins
 1¼ cups water
 ½ cup shortening
 1 teaspoon ground cinnamon
 ½ teaspoon each ground nutmeg and allspice
 2 cups sifted all-purpose flour
 1 teaspoon each baking soda and baking powder
 ½ teaspoon salt

Boil sugar, raisins, water, shortening, and spices for 5 minutes; chill. Sift flour, baking soda, baking powder, and salt together; stir into first mixture. Pour into greased loaf pan 9 x 5 x 3 inches, lined with wax paper. Bake in preheated moderate oven (350°F.) for 55 to 60 minutes. Turn out onto cake rack, remove paper; cool. Makes 1 loaf cake.

RAISIN PIE

 2 cups seeded raisins
 1 cup water
 ½ cup corn syrup
 ¼ cup cornstarch
 ½ teaspoon salt
  Pastry for 1-crust, 9-inch pie with lattice topping

Combine raisins and water; simmer for 10 minutes. Add corn syrup mixed with cornstarch and salt; cook for 3 minutes, stirring constantly. Cool; pour into pastry-lined pie pan; arrange strips of pastry over top. Bake in preheated hot oven (425°F.) about 20 minutes. Makes 6 servings.

SPICED RAISINS

 2 cups firmly packed light brown sugar
 1 teaspoon ground allspice
 ½ teaspoon each ground ginger and cloves
 1 cup water
 2 cups raisins (golden, seeded or seedless)
 1½ cups granulated sugar

Cook brown sugar, spices, and water until a small amount of syrup dropped into very cold water spins a 2-inch thread when dripped from fork or spoon (232°F. registers on candy thermometer). Stir in raisins; cook for 2 minutes. Remove from heat and put pan in bowl of warm water while working. Drain raisins, ½ cup at a time, on paper towel and roll in granulated sugar. When thoroughly cool, store in covered jar. Makes 2 pounds.

RAISIN, APPLE, AND NUT RELISH

1 tablespoon prepared mustard
1 cup sugar
⅓ cup cider vinegar
⅔ cup water
⅛ teaspoon ground allspice
2 cinnamon sticks
1 piece of whole gingerroot
4 medium cooking apples
½ cup seedless raisins
¼ cup chopped nuts

In saucepan blend mustard and sugar. Add vinegar, water, and spices. Bring to boil and simmer for 10 minutes. Pare apples, core, and cut each apple into eighths. Cut each eighth into quarters crosswise. Remove cinnamon and ginger from hot mixture. Add apples, raisins, and nuts; bring to boil and simmer for 10 minutes. Cool. Serve with poultry or ham. Makes about 3 cups.

RAMEKIN or RAMEQUIN—A French word which originally referred to toasted cheese but has developed two different meanings: 1) A certain type of cheese tart or tartlet and 2) an individual baking dish in which food is baked and served. The word ramekin comes from the Flemish *rammeken* which means "a little bit of cream."

In modern culinary usage, the cheese dish called a ramekin is a pastry filled with a creamy mixture of cheese, eggs, milk, or cream. Ramekins are eaten hot or warm, never cold. They can be made in one- or two-bite sizes, and are an excellent hors-d'oeuvre.

Ramekin dishes are usually white, with straight fluted sides, resembling miniature soufflé dishes.

RAMEKINS

Pastry (2 cup flour recipe) unbaked
2 cups grated Swiss cheese (½ pound)
1 tablespoon all-purpose flour
3 eggs, well beaten
1 cup light cream
Salt and pepper

Line ramekin with pastry dough rolled ⅛ inch thick. Chill. Dredge cheese with flour and place on pastry. Beat together eggs, cream, and salt and pepper to taste. Pour over cheese—filling pans not more than three quarters full. Bake in preheated hot oven (425°F.) for 15 to 25 minutes, depending on size of the ramekin. Serve hot or warmed up. Makes eight 4-inch ramekins.

RAMPION—A bellflower, *Campanula rapunculus*, which grows wild in Europe and is sometimes cultivated for its edible tuberous root. The root, about a foot in length, looks like a long white radish. It and the tender young leaves of the plant are used raw in salads and cooked as vegetables.

RAREBIT—Another name for Welsh rabbit, a popular cheese dish.

RASPBERRY—The fruit of a bush of the *Rubus* genus which is a member of the rose family. Raspberries grow wild in woods and are also cultivated. The berry is made up of many small drupelets. In contrast to blackberries, which retain their stems or receptacles when the fruit is picked, the stem of a raspberry separates from the berry and remains on the plant. Raspberries may be red, purple, black, or amber in color. They are a delicately flavored fruit and can be eaten raw either plain or with cream, and can be used for jellies, jams, puddings, pies, etc. Berries of any color can be used interchangeably in recipes and can also be used in most strawberry recipes.

Availability—Fresh raspberries are available from June through November, with July the peak month. They are also canned and frozen in syrup, and are available as raspberry jam and apple-raspberry sauce.

Purchasing Guide—Select berries that are bright, fresh, plump, well-shaped, and solid in color. Avoid wet or leaky berries. A stained container is an indication of overripe or damaged berries.

Storage—Sort berries and refrigerate uncovered. Use as soon as possible.
Refrigerator shelf: 1 to 2 days
Fresh, prepared for freezing; or frozen, refrigerator frozen-food compartment: 2 to 3 months
Fresh, prepared for freezing, or frozen, freezer: 1 year
Canned, kitchen shelf: 1 year

Nutritive Food Values—A fair source of iron and vitamin C.
Fresh red, ½ cup (2½ ounces) raw = 41 calories
Fresh black, ½ cup (2.5 ounces) raw = 49 calories
Canned red 4 ounces, water pack, solids and liquid = 40 calories
Canned black, 4 ounces, water pack, solids and liquid = 58 calories
Frozen red, ½ cup (4.4 ounces) sweetened, unthawed = 122 calories

Basic Preparation—Wash berries just before using. Do not allow berries to soak in water

To Freeze—Use firm ripe berries. Wash in ice water quickly without bruising berries. Spread berries in a single layer on a cookie sheet and freeze until firm. Pour into freezer container. Seal, and freeze.

Or add ¾ cup sugar to every 4 cups berries. Stir gently until sugar is partly dissolved. Spoon into containers, allowing ½-inch headspace. Freeze.

Or pour berries into freezer container. Cover with cold syrup made by cooking 4 cups water with 6 cups sugar and cooling; allow ½-inch headspace. Seal.

RASPBERRY

RASPBERRY PUDDING

- 2 cups raspberry juice
- ¼ cup sugar (about)*
- 1 cinnamon stick
- ¼ teaspoon salt
- ¼ cup cornstarch
- ¼ cup cold water
- Red food coloring (optional)
- Cream

Bring juice, sugar, cinnamon stick, and salt to a boil. Mix cornstarch with cold water and stir into the hot juice. Bring mixture to a quick boil and remove from heat as soon as it thickens. Add a few drops of red food coloring if necessary. Pour into pudding dish or individual glasses. **Sprinkle the top with additional sugar to keep a skin from forming.** Chill. Serve with cream. Makes 4 servings.
*Sugar should be used to taste, depending on tartness of juice. The pudding should be tart rather than sweet.

FROZEN CHEESE AND RASPBERRY DESSERT

- 2 cups creamed cottage cheese
- Juice of 1 lemon
- 1 cup sugar
- 2 cups dairy sour cream
- 2 packages (10 ounces each) frozen raspberries, partially thawed

Turn refrigerator control to coldest setting. Force cheese through food mill or fine sieve. Add lemon juice and sugar and beat until smooth. **Add sour cream and mix well.** Pour into refrigerator tray and freeze until firm. Cut into serving pieces and serve with raspberries. Makes 8 servings.

RASPBERRY CAKE

- ½ cup margarine, softened
- 1½ cups sugar
- 2 eggs, separated
- 1¾ cups all-purpose flour
- 2 teaspoons baking powder
- ¼ teaspoon salt
- ¾ cup milk
- 1 teaspoon vanilla extract
- Raspberry Filling and Frosting

Beat margarine in electric mixer until creamy. Gradually add sugar and beat until well blended. Beat egg whites until stiff and set aside. Then beat egg yolks until thick. Add to sugar mixture and blend well. Mix dry ingredients and add to first mixture alternately with milk, beating after each addition until smooth. Add vanilla, then fold in egg whites. Divide evenly among 3 greased and floured 9-inch layer-cake pans. Bake in preheated hot oven (450°F.) about 10 minutes. Turn out on racks to cool. Spread Raspberry Filling and Frosting between layers and on top. Refrigerate leftover cake. Makes 8 to 12 servings.

Raspberry Filling and Frosting

Defrost until barely thawed 1 box (10 ounces) frozen raspberries. Drain quickly, reserving syrup for other use. Put berries in small bowl of electric mixer and add 1 egg white and 1 cup sugar. Beat until mixture forms peaks.

CHAMPAGNE RASPBERRY CUP

- 2 cups fresh raspberries or 1 package (10 ounces) frozen raspberries
- 1 cup orange juice
- 1 cup brandy
- Few orange slices
- 1 quart champagne, chilled

Put first 4 ingredients in crystal pitcher. Put in refrigerator to marinate 1 hour or longer. Just before serving, add about 1 dozen large ice cubes and champagne. Stir and serve in goblets. Makes 8 to 10 servings.

RASPBERRY PEACH GLACÉES

- 2 egg whites
- ⅛ teaspoon salt
- ½ teaspoon cream of tartar
- ½ cup sugar
- ⅛ teaspoon almond extract
- 1 pint peach ice cream
- Raspberry Sauce

Have egg whites at room temperature; beat with rotary or electric beater until foamy. Add salt and cream of tartar and beat until just stiff enough to stand in peaks. Gradually add sugar and continue beating until very stiff. Add almond extract. Spoon 4 small mounds onto lightly buttered unglazed brown paper on cookie sheet; flatten each mound to make a thin base about 1½ inches in diameter. With a pastry tube or spoon, surround bases with more meringue to height of 2 inches, leaving center unfilled. Bake in preheated slow oven (250°F.) for 1¼ hours. Transfer paper to a damp board; remove meringues. When cold, fill with ice cream and top with Raspberry Sauce. Makes 4 servings.

Raspberry Sauce

- 1 pint raspberries
- Water
- ¼ cup sugar
- 1 tablespoon cornstarch
- Few drops of lemon juice

Mash and sieve berries; add water to make 1 cup. Add sugar and cornstarch, mixed. Cook until thickened, stirring constantly. Add lemon juice. Cool; chill.

RASPBERRY CREAM PIE

6 cups fresh raspberries
Water
⅔ cup sugar
3 tablespoons cornstarch
Dash of salt
1 baked 9-inch pie shell
1 cup heavy cream, whipped
Mint sprigs

Mash 2 cups berries and force through sieve; add water to make 1½ cups. Mix sugar, cornstarch, and salt; add to sieved berries. Cook, stirring constantly, for 5 minutes, or until thickened. Cool. Reserve a few berries for garnish. Put remaining 4 cups berries in baked pie shell. Pour on cooked cornstarch mixture. Chill. Garnish with whipped cream, reserved berries, and mint. Makes 6 to 8 servings.

FRESH RASPBERRY PASTRIES

2 cups fresh raspberries
5 tablespoons sugar
1 teaspoon lemon juice
1 cup sifted all-purpose flour
¼ teaspoon salt
½ teaspoon baking powder
⅓ cup butter or margarine
3 tablespoons cold water
½ cup heavy cream, whipped

Reserve 5 whole berries for garnish. Mix remaining raspberries with 3 tablespoons sugar and lemon juice. Chill until ready to use. Sift flour with salt, baking powder, and 1 tablespoon sugar. Cut in butter until mixture resembles coarse meal. Add water and mix only until all flour is moistened. Turn out on lightly floured board. Shape into a ball. Roll into a sheet ⅛ inch thick. Cut into round with 3-inch cookie cutter (scalloped edge is attractive). Bake on ungreased cookie sheets in preheated hot oven (425°F.) for 12 to 15 minutes, or until lightly browned. Cool on a wire rack. When ready to serve, place a pastry circle on a plate. Cover with 2 tablespoons drained raspberries and 1 tablespoon whipped cream sweetened with remaining 1 tablespoon sugar. Cover with another pastry circle and tip with additional berries and whipped cream. Garnish each with a whole fresh raspberry. Makes 5 servings.

RATATOUILLE—The word is French and describes a stew or casserole which most frequently contains a well-seasoned combination of eggplant, zucchini, tomato, and green pepper. Occasionally meat is added.

RATATOUILLE

2 garlic cloves, minced
1 onion, sliced thin
½ cup cooking or olive oil
1 medium eggplant, diced
3 medium zucchini, sliced
1 green pepper, sliced
1 can (29 ounces) Italian-style tomatoes
1 teaspoon dried oregano or basil
Salt and pepper to taste

Sauté garlic and onion in oil until clear. Add eggplant and toss. Add zucchini and pepper and cook for 10 minutes. Add remaining ingredients and simmer, covered, for 30 minutes. Uncover and simmer for 30 minutes longer. Makes 6 servings.

RAVIGOTE—A well-seasoned classic French sauce consisting of green herbs, butter, and tarragon vinegar added to béchamel sauce. The name is derived from the French *ravigoter,* "to revive, refresh."
Ravigote sauce is served with hot or cold fish, meat, poultry, and vegetables.

RAVIGOTE SAUCE

2 tablespoons butter or margarine
1 tablespoon all-purpose flour
1 cup milk
¼ cup lemon juice
1 tablespoon tarragon vinegar
1 tablespoon each minced shallot, chervil, tarragon, and chives
Salt and pepper to taste

Melt 1 tablespoon butter and blend in flour. Gradually add milk and cook, stirring constantly, until slightly thickened. Add remaining ingredients and let stand for 5 minutes. Strain and serve hot or cold. Makes about 1¼ cups.

RAVIOLI—Shells or cases of noodle dough filled with meat, chicken, cheese, or spinach.
Although the word ravioli is Italian, this type of food preparation is by no means a uniquely Italian dish. It occurs under different names in the cookery of many lands. The Chinese know ravioli as *won ton,* the Jews as *kreplach,* and the Russians as *pelmeni.* It all goes to show that ravioli, filled one way or another, make an excellent dish.
Ravioli dough is not difficult to prepare if the liquid is added to the flour until the dough cleans the bowl but is not sticky. The dough should then be kneaded to develop gluten strands which will make the dough elastic.

RAVIOLI

Let the dough rest for 30 minutes before rolling as this will also help develop gluten strands. The dough should be rolled as thinly as possible on a pastry cloth or board using as little flour as possible. Extra flour at this point in preparation makes the dough tough. The filling must be thick and pasty, not wet, or the dough around the filling will absorb moisture and become sticky. The filling should be thick enough to be shaped into balls with the fingers or a spoon. Once the filling has been placed on the dough, the edges of the dough should be moistened with water to prevent the ravioli from opening during cooking. The ravioli should be dried only for a short time, about 2 hours, before cooking. Uncooked ravioli can be frozen successfully. The ravioli should be dried slightly, then packed into freezer containers with a layer of freezer paper between each two layers of ravioli. Cover and seal. When ready to prepare, cook the ravioli only from the frozen state as defrosting makes them difficult to handle. Remove cooked ravioli from the cooking liquid with a slotted spoon and serve with hot sauce or hot sautéed buttered bread crumbs and Parmesan cheese.

Canned beef or cheese ravioli is available in most food stores. Frozen cheese, beef, or spinach ravioli is available in Italian food stores and some general food stores.

RAVIOLI

- 2 cups sifted all-purpose flour
- ½ teaspoon salt
- 2 eggs, slightly beaten
- 6 tablespoons lukewarm water
- Hamburger Filling
- 2 cups spaghetti sauce
- Grated Parmesan cheese

Sift flour and salt. Add eggs and stir with a fork until thoroughly mixed. Gradually add lukewarm water and stir until mixture forms a smooth ball. Turn out on lightly floured board and knead for a few minutes, or until smooth and elastic. Put in bowl and sprinkle with a little flour. Cover and let stand for 30 minutes. Roll out half of dough on lightly floured board to an oblong 10 x 16 inches. Put small teaspoons of Hamburger Filling about 2 inches apart on the dough. Roll out remaining dough and brush with water. Put dough, moistened side down, over the hamburger. Press edges of dough firmly around each teaspoon of filling. With a sharp knife or a pastry jagger or ravioli cutter, cut ravioli into 2-inch squares. Set aside and let dry for 2 hours. Drop ravioli into boiling salted water and cook for 15 minutes, or until ravioli are tender. Put ravioli in a shallow casserole, cover with hot spaghetti sauce, and sprinkle with Parmesan cheese. Bake in preheated moderate oven (375°F.) for 25 minutes, or until sauce is bubbly. Makes 6 servings.

Hamburger Filling

- ¾ pound ground beef
- ½ teaspoon salt
- ⅛ teaspoon pepper
- 1 tablespoon grated Parmesan cheese
- 2 parsley sprigs, chopped
- 1 egg, slightly beaten
- 1 tablespoon fine dry bread crumbs
- 2 teaspoons grated onion

Cook beef, stirring with a fork, until it loses its red color. Drain off fat. Add remaining ingredients. Mix well and cool.

RAVIOLI ITALIAN STYLE

- 3½ cups sifted all-purpose flour
- 3 egg yolks
- 1½ teaspoons salt
- ⅔ cup water, about
- Meat filling or cheese filling
- 6 quarts beef or chicken bouillon or water
- Tomato Sauce
- 1 cup grated Parmesan cheese

Put flour on a pastry board or in a bowl. Make a well in the center. Put egg yolks, salt, and water into the center of the flour. Stir carefully with a fork until liquid is mixed into flour, forming a soft dough. Knead dough on the board until all flour is incorporated. Continue kneading in a little additional flour until dough becomes smooth and elastic, about 10 minutes. Cover dough with a bowl and let stand for 30 minutes.

Cut dough into 4 pieces and roll out each piece on lightly floured board into the same size sheet. Cover sheets of dough with a towel while rolling to prevent drying. Brush 2 of the sheets lightly with water. On the 2 brushed sheets put small balls of meat or cheese filling about 1½ inches apart. Cover filled sheets with 2 remaining sheets, pushing the dough tightly around each ball of filling. Cut into 2-inch squares. Put ravioli on a lightly floured towel. Sprinkle lightly with flour and let stand for 30 minutes. Cook ravioli in boiling bouillon for 7 to 10 minutes. Remove with a slotted spoon. Put a layer of ravioli into a serving bowl. Spoon some Tomato Sauce over the ravioli and sprinkle with grated Parmesan cheese. Continue layering until bowl is filled. Makes 8 servings.

Meat Filling

- ⅔ cup ground cooked ham or prosciutto
- 1 cup ground cooked white meat of chicken
- 1 cup ground cooked veal
- 2 egg yolks
- 1½ teaspoons salt
- 1 tablespoon olive oil
- 1 tablespoon grated Parmesan cheese
- Salt and pepper

Combine all ingredients and blend well into a smooth paste. Shape mixture into small balls the size of a large olive.

Cheese Filling

- ¾ pound ricotta cheese
- 1 tablespoon chopped parsley
- 2 tablespoons grated Romano cheese
- 1 egg yolk, beaten
- Salt to taste

Combine all filling ingredients and put small spoonfuls about 2 inches apart on dough.

RECIPE

Tomato Sauce

- 1 can (6 ounces) tomato paste
- 1½ cups water
- 5 ripe tomatoes, peeled and diced
- ¼ cup olive oil
- 1 garlic clove
- ¼ cup butter or margarine
- ¼ teaspoon crumbled dried basil
- ¼ teaspoon crushed red pepper
- Salt and pepper to taste

Blend tomato paste with water. Add tomatoes, oil, and garlic. Simmer for 25 minutes, stirring occasionally, or until sauce is reduced to one-third of its original amount. Remove garlic and put mixture through a food mill, or whirl in a blender. Add remaining ingredients, season with salt and pepper, and continue simmering until sauce is reduced to half its original volume.

RECIPE—When applied to cooking, a recipe is a formula for preparing a dish. In old-fashioned usage the words "receipt" or "rule" were often used to mean the same thing.

A recipe is made up of two major parts: the list of ingredients and the directions for preparing the dish. In reading and interpreting recipes there are certain points to bear in mind:

1. Read the recipe through thoroughly, making sure you understand what the ingredients are and the method to be used.

2. Before beginning the dish, make sure you have all the ingredients. A good plan is to collect them before beginning.

3. If you are making the dish for the first time, do not alter any ingredients or procedures. If you are an experienced cook, after you have made the dish once, you may want to alter it as far as the seasonings, method of serving, etc., are concerned.

4. Generally speaking, it is unsafe to double or triple recipes, especially cakes and candies. The cooking time, texture, or consistency of the resulting product may be changed.

Ravioli Italian Style

RED SNAPPER

RED SNAPPER—A salt-water fish of a family that includes gray snapper, muttonfish, schoolmaster, and yellowtail. These fishes are caught in the South Atlantic and the Gulf of Mexico. The market weight ranges from two to fifteen pounds although snappers weighing as much as twenty pounds have been caught.

All varieties are considered lean fishes, with juicy meat and a delicate flavor. They can be panfried, steamed, poached, or broiled, and are particularly delicious baked.

Availability and Purchasing Guide—Available year round fresh and frozen, whole, and as steaks and fillets.

Fresh fish should have bright, clear bulging eyes; gills that look and smell clean; scales that are shiny and lie close to the skin; and firm flesh with some spring to it when pressed with a finger.

Storage—Fresh fish is very perishable. Wrap snapper in moisture-proof paper or place in tightly covered container in coldest part of refrigerator.

Keep frozen snapper solidly frozen until ready to use. Once thawed, use immediately. Do not refreeze.
Fresh, refrigerator shelf, raw: 1 to 2 days
Fresh, cooked; or frozen, refrigerator shelf: 3 to 4 days
Fresh, refrigerator frozen-food compartment, prepared for freezing, raw: 2 to 3 weeks
Fresh, refrigerator frozen-food compartment, prepared for freezing, cooked: 3 to 4 weeks
Frozen, refrigerator frozen-food compartment: 2 months
Fresh, prepared for freezing, raw or cooked; or frozen, freezer: 1 year

Nutritive Food Value
4 ounces, raw = 105 calories

Basic Preparation
To Poach—Cut fillets into serving-size portions. Or use steaks. Put fish in a wire basket or on a plate. If plate is used, it should be tied in a piece of cheesecloth. Lower the fish into boiling salted water and simmer for 10 minutes, or until fish flakes easily with a fork. Serve with any desired sauce such as tomato, drawn butter, egg, etc.
To Steam—Sprinkle both sides of fillets or steaks with salt. Put in a well greased steamer pan and steam over boiling water for 10 to 12 minutes, or until fish flakes easily with a fork. Serve with sauce as listed above.
To Panfry—Cut fillets into serving-size portions. Dip into flour and season on both sides with salt and pepper. Panfry in hot butter or margarine until browned on both sides and fish flakes easily with a fork. Serve with lemon wedges, if desired.
To Broil—Cut fillets into serving-size portions. Or use steaks. Sprinkle on both sides with salt and pepper. Put fish on a preheated greased broiler pan about 2 inches from the heat, skin side up, if skin has not been removed from fillets. Brush fish with melted butter or margarine. Broil for 5 to 8 minutes on each side, or until lightly browned, and fish flakes easily with a fork, basting with butter after turning.
To Bake Whole Fish—Wipe fish with damp cloth. Rub inside and out with salt. Put in a greased shallow baking pan. Brush with melted butter or margarine and, if desired, lay 3 slices of bacon over top. Bake in preheated moderate oven (350°F.) for 40 to 60 minutes, or until fish flakes easily with a fork. Baste with melted butter several times during the baking.
To Bake Fillets or Steaks—Cut fillets into serving-size portions. Or use steaks. Sprinkle on both sides with salt and pepper. Dip each piece into a mixture of twice as much melted butter as fresh lemon juice. Put in a greased shallow baking pan. Bake in preheated moderate oven (350°F.) for 25 to 30 minutes, or until fish flakes easily with a fork. Sprinkle with paprika.
To Freeze—Eviscerate fish and wash well. Cut as desired into steaks or fillets or leave whole. Dip pieces of fish into a solution of ¼ cup salt to 4 cups water for 20 to 30 seconds. Wrap in moisture-vapor-proof wrapping, excluding as much air as possible. Seal.

RED SNAPPER STEAKS WITH SHRIMPS

- 2 pounds red snapper steaks
- Salt and pepper to taste
- 4 tablespoons butter or margarine
- Few parsley sprigs, chopped
- 1 small carrot, minced
- 1 celery stalk, minced
- ¼ teaspoon dried basil
- 1 cup Rhine wine
- ¼ pound raw shrimps, shelled and cleaned
- 1 lemon, sliced

Wipe fish with a damp cloth and season on both sides with salt and pepper. Melt 2 tablespoons butter and use to brush the inside of a shallow baking dish. Arrange fish in dish. Top with parsley, carrot, and celery. Sprinkle with basil and add wine. Bake in preheated moderate oven (350°F.) for 20 minutes. Mince shrimps and sauté in remaining 2 tablespoons butter for 3 minutes, or until lightly browned, stirring constantly. Pour over fish and bake for 10 minutes longer, or until fish flakes easily with fork. Garnish with lemon slices. Makes 4 servings.

BAKED RED SNAPPER, FLORIDA STYLE

- 1 whole red snapper (5 to 7 pounds)
- 1 medium onion, minced
- 1 green pepper, minced
- 1 garlic clove, minced
- Bacon fat
- 2 cups soft stale-bread crumbs
- Chopped fresh dill or dill seed
- 3 eggs, beaten
- 6 slices of bacon
- 1½ cups red wine
- 3 tablespoons all-purpose flour
- ½ cup tomato paste
- Salt and pepper
- Chopped parsley

Have fish cleaned and split with head left on. Sauté onion, green pepper, and garlic in 3 tablespoons bacon fat for 5 minutes. Add crumbs and season with chopped fresh dill to taste. Stir in eggs. Stuff fish with the mixture and sew or secure opening with toothpicks. Put fish in a greased shallow baking pan and arrange bacon slices on it. Pour in 1 cup red wine. Bake in preheated hot oven (400°F.) about 35 minutes, or until fish flakes easily with a fork. Remove fish to a hot platter. Blend flour into drippings in pan. Add remaining ½ cup wine and tomato paste. Cook, stirring constantly, until smooth and thickened. Season to taste with salt, pepper, and parsley. Serve with fish. Makes 6 to 8 servings.

RED SNAPPER AMANDINE

Panfry 2 pounds red snapper fillets, cut into serving-size portions, as directed in To Panfry (on p. 22). Put cooked fillets in a shallow baking dish. Put ¾ cup sliced almonds in a skillet with ¾ cup butter. Cook, stirring, until golden brown. Pour over fish and sprinkle with the juice of 1 lemon. Put in preheated moderate oven (375°F.) for 5 minutes to heat and blend flavors. Makes 4 to 6 servings.

REDUCE, TO
—As a culinary process, the phrase means to cook a liquid until a certain amount of it is cooked away, thus concentrating the flavor in, and thickening the consistency of, that which remains.

Reducing is most commonly done in sauces, stews, and syrups. It is one of the simplest cooking processes; all it requires is that one watches to make sure that there is not *too* much evaporation.

REINDEER
—Any of several varieties of deer of the genus *Rangifer* that live in Arctic and subarctic Europe, Asia, and America. The American variety is called caribou. Their chief characteristics are large hoofs and the possession of crescent-shape antlers in both sexes, which is not usual with deer. However, the antlers of the male reindeer are much larger than those of the female and present a most imposing sight. In the winter their fur is long and grayish-brown on the body while the neck, hindquarters, and belly are white. In the summer the animal becomes a darker gray and brown. The winter furs are especially prized because of their thickness and softness. The meat is sweet, dark red, with clear white fat.

Reindeer have been domesticated and used as a source of food and as draft animals. They are still an essential part of the economy of Laplanders.

Reindeer meat is highly prized in all Scandinavian countries and wherever reindeer are raised. Fresh or smoked, it is excellent. Its flavor is much more delicate than that of other venison, but it is apt to be tough and should be well hung. Reindeer meat can be prepared like any venison. In Scandinavia the meat is often marinated first and then pot-roasted. The sauce usually contains cream.

Availability—Frozen reindeer imported from Norway is available as leg steaks, backs, rump roast, and boneless stew meat in specialty food stores in a very limited area of the Northeast. Canned reindeer meatballs in brown gravy are also available imported from Norway.

RELISH

NORWEGIAN REINDEER POT ROAST WITH MUSHROOMS, TOMATOES, GRAPES, AND PINEAPPLE

- 1 reindeer roast (about 5 pounds) boned and rolled
- 4 cups dry red wine
- 1 large onion, sliced
- 1 celery stalk
- 10 peppercorns
- 1 tablespoon salt
- 2 bay leaves
- ½ pound salt pork or bacon, cut into slices
- ½ cup butter
- 1 cup dairy sour cream
- ½ cup heavy cream, whipped

Garnish

- 1 pound mushroom caps, sautéed in butter
- 6 tomatoes, cut into halves and grilled
- ½ pound dark-blue grapes, stemmed
- 1 cup chopped pineapple, sautéed in butter

Place meat in deep bowl. Combine wine, onion, celery, peppercorns, salt, and bay leaves. Pour over meat and marinate for 24 to 48 hours. Turn meat several times. Drain and wipe dry. Strain marinade and reserve. Lard meat with salt pork, or wrap larding around meat, tying with string. Heat butter in large heavy casserole or Dutch oven. Brown meat on all sides. Reduce heat as low as possible. Pour half of marinade over meat. Simmer, covered, for 2 to 3 hours (depending on toughness of the meat), or until meat is tender. To test for doneness, lift meat and test with a skewer; it should not draw blood. Baste occasionally during cooking time with pan juices; if necessary, add a little more marinade. When done, transfer meat to hot platter and keep hot. Remove string and salt pork or bacon. Make gravy by swirling sour cream in pan in which meat was cooked, but do not boil. If necessary, thicken gravy with a little flour mixed with water to a smooth paste. Begin with 1 tablespoon and cook for 2 or 3 minutes over lowest possible heat. Add whipped cream to finished gravy and spoon a little over meat on platter. To garnish, surround meat with mushroom caps in rows and alternate mounds of grilled tomatoes, grapes, and pineapple. The arrangement should be decorative. Serve remaining gravy separately. Serve with browned potatoes. Makes 6 to 8 servings.

RELISH
—As a verb "to relish" means "to enjoy," and when the word relish is used as a culinary term it can be, and is, applied to a wide range of foods and food preparations served as accompaniments to add zest, flavor, and variety to the main dishes of a meal. Olives and such vegetables as celery, radishes, cucumbers, carrots, and cauliflower, when served raw, are one major type of relish.

A second major type includes such widely used condiments as catsup and chutney, and all the other savory foods prepared from mixed chopped vegetables or fruits, either uncooked, pickled, or preserved.

RELISH

Many commercially prepared relishes are available. When making preserved relishes at home it is important to cook them in an enamelware, glass, or stainless-steel container which will not discolor the food, and to stir the preparation almost constantly to prevent burning.

APPLE RELISH

- 12 apples, peeled and chopped
- 1 onion, chopped
- 2 green peppers, seeded and chopped
- 1 cup sugar
- 2 cups cider vinegar
- 1 lemon, sliced thin and seeded
- 1½ teaspoons each salt and ground ginger
- 1 cup seeded raisins

Combine all ingredients in a large saucepan and cook for 2 hours, stirring occasionally, until mixture is thick. Spoon mixture into hot sterilized jars, seal, and cool. Makes about 2 quarts.

DILLED GREEN BEAN-AND-CARROT RELISH

- 2 pounds green beans, washed and cut in 1-inch pieces
- 1 package (1 pound) carrots, peeled and cut in 1-inch pieces
- 3 tablespoons salt
- 2 teaspoons mustard seed
- 2 teaspoons dillweed
- 1 teaspoon crushed hot red pepper
- 1 teaspoon dillseed
- 4 garlic cloves
- 2 cups white vinegar
- 2 cups water
- ½ cup sugar

Soak beans and carrots in ice water to cover about 30 minutes. Cook beans and carrots in 1 quart boiling water with 1 tablespoon salt 5 minutes, or until of desired tenderness. Drain and pack in hot sterilized jars. Put ½ teaspoon each mustard seed and dillweed, ¼ teaspoon each crushed hot red pepper and dillseed and 1 clove garlic in each jar. Combine remaining 2 tablespoons salt, vinegar, water and sugar and heat to boiling. Pour over beans, filling to within ½ inch of top, and seal. Makes 4 pints.

BEET RELISH

- 1 quart finely chopped cabbage
- 1 quart cooked beets, cut in strips
- 1 cup chopped onion
- 2 cups sugar
- 1 tablespoon black pepper
- 1 teaspoon salt
- ¼ teaspoon cayenne
- 1 cup grated fresh horseradish
- White vinegar

Mix all ingredients, except vinegar. Add enough cold vinegar to cover mixture. Store, covered, in refrigerator (the flavor improves on standing). Makes 4 pints.

CORN AND PEPPER RELISH

- 7 cups corn cut from cobs
- 2 cups chopped cabbage
- 2 green peppers, chopped
- 2 sweet red peppers, chopped
- 1 cup each sugar and water
- 4 cups cider vinegar
- 1 tablespoon each celery seed and whole pickling spice
- 2 tablespoons salt

Mix all ingredients and cook for 30 minutes, stirring frequently to prevent sticking. Pack into hot sterilized jars; partially seal; process in hot-water bath for 20 minutes; complete seals. If closures are self-sealing type, do not tighten after processing. Makes about 6 pints.

QUICK CORN RELISH

- 1⅓ cups cooked whole-kernel corn
- ½ cup finely diced celery
- 1 tablespoon chopped green pepper
- 3 tablespoons wine vinegar
- 2 tablespoons firmly packed brown sugar
- ½ teaspoon salt
- ⅛ teaspoon each pepper and ground turmeric
- 1 tablespoon chopped canned pimiento

Combine all ingredients except pimiento in saucepan and mix well. Heat thoroughly. Add pimiento. Cool, and refrigerate. Makes 2 cups.

CRANBERRY-FILBERT RELISH

- 1 can (20 ounces) crushed pineapple
- Water
- 2 cups sugar
- 1 pound (4 cups) cranberries
- 2 oranges
- ½ cup seedless raisins
- ½ cup chopped candied gingerroot
- ½ cup chopped toasted filberts

Drain pineapple. Measure juice and add enough water to make 2 cups. Add sugar to liquid and bring to boil, stirring until sugar is dissolved. Add cranberries and cook for 5 minutes. Grate rind of 1 orange. Remove segments of both oranges. Add grated rind, segments, raisins, and gingerroot to cranberry mixture. Simmer, stirring frequently, for 25 minutes, or until thick. Add nuts and pour into hot sterilized ½-pint jars; seal immediately. Makes about 6 jars.

SWEET CUCUMBER RELISH

- 8 large ripe cucumbers
- ¼ cup salt
- 4 sweet red peppers, seeded and cored
- 4 large onions, quartered
- 1½ tablespoons each celery seeds and mustard seeds
- 2½ cups sugar
- 1½ cups white vinegar

Peel cucumbers and slice into crock or glass bowl. Add salt and mix well. Let stand overnight in refrigerator. Drain and force through coarse blade of food chopper with peppers and onions. Put in kettle; add remaining ingredients. Bring to boil and cook, uncovered, stirring occasionally, about 30 minutes. Pack into hot sterilized jars and seal. Makes 3 pints.

SPICED-FRUIT RELISH

5 peaches, peeled
3 firm pears, peeled
1 large onion
9 ripe tomatoes, peeled
1 bunch celery
1 sweet red pepper
1 sweet green pepper
1 tablespoon mixed pickling spice
1 hot pepper
2½ cups sugar
1 tablespoon salt
1 cup white vinegar

Cut all fruits and vegetables, except hot pepper, in small pieces and put in kettle. Tie pickling spice in cheesecloth bag and add to mixture with hot pepper, sugar, salt and vinegar. Bring to boil and simmer 2 hours, or until thick. Remove hot pepper and spice bag; pour mixture into hot sterilized jars and seal. Process in hotwater bath 20 minutes. Makes 4 pints.

LEMON RELISH

6 thin-skinned lemons
  Boiling water
1 teaspoon ground sage
1½ cups sugar

Trim yellow peel from 2 lemons. Cut in fine strips and cover with boiling water; drain and reserve. Cut peel and white membrane from all lemons and cut lemons in thin slices. Remove seeds and put slices in bowl. Mix sage and sugar in small saucepan. Add 1 cup reserved water, bring to boil and boil 4 minutes, or until thick. Add lemon strips and pour over lemon slices, cover and chill. Serve with roast pork or other meats. Makes about 2⅔ cups.

ORANGE-CUCUMBER RELISH

1⅔ cups chopped sweet red pepper
1⅔ cups chopped green pepper
4 cups chopped peeled cucumber
¼ cup salt
½ cup water
3 oranges
2 cups white vinegar
2 cups firmly packed brown sugar
½ teaspoon mustard seed
½ teaspoon celery seed

Mix peppers, cucumber, salt and ½ cup water and let stand overnight. In morning, drain and discard liquid. Squeeze most of juice from oranges and reserve for other use. Force pulp and rind through coarse blade of food chopper. Combine all ingredients and bring to boil. Simmer about 10 minutes. Pour into hot sterilized jars and seal. Makes 3 to 4 pints.

LIME RELISH

12 limes
1½ cups sugar
1 cup vinegar
½ cup water

Wash limes and soak them in water to cover for 24 hours. Drain, cover with fresh water, and cook for 15 to 20 minutes, or until limes are just easily pierced. Drain. Cool; cut limes into eighths. Remove seeds. Cook remaining ingredients about 15 minutes, or until syrupy. Spoon limes into hot sterilized jars and cover with syrup. Seal and cool. Makes 2 pints.

PEACH RELISH

16 medium peaches
1 cup seedless raisins
1½ cups firmly packed light brown sugar
¾ cup cider vinegar
1 teaspoon ground cinnamon
½ teaspoon ground cloves
2 teaspoons mustard seeds
½ cup coarsely chopped nuts

Peel, pit, and slice peaches. There should be 8 cups. Combine in kettle with remaining ingredients except nuts. Bring to boil and cook, uncovered, for 45 minutes, or until thick, stirring frequently. Add nuts and cook for 2 minutes. Fill hot sterilized jars and seal. Makes 3 pints.

RED AND GREEN PEPPER RELISH

6 red peppers
6 green peppers
6 onions, peeled
2 cups white vinegar
1½ cups sugar
2 tablespoons salt
1 tablespoon mustard seed
1 tablespoon celery seed

Split peppers and remove seeds. Chop peppers and onions coarsely, cover with boiling water and let stand 5 minutes; drain. Cover again with boiling water and let stand 10 minutes; drain. Combine remaining ingredients and boil 5 minutes. Add vegetables and boil 10 minutes. Pack into hot sterilized jars; seal. Makes 4 pints.

Hot Pear Relish
Dilled Green Bean and Carrot Relish
Red and Green Pepper Relish
Gingery Yellow Tomato Relish
Beet Relish
Orange-Cucumber Relish
Chop-Suey Relish
Turnip Relish

RELISH

HOT PEAR RELISH

- 6 firm pears
- 3 onions
- 3 green peppers
- 1 sweet red pepper
- 1 small hot pepper or ½ teaspoon crushed dried red pepper
- 2 tablespoons salt
- 1 cup sugar
- 1 cup white vinegar

Remove cores from pears and force, with next 4 ingredients, through coarse blade of food chopper. Sprinkle with salt and let stand 2 hours. Drain thoroughly. Bring sugar and vinegar to boil in kettle and add vegetables. Bring again to boil and simmer about 15 minutes. Pour into hot sterilized jars and seal. Makes about 5 half-pints.

GREEN-TOMATO RELISH

- 2 quarts chopped green tomatoes (4 to 5 pounds)
- 2 medium onions, chopped
- 2 quarts cold water
- ½ cup salt
- 1½ cups white vinegar
- ½ cup boiling water
- 1½ cups sugar
- 1½ teaspoons celery seeds
- 1 tablespoon mustard seeds
- ½ teaspoon each ground turmeric and cinnamon
- ¼ teaspoon dry mustard

Combine tomatoes and onions with water and salt in crock or bowl; soak for 3 hours. Drain and rinse thoroughly with cold water. Combine remaining ingredients and boil for 3 minutes. Add tomatoes and onions, bring to boil, and simmer, uncovered, for 10 minutes. Pack into hot sterilized jars and seal. Makes 2 or 2½ pints.
NOTE: For a colorful addition, tuck in red-pepper strips among the green tomatoes and white onions.

TOMATO-APPLE RELISH

- 3 medium onions, peeled and quartered
- 4 medium-large tart apples, cored and cut in eighths
- 1 outer stalk celery, cut in pieces
- 2½ cups white vinegar
- ¾ cup seedless raisins
- 2 tablespoons mustard seed
- 1 tablespoon ground ginger
- 2 ounces candied or preserved ginger, finely chopped
- 3 cups firmly packed light-brown sugar
- 1 tablespoon salt
- 4 large ripe tomatoes, peeled, cored and cut in eighths
- 1 sweet red pepper, minced

Force first 3 ingredients through coarse blade of food chopper. Put in kettle with remaining ingredients, except pepper. Bring to boil and simmer 1¾ hours uncovered, stirring frequently. Add pepper and simmer, stirring very frequently, about 15 minutes longer. Pour into hot sterilized jars and seal. Makes 3 to 4 pints.

CHILI RELISH

- 2 quarts chopped peeled tomatoes
- 1 cup chopped green onion
- ½ cup each coarsely ground sweet red and green pepper
- 1 teaspoon crushed dried red pepper
- 1 cup sugar
- 1½ teaspoons salt
- 1½ teaspoons white mustard seed
- ½ teaspoon ground cinnamon
- 1¼ cups white vinegar

Combine all ingredients in large kettle, bring to boil and simmer, stirring frequently, 3 to 4 hours, or until thick. Pour into hot sterilized jars and seal. Makes about 4 half-pints.

GINGERY YELLOW-TOMATO RELISH

- 2 quarts small yellow tomatoes (about 2½ pounds)
- 1 lemon, cut in thin slices
- ¼ pound candied ginger, chopped
- 5 cups sugar
- 1 cup water

Wash tomatoes and remove stems but do not peel or slice. Combine all ingredients, bring to boil and simmer 2 hours, or until thick. Pour into hot sterilized jars and seal. Process in hotwater bath 20 minutes. Makes 3 pints.

CHUCK'S BARBECUE SAUCE RELISH

- 3 garlic cloves, minced
- 1 cup malt vinegar
- 2 teaspoons each pepper and chili seasoning
- 2 tablespoons dry mustard
- 2 cups ground onions
- 2 quarts ground tomatoes
- ¼ cup each Worcestershire and sugar
- 1 tablespoon salt

Mix all ingredients; cook until thick, stirring frequently. Pour into hot sterilized jars and seal. Makes 3 pints.

TURNIP RELISH

- 15 medium white turnips (about 3 pounds)
- 3 sweet red peppers
- 6 green peppers
- 3 large onions
- ½ cup salt
- 1 pint white vinegar
- 3 cups sugar
- 1 tablespoon white mustard seed
- 1 tablespoon celery seed
- ½ teaspoon crushed dried red pepper

Peel turnips and cut in pieces. Remove seed and white membrane from red and green peppers and cut peppers in pieces. Peel and cut up onions. Force all through coarse blade of food chopper. Sprinkle with salt and let stand 2 hours. Drain and squeeze dry. Mix remaining ingredients in kettle and bring to boil. Add vegetables, bring to boil and simmer, uncovered, about 1 hour. Pour into hot sterilized jars and seal. Makes 4 half-pints.

ZUCCHINI-ONION RELISH

- 2 pounds zucchini
- 2 small onions
- ¼ cup salt
- 2 cups white vinegar
- 2 cups sugar
- 1 teaspoon celery seed
- 1 teaspoon turmeric
- 2 teaspoons mustard seed

Cut zucchini in thin slices. Peel and quarter onions and cut in thin slices. Cover vegetables with water and add salt. Let stand 2 hours, then drain thoroughly. Bring remaining ingredients to boil and pour over vegetables. Let stand 2 hours, then bring to boil and boil 5 minutes. Pack in hot sterilized jars and seal. Makes about 3 pints.

CHOP-SUEY RELISH

- 6 large cucumbers, peeled, seeded and diced
- 11 medium onions, diced
- 3 large sweet red peppers, diced
- 3 large sweet green peppers, diced
- ½ cup salt
- 3 tablespoons mixed pickling spice
- 1 tablespoon celery seed
- 1 to 2 teaspoons curry powder
- 1 pint white vinegar
- 4 cups sugar
- 1 cup water

Mix first 5 ingredients in large bowl and refrigerate, covered, overnight. In morning, rinse several times in cold water and drain thoroughly. Tie spices in cheesecloth bag and put with remaining ingredients in large kettle. Bring to boil and add vegetables. Bring again to boil and simmer 1 hour, or until thickened. Pour into hot sterilized jars and seal. Makes about 4 pints.

HOT DOG AND HAMBURGER RELISH

- 3 pounds (about 10) medium green tomatoes
- 4 medium red apples
- 3 sweet red peppers
- 4 onions
- 1½ tablespoons salt
- 1½ teaspoons each pepper and ground cinnamon
- ¾ teaspoon ground cloves
- 2½ cups sugar
- 2 cups white vinegar

Wash tomatoes and remove stem ends. Core apples; do not peel. Remove cores and seeds from peppers. Force apples and all vegetables through coarse blade of food chopper. Combine remaining ingredients and bring to boil in kettle. Add vegetables and simmer, uncovered, for 30 minutes, or until thick, stirring occasionally. Pack into hot sterilized jars and seal. Makes 4 or 5 pints.

LADY ROSS RELISH

- 4 cups chopped peeled cucumber (2 large)
- 4 cups chopped onion
- 1 large cauliflower, chopped
- 1½ green peppers, chopped
- 1½ sweet red peppers, chopped
- ¼ cup salt
- 4 cups firmly packed brown sugar
- 3 cups white vinegar
- 2 tablespoons mustard seed
- ¼ cup dry mustard
- 1½ teaspoons turmeric
- ¼ cup all-purpose flour
- ¼ cup cold water

Mix first 6 ingredients and let stand overnight. Drain thoroughly. Bring next 5 ingredients to boil in kettle. Blend flour with water to make a smooth paste. Stir into boiling mixture. Add vegetables, bring again to boil and simmer 10 minutes. Pour into hot sterilized jars and seal. Makes about 5 pints.

MINT RELISH

- ½ cup fresh mint leaves
- 3 large apples, cored
- 1½ cups seedless raisins
- 12 ripe tomatoes
- 2 red peppers, seeded
- 4 large onions, peeled
- 2 tablespoons white mustard seeds
- ½ cup salt
- 2 cups sugar
- 6 cups cider vinegar

Put mint, apples, raisins, tomatoes, peppers, and onions through coarse blade of food chopper. Add remaining ingredients. Mix well and store the mixture in a crock for 10 days, stirring occasionally. Pour into sterilized jars, seal, and store. Makes about 3 quarts.

RED-HOT SAUCE RELISH

- 10 pounds (about 30) ripe tomatoes
- 8 medium onions
- 2 hot red peppers
- 1 cup cider vinegar
- 1 cup sugar
- 1 teaspoon ground cinnamon
- 1½ tablespoons salt

Wash and quarter tomatoes; peel and quarter onions; seed peppers and cut into pieces. Cook together until soft; rub through sieve. Add remaining ingredients and boil until mixture begins to thicken. Reduce heat and simmer, stirring frequently, until quite thick. Pour into hot sterilized jars and seal. Makes about 5 pints.

RÉMOULADE

RÉMOULADE, RÉMOLADE—A highly seasoned classic French sauce based on a blend of mustard, flour, water, oil, and vinegar with other seasonings. It is served cold with fish and seafood, cold meats, poultry, and vegetable salads. For a recipe, see the section Sauce Cookbook.

RENDER, TO—To melt down or try out meat fat, especially pork, in order to separate the portions of lean or connective tissues from the clear fat. Rendering is done in a heavy pan over low heat. If the rendered fat is to stored for later use it should be strained and refrigerated. The crisp bits of connective tissue left after the fat has been rendered are known as cracklings. Cracklings from rendering chicken or goose fat are sometimes called greben or grebenes. They are excellent when added to mashed potato or to chopped liver dishes. Diced salt pork is often rendered for making chowders. The fat is used for browning the onion and the crisp cracklings are added to the chowder just before serving.

Bacon cracklings are available canned as a cocktail snack.

RENNET—A combination of two inorganic enzymes or ferments, rennin and pepsin, obtained from the membranes of the stomachs of young mammals. The best quality is that from an animal so young that it has received no other food than milk, the most desirable coming from a calf's stomach. Rennet's chief importance from a food standpoint is its property of coagulating milk and its widest food use is in the manufacture of cheese. Available commercially are packaged rennet-custard desserts in powder form in vanilla, chocolate, maple, lemon, orange, and raspberry flavors. Tablets in vanilla flavor are also available. These desserts are easily digested and are used for children and invalids as well as a basis for other desserts.

RHUBARB—A hardy perennial plant of the genus *Rheum* native to northern Asia and now grown chiefly for its thick succulent leaf stalks. The plant has large clumps of broad green leaves, up to two feet across, growing on thick fleshy red and green leaf stalks which average twelve to eighteen inches in length, but can be much longer.

There are many varieties of rhubarb, but the only important distinction in the edible types is between forced or hot-house rhubarb and field rhubarb. The first usually has slender pink to light red stalks with yellow-green leaves and the second deep red stalks and green leaves.

Only the leaf stalks of the rhubarb are edible. Leaves and root contain a substance that can sometimes be poisonous. But the stalks are so delicious in pies that rhubarb has also been known as pie plant. Stewed rhubarb and desserts of many kinds, as well as jam and wine, are equally delicious.

Rhubarb is extremely popular in northern Europe and in the Scandinavian countries. Apart from the fact that it is easily grown, it is also the first fresh fruit of the year and the harbinger of summer's bounty.

Like so many other plants, rhubarb crossed the Atlantic Ocean with the colonists, but it wasn't until the late 18th century that it was used much. The early Indians cooked the stalks like asparagus, and the new Americans learned from them to prepare the plant for eating.

Availability—Fresh rhubarb is available from February to August with the peak season in May and June.

Rhubarb is also available canned and frozen.

Purchasing Guide—Rhubarb is sold by the bunch, or by weight. Select fresh, firm, large, crisp, straight stalks with bright dark-red or cherry color. Rhubarb may be field grown or forced. The forced variety is lighter in color and has yellowish-green leaves. Avoid wilted, oversized, or very thin stalks.

1 pound = 2 cups cooked

Storage—Fresh rhubarb is perishable. Refrigerate and use as soon as possible.
Fresh, refrigerator shelf, uncooked: 1 to 3 days
Fresh, cooked; or canned, opened, refrigerator shelf: 4 to 5 days
Fresh, prepared for freezing; or frozen, refrigerator frozen-food compartment: 2 to 3 months
Fresh, prepared for freezing; or frozen, freezer: 1 year
Canned, kitchen shelf: 1 year

Nutritive Food Values—Fair source of vitamin A.
Fresh, ½ cup (4 ounces), cooked with added sugar = 169 calories

Basic Preparation—Wash; remove leaves and stem ends. If tender, do not peel. Cut stalks into inch-long pieces. Add only enough water to cover and cook until just tender. Stir in sugar to taste. Cool, and serve warm or chilled.

To Freeze—Use tender red crisp stalks. Trim stems and cut into 1-inch lengths. Wash and pack into freezer containers. Cover with cold syrup made by cooking 3½ cups sugar with 4 cups water. Allow ½-inch headspace. Seal.

Rhubarb can also be packed into containers without syrup, or can be mixed with sugar, 1 cup to 4 cups rhubarb, and spooned into freezer containers, allowing ½-inch headspace.

BAKED ROSY RHUBARB

Cut 1 pound unpeeled rhubarb into 1-inch lengths. Mix in shallow baking dish with 1 cup sugar and ¼ cup water. Bake in preheated moderate oven (350°F.) for 35 minutes, or until rhubarb is just tender. Chill; serve. Makes 4 servings.

RHUBARB TANGY FRESH APPLESAUCE

Diced fresh rhubarb added to the apples when making fresh applesauce gives it a rosy red color and a tangy flavor.

FRESH RHUBARB BETTY

- 6 cups diced fresh rhubarb
- 1¼ cups sugar
- 2½ tablespoons quick-cooking tapioca
- 1 teaspoon grated lemon rind
- 1 tablespoon grated orange rind
- ¼ teaspoon salt
- 2⅔ cups soft bread crumbs
- ⅓ cup melted butter or margarine
- 1 teaspoon vanilla extract

Combine first 6 ingredients and set aside. Mix bread crumbs with melted butter and vanilla. Fill buttered 1½-quart casserole with alternate layers of rhubarb and bread crumbs, having rhubarb as the bottom layer and bread crumbs as the top layer. Cover and bake in preheated hot oven (400°F.) for 25 minutes. Remove cover and bake until crumbs are brown, about 10 minutes. Serve warm. Makes 6 to 8 servings.

DOUBLE-BOILER RHUBARB

Cut 1 pound rhubarb in 1-inch pieces. Put in top part of double boiler over boiling water. Cover and cook without added water 20 minutes, or until tender. Remove from heat and add sugar or honey to taste, stirring gently. Makes about 1½ cups.
NOTE: Sweetening can be added to rhubarb before cooking, if preferred.

JELLIED RHUBARB

Drain 1 cup sweetened cooked rhubarb and add water to the liquid to make 1 cup; heat to boiling and pour over ½ box (3-ounce size) lemon-flavored gelatin; stir until dissolved. Cool; then chill until syrupy. Stir in rhubarb. Chill until firm. Makes 2 servings.

RHUBARB AND STRAWBERRY PIE

- Pastry for 2-crust 9-inch pie
- 1 cup sugar
- ¼ cup all-purpose flour
- ¼ teaspoon salt
- 2 cups diced rhubarb
- 1 pint strawberries, hulled
- 2 tablespoons butter

Roll a little more than half of pastry ⅛ inch thick and line 9-inch pie pan. Mix sugar, flour, and salt and sprinkle a small amount in pastry-lined pan. Combine remaining sugar mixture with rhubarb and berries. Put in pie pan and dot with butter. Roll remaining pastry ⅛ inch thick. Put on pie, trim edges and flute. Cut a few slits for steam to escape. Bake in preheated hot oven (425°F.) for 40 to 50 minutes. Makes 6 to 8 servings.

RHUBARB CRUNCH

- 1 cup rolled oats
- ½ cup all-purpose flour
- ¾ cup firmly packed light-brown sugar
- ½ cup butter or margarine
- 1 cup granulated sugar
- ½ cup water
- 4 cups rhubarb, cut in 1-inch pieces

Mix first 3 ingredients. Cut in butter until crumbly. Pat half the mixture on bottom of greased 8-inch baking pan. In saucepan, mix granulated sugar and water and bring to boil. Add rhubarb and simmer 8 to 10 minutes, or until soft. Drain, reserving syrup. Whirl rhubarb in blender or press through sieve (there should be about 2 cups purée). Cover oatmeal mixture in pan with purée and top with remaining oat mixture. Bake in preheated moderate oven (350°F.) about 45 minutes. Serve warm with reserved syrup. Makes 6 to 8 servings.

RHUBARB UPSIDE-DOWN PUDDING

- 2 cups diced rhubarb
- All-purpose flour
- Honey
- 1 teaspoon grated orange rind
- 1 teaspoon ground cinnamon
- 2 teaspoons baking powder
- ½ teaspoon salt
- ¼ cup shortening
- 1 egg, beaten
- 3 tablespoons each milk and orange juice
- Light cream (optional)

Mix rhubarb, 1 tablespoon flour, ⅔ cup honey, orange rind and cinnamon and put in well-greased 8-inch square baking pan. Mix 1 cup flour, baking powder and salt. Cut in shortening. Mix 2 tablespoons honey, egg and milk. Add to flour-shortening mixture and stir only until dry ingredients are moistened. Spread on rhubarb and bake in preheated moderate oven (350°F.) 25 minutes. Mix 1 tablespoon honey and orange juice and drizzle over cake. Bake about 15 minutes longer. Turn out and serve warm, with cream, if desired. Makes 6 servings.

RICE

RHUBARB-PINEAPPLE JAM

3½ pounds rhubarb
1 medium-size fresh pineapple, peeled
5 cups sugar

Chop rhubarb and pineapple fine. Add 2½ cups sugar, bring to boil and cook 15 minutes. Add remaining 2½ cups sugar and simmer, uncovered, 2 hours, or until thick. Pour into 8 hot sterilized half-pint jars; seal.

RHUBARB AND STRAWBERRY JAM

1 quart rhubarb, cut into ½-inch pieces
1 quart strawberries, cut into pieces
4 cups sugar

Mix fruit and sugar and let stand for 1 hour. Bring to boiling point and cook rapidly about 30 minutes, or until thick. Stir frequently to prevent burning. Turn into hot fruit jars and seal, or put in jelly glasses and seal with paraffin. Makes about four 8-ounce glasses.

FRESH RHUBARB FRUIT PUNCH

To give fruit punch extra flavor and color, too, add rhubarb to the fruit juices. Cook diced fresh rosy rhubarb in enough water to cover until soft. Strain, and cool.

RICE—An annual cereal grass the seed of which provides the chief source of food for half the world's population.

Although wheat, barley, and millet were domesticated before it, rice is an ancient grain. Its wild ancestor has been identified as *Oryza sativa,* a semiaquatic marsh grass native to India and southeast Asia. Most cultivated rice, known as aquatic rice, is grown in marshy or flooded lands, the sort of terrain found throughout much of the southern Orient and southeastern United States. It can also be grown, but with a lesser yield of lower quality, in areas with a long growing season and a great deal of steady rainfall. This type is called hill rice. (American wild, or Indian, rice is not a member of the true rice family at all, but is an aquatic perennial grass, *Zizania aquatica*. It has never been successfully domesticated for large-scale cultivation, although it has a long history of use by the Indians, and is considered a culinary delicacy today.)

Rice is a giving food. It will grow where wheat hesitates to grow. It yields much more per acre than wheat or corn. Where wheat or barley must be ground first, rice can be eaten as a grain, eliminating the need for elaborate tools, mills, yeasts, and baking ovens. Rice is a highly nutritious and easily digested food, too. Almost all of it is completely assimilated. When milled so that only the husks are removed, producing "whole" or "brown" rice, eighty-eight per cent of it is nutrients: about eight per cent protein and seventy-nine per cent carbohydrates (chiefly starch) with very small amounts of fat. The peoples who rely on rice as a mainstay of their diet always eat it in this state since further milling reduces its food value.

The grain seems to invite controversy. The fight over the proper way to cook it—covered or uncovered, in lots of water or a little, stirred or unstirred—is still being fought. The didactic tone of those instructing others on how to cook rice is evident in the voice of Charles Gayarré, a gourmet writing in the 1880's about an old southern cook: "Who but Valentin knew how to bake rice in an iron pot? I say *iron,* because it must be nothing else, and that rice must come out solid, retaining the exact shape of the pot, with a golden crust about its top and sides."

In modern processing, rice when harvested goes to a drying plant where hot air is blown through it to "cure" it and reduce its moisture content, assuring good keeping quality. The first step in the milling process is the removal of the husk, leaving what is known as "natural brown rice." If the milling is carried further the next step involves the grinding away of several outer layers of the grain. This results in white rice. It also produces such by-products as rice bran and rice polishings, used mainly as stock feeds. In the next step all broken particles and any foreign seeds or defective grains are screened out, leaving clean white rice. Finer particles of broken rice are used in making beer. Larger broken particles are sometimes mixed with whole grains for extremely low-cost table rice, where economy is the main factor. Years ago rice was given a coating of talc or glucose, which is why old recipes say "wash rice until the water runs clear." Nowadays this is not necessary. Rice no longer requires washing when it comes from a package.

Brown rice is rich in the vitamins of the B complex, thiamine, niacin, and riboflavin, and in iron and calcium. It is higher in many of these vitamins and minerals than enriched, parboiled, or other processed rice. Cooking time for brown rice is about 40-45 minutes.

Availability and Purchasing Guide—Packaged rice is available year round. The varieties include **brown rice,** which has a nutlike flavor and requires a comparatively long cooking time; and **short-** and **long-grain** white rice. Most rice is short grain unless the package specifically states otherwise. When cooked, short-grain rice is moister and more tender than long-grain rice, which cooks more quickly and is drier and fluffier. Carolina and Honduras types are long-grain rices.

Parboiled white rice is a long-grain rice parboiled, steamed, and dried, a process designed to retain many of the nutrients otherwise lost in milling. It takes longer to cook than regular rice. **Precooked rice** is long-grain rice that has been cooked, rinsed, and dried, and requires only a short heating period before serving. **Enriched rice** has had iron and B vitamins added to it.

Other rice products are available. Spanish rice, chicken and rice dinners, soup, and pudding are available in cans. Fried rice is included in frozen Chinese dinners. Mixes are available for rice pudding and for a rice and vermicelli product with meat, cheese, or vegetable flavoring. Regular, quick-cooking, and ready-to-eat rice cereals are also available. There is a waxy rice flour which is used by persons allergic to wheat flours. It has also found use as a stabilizer in frozen sauces and gravies.

1 cup regular rice = 3 cups cooked
1 cup parboiled rice = 4 cups cooked

1 cup brown rice = 4 cups cooked
1 cup precooked rice = 2 cups cooked

Storage—Store in covered container in a cool dry place. Rice will keep almost indefinitely.

Nutritive Food Values—Rice contains some calcium and iron, and the B-complex vitamins thiamine, riboflavin, and niacin. Brown rice is richer in these minerals and vitamins than the other types of rice.
Brown rice, ⅔ cup (3½ ounces), cooked = 119 calories
White rice, all types, ⅔ cup (3½ ounces), cooked = 109 calories
Parboiled white rice, ⅔ cup (3½ ounces), cooked = 106 calories
Rice, granulated, breakfast cereal, 3½ ounces, cooked = 50 calories
Rice flakes, 1 ounce = 109 calories
Rice, puffed, 1 cup (½ ounce) = 60 calories

HOW TO COOK SUPERBLY: RICE

by HELEN EVANS BROWN

The Indians and Chinese are probably born knowing how to cook rice perfectly, but it's an art that doesn't come as easily to many of us. However, we can learn to cook it so that each grain is separate and dry, yet tender, not gummy or sticky. There are several ways to accomplish this and good cooks have been known to come to blows over which is the right one. I think perhaps you should decide for yourself, so I'll give you several recipes for cooking plain rice. But before we begin I should warn you that there are even more kinds of rice than there are ways of cooking it. In this country, long-grain rice from Louisiana and Texas is usually the most satisfactory, as it cooks into fluffy white grains, but short-grain rice from California is fine for puddings and soups. Then there is Spanish-type rice, which has a short plump grain, Patna rice from India, with a long narrow grain, Japanese rice, Chinese rice, Italian rice, hundreds of rices; not counting wild rice, which is the seeds of a tall wild aquatic grass which the Indians have harvested in northwestern North America for many hundreds of years. It has become very expensive and is often mixed with long-grain rice for economy. There's also parboiled rice, which is uncooked but is treated to preserve the food values lost in polishing, and precooked rice, which is quick to prepare. Most white rice today is lightly milled so that it retains its natural qualities. Brown rice has only the husks removed. Most rices may be cooked the same way, but some require a longer cooking time than others. Long-grain Louisiana rice was used in these recipes, so if you are using other varieties, start testing for tenderness sooner, and if necessary, cook longer. In these recipes the rice was not washed first, but if you prefer to do it that way, go ahead.

TO TEST FOR TENDERNESS
The easiest way is to taste. Scoop out a few grains and bite into them. The grains should have no hardness in the center. As soon as the grains are tender all through but still firm, the rice is done.

RICE MEASUREMENTS
A pound of rice measures 2¼ cups; 1 cup rice weighs about 6¾ ounces; ¼ pound rice is a heaping ½ cup. Rice increases in bulk a little over three times when cooked. Allow 1 cup rice for each 3 to 6 servings, depending upon whether it is an accompaniment to meats and vegetables or the basis of a one-dish meal.

EQUIPMENT
You won't need any special equipment when cooking rice recipes. The usual casseroles, skillets, saucepans, molds, measures, spoons, double boiler, rotary beater, and strainer are all that will be necessary.

BASIC PREPARATION
To Boil—Add 1 teaspoon salt to 8 cups rapidly boiling water in a large pot, then slowly dribble in 1 cup rice. Do not cover and do not stir. Start testing at about 15 minutes (18 minutes is usually right for long-grain; 15 minutes for short-grain). Drain rice and then rinse in hot water and put in a warm oven to dry out more, or serve as is. I find that rice cooked this way, then rinsed in cold water and put overnight in the refrigerator in an uncovered dish, becomes marvelously dry. It reheats easily in double boiler or in a lightly buttered casserole in a preheated moderate oven.

To Cook Oriental Style—Add ½ teaspoon salt to 2 cups rapidly boiling water, then slowly add 1 cup raw rice. Shake pot to level rice, cover, and reduce heat as low as possible. Cook for 18 to 25 minutes. Don't remove cover until first testing.

To Bake—Preheat oven to slow (300°F.). Put ½ teaspoon salt, 1 cup raw rice, and 1 tablespoon butter in a 1½- or 2-quart casserole. Pour on 2 cups rapidly boiling water, cover, and put in the oven for 30 minutes. Turn off oven, remove cover, put a folded paper towel over the top of the casserole, and leave the oven door open to dry out rice. Bouillon may be used in place of water, and butter and salt omitted.

To Toast—Distribute 1 cup raw rice as evenly as possible on a cookie sheet and put in preheated hot oven (400°F.) for 6 to 10 minutes, or until golden brown, stirring occasionally so that it will color evenly. Proceed exactly as for Baked Rice, above. Rice may also be toasted before boiling or steaming.

Variations for Plain Rice—Either of the following, added to cooked rice, gives it added interest. To each 3 cups cooked rice (1 cup raw), add:

1 cup mushrooms which have been sliced and sautéed in 3 tablespoons butter for 6 minutes.

½ cup slivered almonds which have been stirred over heat with 3 tablespoons butter until golden.

RICE COOKBOOK

NOTE: If you don't have chicken broth, make some by covering 3 pounds of chicken backs, wing tips, and necks with 2 quarts boiling water; add 2 teaspoons salt and an herb bouquet, and simmer for 1½ hours, or until reduced to 6 cups. Strain, and discard bones. Chill, and remove hardened fat on top.

SOUPS

PURÉE OF RICE

- ½ cup chopped onion
- 2 tablespoons butter or margarine
- ½ cup chopped carrot
- 2 tablespoons raw rice
- 3 cups bouillon, preferably chicken
- 1 cup cream, light or heavy
- Salt and pepper
- Rice Balls

Cook onion in butter until golden. Add carrot, rice, and bouillon and bring to a boil. Turn heat low and simmer for 30 to 40 minutes, or until rice is very soft. Strain, pressing rice and vegetables through a strainer, or whirl smooth in a blender (you'll have to do this in two batches). Return to pot, add cream, and season to taste. Serve with Rice Balls or croutons. Makes 4 servings.

Variations—This may be seasoned with 1 to 3 teaspoons curry powder, or with 2 tablespoons minced chives, or ½ cup cooked sorrel, chopped fine, or with anything else that appeals to you. Make up your own version, and serve it hot or cold.

Rice Balls

Mix ¾ cup cooked rice with 2 tablespoons butter, 1 egg yolk, 2 tablespoons grated Parmesan cheese, ¼ teaspoon salt, and a dash of cayenne. Cook, stirring, over low heat for 4 minutes, then cool. Form into tiny balls, roll them in 2 tablespoons all-purpose flour, then dip into slightly beaten egg. Fry in deep hot fat (370°F. on a frying thermometer) until golden-brown and crispy. Drain on paper towels.

GREEK RICE SOUP

- 6 cups seasoned chicken broth (See note)
- ⅓ cup raw rice
- 2 eggs
- 3 tablespoons lemon juice
- Salt and pepper

Heat broth, add rice, and cook for 20 minutes. Beat eggs well, then beat in about ½ cup hot chicken broth. Add lemon juice and pour into remaining broth and rice. Mix well, correct seasoning, and serve hot. Makes 6 servings.

MAIN DISHES

SHRIMP AND RICE JAMBALAYA

- 4 slices of bacon, diced
- 1 medium onion, minced
- ½ medium green pepper, diced
- 2 cups chicken bouillon
- ½ cup catsup
- 2 tablespoons firmly packed brown sugar
- 1 package (10 ounces) frozen shelled shrimps, cooked
- 1 cup finely diced cooked ham
- 2 tablespoons cornstarch
- 3 tablespoons cold water
- Salt and pepper to taste
- Hot cooked rice

Cook bacon until crisp. Remove bacon, and cook onion and pepper in the fat for 5 minutes. Add next 3 ingredients. Simmer, covered, for 15 minutes. Cut shrimps into pieces. Add with ham to first mixture. Heat well; thicken with blended cornstarch and water; season; serve on rice. Makes 4 servings.

HAM-CHEESE RICE BAKE

- 1 small onion, minced
- 6 tablespoons butter or margarine
- 3 tablespoons all-purpose flour
- 1 teaspoon salt
- ⅛ teaspoon pepper
- ½ teaspoon dry mustard
- 1 teaspoon Worcestershire
- 2 cups milk
- ½ pound sharp Cheddar cheese
- ½ cup diced cooked ham
- 1 can (8 ounces) peas, drained
- 4 cups hot cooked rice
- 3 tablespoons fine dry bread crumbs

Cook onion in ¼ cup butter for 5 minutes. Blend in flour and seasonings; add milk. Cook, stirring constantly, until thick and smooth. Dice half of cheese and add to mixture. Stir until blended. Add ham and peas. Slice remaining half of cheese. Put half of rice in greased shallow baking dish. Cover with layer of sliced cheese; pour half of hot mixture over top. Repeat. Sprinkle with crumbs; dot with remaining 2 tablespoons butter. Bake in preheated hot oven (400°F.) for 20 minutes, or until lightly browned and bubbly. Makes 4 to 6 servings.

HAM- AND RICE-STUFFED PEPPERS

- 4 large green peppers
- 2¾ cups boiling water
- 1 cup raw rice
- 1 medium onion, minced
- 2 tablespoons butter or margarine
- ½ pound process American cheese, diced
- 1 cup diced cooked ham
- 2 tablespoons minced parsley
- Salt and pepper

Cut peppers into halves crosswise. Remove seeds. Cook peppers in 2 cups boiling water for 5 minutes. Drain, reserving liquid. Cook rice until tender; drain. Sauté onion in hot butter for 5 minutes. Add remaining ¾ cup water and diced cheese. Stir until blended. Add rice, ham, parsley, and salt and pepper to taste. Fill pepper halves. Put on rack in skillet with 1½ cups pepper liquid in bottom. Simmer, covered, about 15 minutes. Makes 4 servings.

BAKED RICE, PORK, AND CABBAGE

- ¾ pound boneless lean pork
- ½ cup raw rice
- 1½ teaspoons salt
- ¼ teaspoon pepper
- 8 cabbage leaves
- 1 small onion, minced
- 1 tablespoon cooking oil
- 1 can (10½ ounces) condensed tomato soup
- ¾ cup water

Cut pork into ½-inch cubes and mix with rice, salt, and pepper. Cook cabbage leaves in boiling salted water until limp. Fill each leaf with about ⅓ cup meat mixture and roll up loosely. Put seam side down in greased baking dish. Cook onion in oil for 5 minutes. Add soup and water; mix well, and pour over cabbage rolls. Bake, covered, in preheated moderate oven (375°F.) about 1½ hours. Makes 4 servings.

BAKED TURKEY AND RICE

- 1½ cups packaged precooked rice
- 1½ cups boiling water
- ¾ teaspoon salt
- 2 tablespoons instant minced onion
- 1 teaspoon curry powder
- 2 cups diced cooked turkey
- 6 olives, sliced
- 1 can (10½ ounces) condensed cream-of-mushroom soup
- ½ cup milk
- ½ cup grated Cheddar cheese
- ¼ cup corn-flake crumbs

Prepare rice with water and salt as directed on the label. Add onion and curry powder; put in greased shallow baking dish. Cover with turkey and sprinkle with olives. Mix soup and milk; pour over top. Sprinkle with cheese and crumbs. Bake in preheated moderate oven (350°F.) about 30 minutes. Makes 6 servings.

RICE AND PORK CASSEROLE

- 4 pork chops
- Salt and pepper to taste
- 2 chicken bouillon cubes
- 2 cups hot water
- 1 cup raw rice
- ½ green pepper, chopped
- 2 green onions, sliced
- 1 tomato, peeled and diced
- Paprika

Brown chops and put in shallow baking dish. Season with salt and pepper. Dissolve bouillon cubes in water; pour over chops. Add next 4 ingredients. Sprinkle top with pepper and paprika. Cover tightly, with foil if cover is not available, and bake in preheated moderate oven (350°F.) about 1 hour. Makes 4 servings.

BOK YOU GUY

- 1 frying chicken (about 2½ pounds), cut up
- 1½ cups water
- 3 tablespoons soy sauce
- 3 tablespoons cornstarch
- 1 cup raw rice, cooked
- ½ cup seedless raisins
- ½ cup peanuts
- Flaked coconut

Simmer chicken in water with soy sauce for 45 minutes, or until tender. Thicken liquid with cornstarch mixed with a little cold water. Combine hot rice and raisins; sprinkle with peanuts and coconut. Serve with chicken and gravy. Makes 4 servings.

SPANISH CHICKEN WITH RICE

- 1 frying chicken (about 2½ pounds), cut up
- Salt
- 3 tablespoons olive oil
- 1 large onion, chopped
- 1 garlic clove, minced
- 1 medium green pepper, chopped
- 1 can (1 pound 3 ounces) tomatoes
- ⅓ cup sherry
- ¼ teaspoon pepper
- Dash of ground saffron
- ½ teaspoon paprika
- 2 whole cloves
- 1 crumbled bay leaf
- 1 cup water
- 1¼ cups raw long-grain rice
- 1 cup cooked peas
- 1 pimiento, cut up

Season chicken with salt. Brown in oil. Add onion, garlic, and green pepper, and brown about 5 minutes longer. Add remaining ingredients except rice, peas, and pimiento; simmer, covered, for 15 minutes. Add rice, bring to boil, stirring constantly. Cover, and simmer about 30 minutes. Garnish with peas and pimiento. Makes 4 to 6 servings.

RICE

SALADS

MAIN-DISH RICE SALAD

1½ cups packaged precooked rice
1½ cups boiling water
¾ teaspoon salt
2 tablespoons dry mustard
2 tablespoons cold water
1½ teaspoons sugar
2 tablespoons wine vinegar
¼ cup cooking oil
½ green pepper, chopped
1 cup diced cooked ham
½ cup cooked peas
   Chopped parsley
   Salad greens

Prepare rice with boiling water and salt as directed on the label. Mix next 4 ingredients and gradually beat in oil. Stir lightly into warm rice. Cool; add next 3 ingredients. Add more salt if necessary. Sprinkle with parsley and serve with greens. Makes 4 servings.

RICE-TUNA SALAD SUPREME

1 can (7 ounces) tuna, drained and flaked
3 cups cold cooked rice
6 pimiento-stuffed olives, sliced
⅓ cup chopped sweet pickle
2 tablespoons minced green pepper
1½ cups finely chopped celery
2 tablespoons minced parsley
½ cup mayonnaise
½ cup dairy sour cream
2 tablespoons lemon juice
½ teaspoon salt
¼ teaspoon pepper
   Dash of cayenne
2 pimientos, diced
   Mask
1 hard-cooked egg yolk
   Salad greens

Combine first 7 ingredients. Mix mayonnaise and next 5 ingredients, add to tuna mixture and toss well. Gently stir in pimiento. Pack in 1-quart bowl and chill. Unmold on serving plate. Spread with Mask and sprinkle with sieved hard-cooked egg yolk. Garnish with chicory or other salad greens. Makes 6 to 8 servings.
Mask: Mix ¼ cup each sour cream and mayonnaise.

Rice-Tuna Salad Supreme

RICE AND SEAFOOD SALAD

- 1 cup raw rice, cooked
- ¼ cup salad oil
- 1 tablespoon cider vinegar
- 1½ teaspoon salt
- ½ teaspoon pepper
- 1 cup cooked green peas
- ¼ cup each chopped pimiento, chopped parsley, and minced onion
- 2 tablespoons chopped green pepper
- 1 cup cooked flaked crabmeat
- 1 cup shelled and deveined cooked shrimps
- 1 cup cooked flaked lobster
- ⅔ cup mayonnaise
- 1 tablespoon lemon juice
- Salad greens
- Black olives

Cook rice until tender according to package directions. In the meantime combine oil, vinegar, and salt and pepper to make a French dressing. Drain rice and toss immediately with French dressing; cool. Gently mix in vegetables, crabmeat, shrimps, and lobster; chill. Just before serving time combine mayonnaise with lemon juice. Fold into salad. Pile pyramid fashion on salad greens and decorate with black olives. Makes 8 servings.

GOLDEN GATE SALAD

- 3 cups cold cooked rice
- 2 cups diced cooked chicken
- 1½ cups thinly sliced celery
- 1 cup seedless grapes, halved
- ½ cup mayonnaise
- 3 tablespoons lemon juice
- 1 teaspoon curry powder
- Salt and onion salt
- Salad greens
- Peach halves (optional)

Combine first 4 ingredients. Mix mayonnaise, lemon juice and curry powder and toss lightly with rice mixture. Season to taste with salt and onion salt. Chill until serving time. Serve on salad greens, surrounded with peach halves, if desired. Makes 6 to 8 servings.

RICE-EGG SALAD

- 2 cups cold cooked rice
- 1 cup thinly sliced celery
- ¼ cup diced sweet pickle
- ¾ cup mayonnaise
- 2 tablespoons cider vinegar
- 6 hard-cooked eggs, coarsely chopped
- Salt and pepper
- Salad greens
- Paprika

Combine first 5 ingredients and mix well. Mix in eggs lightly and season to taste with salt and pepper. Refrigerate until serving time. Garnish with salad greens and sprinkle with paprika. Good with ham, frankfurters or cold cuts. Makes 6 servings.

BROWN-RICE SALAD

- 1 cup raw brown rice
- 1 small onion, minced
- ¾ teaspoon salt
- ⅛ teaspoon pepper
- 1 teaspoon sugar
- ⅓ cup cider vinegar
- 3 tablespoons salad oil
- 1½ cups finely chopped celery
- 3 tablespoons minced parsley
- 4 slices bacon, cooked until crisp

Cook rice according to package directions. Put next 5 ingredients in large bowl and let stand about 10 minutes. Add salad oil, then stir in hot rice, celery and parsley. Sprinkle with crumbled bacon and serve warm. Good with cold cuts, frankfurters or sautéed liver. Makes 6 servings.

ITALIAN RICE SALAD WITH VEAL

- 3½ pounds veal cut from the leg
- 4 celery stalks
- 1½ cups olive oil (about)
- 1 carrot
- 10 anchovy fillets
- ½ sour pickle
- 2 cans (7 ounces each) tuna fish
- 1 cup dry white wine
- 2 garlic cloves
- Salt, pepper, dried thyme
- 2 egg yolks
- 1½ cups raw rice
- 2 carrots, chopped
- 1 cup diced celery
- 6 green onions, sliced
- 1 red onion, chopped
- ½ green pepper, chopped
- 12 each ripe and green olives, chopped
- ¼ cup minced parsley
- Tarragon vinegar

Simmer veal, celery stalks, ½ cup olive oil, next 6 ingredients, and seasonings to taste for about 3 hours. When tender, cool in pot. Remove meat and purée mixture in a blender, or force through a food mill. Season to taste with salt, pepper, and thyme. Beat egg yolks. Stir in ½ cup oil, a few drops at a time. When thickened, beat in puréed mixture. Cook and cool rice. Add chopped carrots, diced celery, green and red onion, green pepper, olives, and parsley. Dress to taste with remaining ½ cup oil, vinegar, and additional salt and pepper, if desired. Add a little purée. Serve veal sliced very thin, with the purée as a sauce, and with the rice salad. Garnish with artichokes and pimientos if desired. Makes 8 servings.

RICE

FRENCH RICE SALAD

1 cup raw rice
Oil and vinegar
Salt and pepper
½ pound Port-Salut cheese, cubed
12 radishes, sliced
2 tablespoons chopped walnuts
½ cup chopped watercress

Cook rice; while still warm, dress to taste with oil, vinegar, salt, and pepper. Chill, add other ingredients, and serve. Makes 4 servings.

RICE-VEGETABLE SALAD

1 cup raw rice
2 cups coarsely shredded carrot
½ cup thinly sliced celery
1 green pepper, cut in thin 2-inch strips
3 green onions, thinly sliced
1 cup cooked peas
2 pimientos, diced
½ cup bottled French dressing or other preferred dressing (about)
Salt and pepper

Cook rice according to package directions; cool to room temperature. Add next 6 ingredients. Stir in dressing, and salt and pepper to taste; chill. Makes 6 to 8 servings.
NOTE: Cut-up cooked ham, beef or pork can be added to salad, if desired. Or surround salad with cold-cut slices, folded in half and rolled.

HAWAIIAN RICE SALAD

1 cup raw rice
1 can (13¼ ounces) pineapple tidbits
2 cups finely chopped celery
¾ cup mayonnaise
¼ cup lemon juice
1 can (8 ounces) mandarin oranges

Cook rice according to package directions, using syrup drained from pineapple for part of the water. Put on plate to cool. Add drained pineapple and celery. Mix mayonnaise, lemon juice and 2 tablespoons syrup from mandarin oranges. Stir into rice mixture and fold in drained mandarin oranges; chill. Good with ham, corned beef or smoked tongue. Makes 6 to 8 servings.
NOTE: A few seedless grapes, halved, or pitted grapes can be added to mixture, if desired.

MEAT ACCOMPANIMENTS

ITALIAN RICE AND PEAS

½ cup chopped onion
3 tablespoons butter or margarine
1½ cups shelled peas*
½ cup chopped cooked ham (optional)
1 cup raw rice
3 to 5 cups chicken or beef bouillon
2 tablespoons grated Parmesan cheese

Cook onion in 2 tablespoons butter until golden. Add peas, cook for 1 minute, then add ham (if used) and rice. Cook, stirring, over low heat until the rice becomes golden; then add 3 cups bouillon. Cover, turn heat low, or put in preheated moderate oven (350°F.), and cook until the rice is tender, adding more bouillon if necessary, and stirring lightly with a fork to prevent sticking. This will take from 18 to 30 minutes. The liquid should be absorbed, the rice tender but not mushy. Stir in remaining 1 tablespoon butter and cheese and serve at once, garnished with a little pimiento if desired. Makes 4 to 6 servings.
*1 package (10 ounces) frozen peas may be used; add when rice is half cooked.
NOTE: This dish is excellent to take the place of a vegetable and farinaceous dish, as it is a combination of both. Add ham and it becomes a main dish.

SURPRISE RICE CROQUETTES

2 cups cooked rice
½ cup grated cheese
1 egg, well beaten
2 teaspoons prepared mustard (optional)
1 teaspoon salt
⅛ teaspoon white pepper
1 tablespoon melted butter or margarine
½ inch cubes of your favorite cheese
Fine bread crumbs
Fat for deep frying

Mix rice and grated cheese. Add egg, seasonings, and melted butter. Blend well. Cover each cube of cheese with the rice mixture. Form into croquettes or balls. Roll in bread crumbs. Fry in hot deep fat or oil (365°F. on frying thermometer) for 5 minutes, or until light brown. Drain on absorbent paper. Serve with meats or as a main dish with tomato sauce. Makes 12 to 14 croquettes depending on size.

CURRIED RICE

2½ cups boiling water
1 teaspoon salt
1¼ cups raw rice
¼ cup butter or margarine
1½ teaspoons curry powder
1 package (10 ounces) frozen peas
1 pimiento, cut into strips

Mix first 5 ingredients in Dutch oven or covered casserole. Bake, covered, in preheated hot oven (400°F.) about 45 minutes. Cook and drain peas; mix lightly into rice with fork. Top with pimiento strips. Good with roast lamb, poultry, or pork. Makes 6 servings.

SAUTÉED BROWN RICE AND MUSHROOMS

- 1 medium onion, minced
- ¼ green pepper, minced
- ¼ cup butter or margarine
- 1 can (3 ounces) mushroom stems and pieces, drained
- 3 cups cooked brown rice
- ¾ teaspoon salt
- ⅛ teaspoon pepper
- ½ teaspoon chili powder

Cook onion and green pepper in butter for 5 minutes. Add remaining ingredients. Cook until lightly browned, stirring gently. Makes 4 servings.

FRIED RICE

- ½ cup minced onion
- 3 tablespoons cooking oil
- 6 cups cooked rice
- ½ cup cooked ham, chicken, pork, or shellfish
- ¼ cup water chestnuts and/or bamboo shoots
  Mushrooms, sliced or chopped
- 1 tablespoon soy sauce
- 2 eggs, slightly beaten
  Salt and pepper to taste

Cook minced onion in oil until it colors slightly. Add rice and cook, stirring, over low heat for 2 or 3 minutes; then add meat and water chestnuts slivered into matchlike pieces or chopped. Add sliced or chopped mushrooms or use alone. Mix well, then add soy sauce, eggs, and seasonings. Cook, stirring, over low heat until the egg is cooked. This will take only 2 or 3 minutes. Put into a bowl, pack down, then unmold on a hot dish. If you wish, sprinkle over the top some chopped green onions or some of the same meat, slivered, that is used in the rice. Makes 6 servings, or twice as many if used as one of the dishes in a Chinese meal.
NOTE: This versatile Chinese recipe is wonderful for using up bits of cooked ham, shrimps, pork, chicken, mushrooms, or such. It makes a good main dish for luncheon or supper. Without the additions, it is a good accompaniment for broiled chicken, pork chops, meat loaf, or seafood.

INDIAN KITCHREE

- 1 onion, chopped
- 3 tablespoons butter or margarine
- 1 cup raw rice
- 1 cup dried lentils
- 5 to 7 cups water
  Salt
- 1 teaspoon each pepper and ground coriander
- ¼ teaspoon each ground caraway, cloves, and cardamom
- ½ teaspoon ground cinnamon

Cook onion in butter until soft. Add rice and lentils and cook, stirring, for 2 minutes, then add 5 cups water. Bring to a boil, reduce heat to low, and simmer for 10 minutes. Add spices and salt to taste. Cover and continue to cook until rice and lentils are tender, adding liquid if necessary, and stirring occasionally. Makes 6 servings.
NOTE: 2½ teaspoons curry powder and ½ teaspoon ground pepper may be substituted for the pepper, coriander, caraway, cloves, cardamom, and cinnamon in this recipe.

MEXICAN RICE

- 1 cup minced onions
- ⅓ cup oil, preferably olive
- 1 cup raw rice
- 1 teaspoon salt
- 1 tablespoon chili powder
- 3 to 4 cups tomato juice (part may be bouillon)
- ½ cup sliced chorizo (Spanish sausage)
- ½ cup sliced sautéed mushrooms (optional)

Cook onions in oil for 2 or 3 minutes. Add remaining ingredients. Bring to boil; cover and simmer for 18 to 25 minutes, or until rice is tender. Makes 4 to 6 servings.

YELLOW RICE

- 1 cup raw rice
- 2 tablespoons butter or oil
- 1 teaspoon salt
  Dash ground saffron, or 1 teaspoon ground turmeric, or 2 teaspoons curry powder
- 3 to 4 cups boiling water or bouillon

Cook rice in butter until opaque. Add salt and seasonings and 3 cups liquid. Cover and cook for 16 to 20 minutes, or until the rice is tender. After 18 minutes, stir lightly and add more liquid if necessary. Makes 3 or 4 servings.
NOTE: If whole saffron is used, pound fine in a mortar or steep in ¼ cup of the liquid for 10 minutes, then strain off liquid and use.

BREADS

RICE PANCAKES

Mix well 1 egg, 1 cup pancake mix, and 1½ cups milk. Stir in 1 cup cooked rice. Fry on hot well-greased griddle until browned on both sides. Serve at once with butter and syrup. Makes about 3 dozen 3-inch pancakes.

RICE WAFFLES

Beat until smooth 4 cups buttermilk biscuit mix, 3⅓ cups milk, 2 eggs, and ¼ cup cooking oil. Add 2 cups cooked rice. Cook on hot waffle iron. Serve hot with butter and syrup. Makes 10 waffles, 11 x 6 inches.

RICE RECIPES

Rich Rice Pudding

Mexican Rice

Purée of Rice with Rice Balls

Rice Pudding

NEW ORLEANS RICE FRITTERS

½ package active dry yeast or ½ cake compressed yeast
½ cup water*
1½ cups very soft cooked rice
3 eggs, beaten
1¼ cups sifted all-purpose flour
¼ cup sugar
½ teaspoon salt
¼ teaspoon ground nutmeg
Fat for deep frying

Sprinkle or crumble yeast into water. *Use very warm water (105°F. to 115°F.) for dry yeast; use lukewarm (80°F. to 90°F.) for compressed. Let stand for a few minutes, then stir until dissolved. Mash rice grains and cool to lukewarm. Stir into yeast mixture and mix well. Cover and let rise overnight. Next morning, add eggs, flour, sugar, salt, and nutmeg and beat until smooth. Let stand in a warm place for 30 minutes. Drop by tablespoonfuls into deep hot fat (360°F.) on a frying thermometer) and fry until golden brown, about 3 minutes. Serve sprinkled with confectioners' sugar or sugar mixed with ground cinnamon. Makes 2 dozen.

Poires à l'Imperatrice

Italian Rice and Peas

DESSERTS

RICE PUDDING

Prepare rice as in Pears Condé, instead of molding, put in a baking dish, brush top with 1 tablespoon heavy cream, and brown under broiler. Serve warm or cold.

RICH RICE PUDDING

Prepare rice as in Pears Condé; instead of molding, cool mixture slightly, add ¼ cup seedless raisins heated in ¼ cup sherry, then drained; ¼ cup candied fruit, and 1 cup heavy cream, whipped. Put into serving dish; chill. Sprinkle top with slivered almonds and mint sprigs if desired. Makes 6 servings.

PINEAPPLE RICE PUDDING

Mix 2 cups cooked rice, 2 tablespoons sugar, dash of salt, and 1 can (1 pound, 14½ ounces) crushed pineapple. Chill; fold in 1 cup heavy cream, whipped. Chill. Makes 6 servings.

41

RICE

OLD-TIME RICE PUDDING

½ cup raw rice (not processed)
½ cup sugar
½ teaspoon salt
½ teaspoon ground nutmeg
2 quarts milk
¾ cup seedless raisins

Mix rice, sugar, salt, and nutmeg in a shallow 2½-quart baking dish. Add 1 quart milk. Then, to prevent spilling, add second quart of milk after placing dish in the oven. Bake in preheated moderate oven (325°F.) for 2½ hours, stirring twice during first hour. Stir the brown crust into pudding several times during the remainder of baking. Add raisins 30 minutes before pudding is done. Then allow crust to form again. Serve with cream if desired. Makes 6 to 8 servings.
NOTE: Can be made with brown rice.

Butterscotch Rice Pudding

In Old-time Rice Pudding recipe, substitute ⅔ cup firmly packed brown sugar for the ½ cup granulated sugar. Omit raisins if desired. Serve cold.

Date Rice Pudding

In Old-time Rice Pudding recipe, substitute ¾ cup chopped pitted dates for the raisins.

CUSTARD RICE PUDDING

½ cup raw rice, cooked
3 eggs, beaten
½ cup sugar
¼ teaspoon salt
1 teaspoon vanilla extract
1½ teaspoons grated lemon rind
½ cup seedless raisins
3½ cups milk
Ground nutmeg

Mix all ingredients except nutmeg. Pour into greased shallow baking dish and sprinkle with nutmeg. Set in pan of hot water and bake in preheated slow oven (300°F.) about 1½ hours. Serve warm or cool. Makes 6 servings.

WALNUT-RICE FRITTERS

1 cup sifted all-purpose flour
1 teaspoon baking powder
1 teaspoon salt
3 eggs, slightly beaten
½ cup milk
2 tablespoons cooking oil
2 cups cooked brown rice
½ cup chopped walnuts
Fat for deep frying
Maple syrup

Sift dry ingredients into a bowl. Add eggs, milk, and oil; beat until smooth. Stir in rice and nuts. Drop by teaspoonfuls into deep hot fat (365°F. on a frying thermometer) and fry until golden brown and done. serve very hot with syrup. Makes about 22.

SWEET SCRAMBLED RICE

¼ cup seedless raisins
¼ cup rum
1 cup raw rice
¼ teaspoon salt
1¼ cups sugar (about)
3 cups milk
2 tablespoons chopped nuts
Grated rind of 1 lemon
1 egg, beaten
½ cup butter
Ground cinnamon

Soak raisins in rum for several hours. Cook rice, salt, and 1 cup sugar in milk in top part of double boiler over boiling water for 30 minutes, or until rice is tender and milk is absorbed, stirring occasionally. Add raisins, nuts, lemon rind, and egg. Melt butter in skillet, add rice mixture, and cook, letting brown crusts form. Turn and brown remainder. Sprinkle with remaining ¼ cup sugar and cinnamon. Makes 4 to 6 servings.

PEARS CONDÉ

1 can (1 pound 13 ounces) pear halves or 6 fresh pears
2 cups water
2⅓ cups sugar
2 teaspoons vanilla extract
4 cups boiling water
¾ cup raw rice
2 cups milk
¼ teaspoon salt
2 tablespoons butter
4 egg yolks
1 cup heavy cream, whipped

You may use either canned or fresh pears for this French dessert. If fresh are used, select 6 firm ones and leave whole. Make a syrup by combining water, 2 cups sugar, and 1 teaspoon vanilla. Bring to a boil, add pears, and cook, turning, for 3 minutes, or until skins loosen. You will probably have to do 3 at a time. Remove from syrup. When cool enough to handle, peel off skins, cut pears into halves, and remove stems and cores. Return to syrup and simmer about 7 minutes, or until a toothpick slips in easily. Drain; you can use the syrup again. Pour boiling water over rice and allow to stand for 10 minutes, then drain. Put 2 cups milk in the top part of a double boiler and scald (cook over direct heat until tiny bubbles form around the edge). Remove from heat, add rice, salt, remaining ⅓ cup sugar, and butter. Cover, put over hot water, and cook for 1 hour, or until the rice is tender. Remove from heat. Beat egg yolks and remaining 1 teaspoon vanilla until well mixed; add a little hot rice, and mix well; then combine with remaining rice. Taste and add more salt and sugar if needed; mix well. Butter a

3- or 4-cup mold, or a ring mold if you have it, and pack in the rice. Chill, and unmold. Surround with poached pears and garnish with whipped cream. If ring mold is used, put cream in center. Makes 6 servings.

RICE À L'IMPÉRATRICE

- 3 cups boiling water
- ½ cup raw rice
- 2 cups milk
- 1 piece (1 inch) vanilla bean or 1 teaspoon vanilla extract
- 1 envelope unflavored gelatin
- 2 tablespoons cold water
- 3 egg yolks
- ⅓ cup sugar
- ¼ teaspoon salt
- ½ to ¾ cup slivered candied fruit
- 3 tablespoons kirsch or other liqueur
- 1 cup heavy cream, whipped
- Additional candied fruit and whipped cream (optional)

Pour boiling water over rice and let stand for 5 minutes. Drain. Put rice into a heavy pan with 1¼ cups milk. Bring to a boil, reduce heat, and simmer without stirring until the rice is tender, 30 to 40 minutes. Heat remaining ¾ cup milk with vanilla bean. In the meantime, soften gelatin in cold water and beat egg yolks with sugar and salt. Pour a little hot milk into egg mixture, then combine both mixtures and gelatin. Heat, stirring, until it begins to thicken. Add rice and chill. Soak candied fruit (mixed peels) in kirsch (or any liqueur or rum or brandy). When the rice starts to set, mix in fruits and whipped cream; pour into 1½-quart mold. Chill until set. Unmold in a fancy dish. Garnish with candied cherries and strips of angelica and more whipped cream, if desired. Makes 6 servings.

POIRES À L'IMPÉRATRICE

Halves of canned pears may be used for this, although the classic version calls for poaching fresh pears in vanilla syrup (see Pears Condé). Make the Rice à l'Impératrice and turn it into 6-cup ring mold. Chill and unmold on a round dish. Arrange pears around the edge, having them small end up, like a crown, and fill the center with sweetened whipped cream. Decorate with mint sprigs, candied cherries, and angelica. Makes 6 servings.

RICE FLOUR—Ground rice made principally from the rice broken during milling. It cannot be used in breadmaking but is used commercially for making ice creams and confections. It is also widely used by the Chinese in making rice cookies, etc. Another use is by persons on allergy diets. It can be purchased in health-food stores or stores selling oriental products.

RICE, TO—To press a vegetable, especially a potato, through a heavy sievelike utensil, which reduces it to ricelike pellets.

ROAST, TO—The phrases "to roast" and "to bake" both refer to a method of cooking by exposing food to dry heat. It can be the enclosed heat of an oven or the open heat of a fire. If an open fire is used, the food to be roasted can be placed on a spit, or buried in hot ashes. Usage determines whether we say "roast" or "bake," and in general roasting is used in reference to the cooking of meats, baking to other foods. There are, however, exceptions: the commercial process of removing the excess moisture from coffee, cocoa, etc., is called "roasting"; and we speak of roasted chestnuts and roasted corn on-the-cob. On the other hand, we say "baked ham."

Whichever word is used, roasting is one of the oldest methods of cooking in the world, if not *the* oldest and most universal. Since it does not necessarily call for a pot or pan, it was easier for primitive man than boiling or frying. The earliest roasting was probably of two kinds: foods were buried in hot ashes or placed on sticks or spits. Spit roasting used to be much more common than it is now. In colonial days, the huge fireplace of every kitchen normally contained a spit. Oven roasting was done in an oven in the wall off the fireplace.

Nowadays, oven roasting is the method most often used, in a range oven, in top-stove ovens, or in portable electric ovens. However, electric rotisseries are popular for both indoor and outdoor cooking. Rotisserie roasting is the modern equivalent of spit roasting.

Poultry and the tender cuts of meat or "roasts" are the foods most often selected for roasting. A large shallow pan and a rack are the best equipment. The rack allows the heat to circulate under and around the roast. A broiler pan and a cake rack can be used. Helpful but not essential are: a bulb-handled baster, a pair of large metal tongs, and a meat thermometer.

Wipe the meat with a damp cloth and dry thoroughly. If the meat is too lean, it may be larded with a larding needle or by pushing strips of bacon or salt pork into it with an ice pick or a knitting needle. Season with salt and pepper, or don't season, as you prefer. Some claim that salting draws the juices out of the roast and that it is better done halfway through the cooking when the outside of the meat has been seared. The uncooked roast may be seasoned with garlic slivers, herbs, and spices by making tiny incisions in the surface of the meat and inserting the seasoning with the point of a knife.

Put the meat, fat side up, on the rack in the pan. Give lean meats, such as veal, lamb, poultry, or birds which have not been larded, a covering of either rubbed-on butter or olive oil, slices of bacon, salt pork, or suet. The fat will baste the meat and prevent it from drying out; this will make the roast more tender.

Insert the shaft of the meat thermometer into the thickest part of the meat. It must *not* touch bone, fat, or gristle. If the roast is slender, insert it on a slant. For a bird, insert the meat thermometer in to the thickest part of the thigh. If the bird is stuffed, place it in the center of the stuffing.

Unless a recipe specifies otherwise, put a roast in a preheated oven for the most accurate timing of cooking period.

Generally speaking, low temperatures of 300°F. to

Roast Loin of Pork with Fruit and Vegetables

350°F. are best for roasting meats since these temperatures keep the meat juicy and tender. However, roasting directions in the individual recipe should be followed.

Cook a roast to about 10° under the meat-thermometer temperature you want, since the meat continues cooking after it has been taken out of the oven. This is particularly important if rare meat is desired. Remove the meat from the oven, stand it on a heated platter or carving board, and let it stand at room temperature for 15 to 25 minutes, depending on the size of the roast. The meat will go on cooking inside, but the connective tissues and juices will have time to settle from the softening which has taken place during cooking, and the meat will be easier to carve.

ROCK CORNISH HEN or CORNISH GAME HEN—A small fowl with small bones and all white meat. It was developed from the Cornish hen, an English breed of domestic fowl with a pea comb, very close feathering, and a compact, sturdy body. Rock Cornish hens weigh from one-half to one and a quarter pounds and are good broiled or roasted.

Availability and Purchasing Guide—Available year round frozen whole, unstuffed or with wild-rice stuffing.

A few producers now sell fresh cornish hens; as they have very little fat they can become dry. Cook and serve them promptly.

Storage—Refrigerator frozen-food compartment: 4 to 5 weeks
Freezer: 6 months
Fresh uncooked, refrigerator shelf: 1 to 2 days

GLAZED ROASTED STUFFED ROCK CORNISH HENS

6 frozen Rock Cornish hens
   Pecan Stuffing
½ cup butter, melted
   Salt and pepper to taste
1 cup beef bouillon
2 tablespoons cornstarch
3 tablespoons cold water

Thaw Cornish hens. Stuff with Pecan Stuffing; secure with toothpicks and tie legs together. Put in shallow roasting pan; pour butter over birds. Sprinkle with salt and pepper. Roast in preheated hot oven (425°F.) for 1 to 1¼ hours, basting twice with drippings in pan. When done, glaze with hot bouillon thickened with cornstarch mixed with water. Makes 6 servings.

Pecan Stuffing

- 1 medium onion, chopped
- ½ cup chopped celery
- ½ cup butter or margarine
- 1 teaspoon salt
- ½ teaspoon paprika
- 5 cups diced stale bread
- 1½ cups chopped pecans
- ½ cup chopped parsley

Sauté onion and celery in butter for about 5 minutes. Add salt and paprika. Mix lightly with remaining ingredients.

ROCKFISH
—The name given to a large genus, *Sebastodes,* of salt-water food fish found along the Pacific coast from California to Alaska. The fish is sometimes mistakenly called the rock cod. Among the best known and most valuable rockfish are the black fish, bocaccio, rasher, red rockfish, Spanish flag, yellow-backed rockfish, and the yellowtail rockfish. The skin varies in color from dark gray to bright orange and the meat from almost a pure white to a deep pink. The texture and flavor of the meat of all the species seem to be the same: texture is firm and when cooked, it is white and flaky, resembling crabmeat; flavor also resembles crabmeat and the fish is often steamed and used for salads, etc., just as crabmeat is. Baking and oven-steaming are favorite methods of preparation. The steamed fish is good with such sauces as Newburg, cheese, herb butter, etc.

Availability—Year round, sold fresh, whole, and dressed, or as fillets.

Storage—See Red Snapper.

Nutritive Food Values—4 ounces, oven-steamed = 121 calories

Basic Preparation—See Red Snapper.
  To Oven-Steam—Wipe fish fillets with damp cloth. Sprinkle lightly with salt and put in a casserole. Cover and bake in preheated moderate oven (350°F.) for 30 minutes, or until fish can be shredded easily with a fork.

ROCKFISH EN PAPILLOTE

- 4 shallots, chopped
- ¼ cup chopped mushrooms
- Butter or margarine
- ¼ cup all-purpose flour
- 1 cup white wine
- 1 cup heavy cream
- 1 egg yolk
- Salt and pepper
- 6 large mushrooms
- 1½ pounds rockfish, cut into serving pieces
- 6 shrimps, cooked, shelled, and cleaned

Sauté shallots and mushrooms in ¼ cup butter for 5 minutes. Blend in flour, wine, and cream. Cook, stirring constantly, until smooth and thickened. Beat in egg yolk and season to taste with salt and pepper. Chill. Cut 6 heart-shape pieces of foil about 11 x 8½ inches, allowing one sheet for each serving. Sauté 6 mushrooms lightly in 1 tablespoon butter. Spread a little chilled wine mixture on one-half of foil heart, put a piece of fish on it, and top with a mushroom and a shrimp. Add about ½ cup more mixture. Fold foil and double-fold the edges, crimping firmly. Bake in preheated very hot oven (450°F.) about 15 minutes. Serve in the foil. Makes 6 servings.

CURRIED ROCKFISH SALAD

Oven-steam 1 pound rockfish fillets. Chill fish, and shred. Add 2 cups diced celery, and mayonnaise to moisten. Season with salt, pepper, and curry powder to taste. Serve in lettuce cups. Makes 6 to 8 servings.

ROCK LOBSTER
—A member of the family of Crustaceans which have crusty outer shells with jointed bodies and limbs. The meat of these sea-creatures is highly valued as a delicacy and is becoming scarce and expensive. Rock lobsters, also known as spiny lobsters in the Caribbean and Gulf of Mexico are the same species as the Cape lobsters of South Africa. They are related to the North American lobster but lack the meaty claws of their Atlantic cousins. For availability, purchasing guide, storage and preparation, refer to LOBSTER.

CURRIED LOBSTER WITH PINEAPPLE

- 6 frozen rock-lobster tails (5 ounces each, or 30 ounces total)
- Salt
- ¼ cup butter or margarine
- ¼ cup all-purpose flour
- 1 teaspoon (or more) curry powder
- 1½ cups chicken broth
- 1 can (8 ounces) pineapple tidbits, drained
- 1 can (2 ounces) water chestnuts, drained and finely diced
- ¼ cup canned pimiento
- ¼ cup chopped green pepper
- ½ cup coarsely chopped cashew nuts
- Hot cooked saffron rice

Drop lobster tails into boiling salted water. Bring again to boil and boil 6 minutes. Drain and drench with cold water. Cut away underside membrane, remove meat and dice coarsely. Melt butter and blend in flour and curry powder. Gradually add broth and cook, stirring, until thickened. Add lobster meat and remaining ingredients, except rice, and heat well. Add salt to taste and serve on bed of rice. Makes 6 to 8 servings.

ROE

ROCK-LOBSTER AND POTATO SALAD

    8 frozen rock-lobster tails (3 ounces each, or 24 ounces total)
    Salt
    6 raw medium potatoes
    1 small onion, minced
    ¼ teaspoon white pepper
    1½ cups mayonnaise
    ¼ cup heavy cream or dairy sour cream

Drop lobster tails into boiling salted water. Bring again to boil and boil 2 minutes. Drain and drench with cold water. Cut away underside membrane, remove meat and chill. Cook and drain potatoes. While still warm, cut in cubes and add onion, 1 teaspoon salt and pepper. Mix mayonnaise and cream and pour over potatoes. Cool, then chill. At serving time, cut lobster meat in bite-size pieces and add to first mixture. Toss until well combined. Makes 8 servings.

ROE—Fish eggs still enclosed in the thin natural membrane in which they are found in the female fish are called roe or hard roe. Roe is taken from many species of fish and is now available in food stores year round in most sections of the country. Shad roe is perhaps the most popular and best known. However, the fish industry is marketing large quantities of roe in fresh, frozen, and canned forms from many different fish including alewife, herring, cod, mackerel, mullet, salmon, shad, and whitefish. The size of roe varies with the fish. Shad roe is usually from five to six inches long, about three inches wide, and an inch or more thick. The canned variety is somewhat smaller in size.

    Sturgeon roe is so scarce that it is widely reserved for the making of caviar, which is hard roe, salted down. A large part of the salmon and whitefish roe is also used for this purpose.

    Soft roe or milt is the male fish's reproductive gland when filled with secretion, or the secretion itself. It has a soft creamy consistency and the vein must be removed before cooking.

    Hard roe has a grainy texture when cooked. It can be poached, broiled, or baked.

Nutritive Food Values—A source of protein.
Cod and shad, 4 ounces, cooked = 143 calories
Canned cod, haddock, or herring, 4 ounces, solids and liquid = 134 calories

Basic Preparation—Before cooking hard roe, the membrane holding the eggs together should be pricked with a needle to prevent its bursting. The roe should be cooked slowly and gently to prevent excessive drying.

DEVILED ROE

    1½ pounds roe
    1½ teaspoons prepared mustard
    1 teaspoon anchovy paste
    1 tablespoon Worcestershire
    Dash each cayenne and dried rosemary
    1 tablespoon butter, melted
    3 tablespoons dry sherry
    3 drops Angostura bitters
    4 slices of hot buttered toast
    Parsley sprigs

Put roe in saucepan and cover with boiling water. Bring to boil and simmer, covered, for 15 minutes. Drain, and cut roe into 1-inch pieces. Blend remaining ingredients except toast and parsley. Arrange toast on an ovenproof platter. Dip roe pieces into seasoning mixture and arrange on the toast. Put in preheated hot oven (400°F.) for 5 minutes to heat. Garnish with parsley. Makes 4 servings.

ROE EN CASSEROLE

    1½ pounds roe
    1 cup dry sauterne
    1 bay leaf
    2 whole cloves
    3 peppercorns
    6 tablespoons butter or margarine
    2 tablespoons all-purpose flour
    1 cup milk
    Salt and pepper
    1 teaspoon grated onion
    Few parsley sprigs, minced
    1 tablespoon fresh lemon juice
    1 cup toasted soft-bread crumbs
    Paprika

Put roe in saucepan. Add sauterne, bay leaf, cloves, and peppercorns. Bring to boil, cover, and simmer for 15 minutes. Drain, and break roe into pieces with fork. Put a layer in greased 1½-quart casserole. Melt 2 tablespoons butter and blend in flour. Gradually add milk and cook, stirring, until thickened. Season with salt and pepper to taste. Sprinkle roe lightly with salt and pepper, onion, parsley, lemon juice, and crumbs. Pour some of white sauce over crumbs. Continue making layers until all ingredients are used, ending with crumbs. Dot with remaining ¼ cup butter and sprinkle with paprika. Bake in preheated moderate oven (350°F.) for 20 minutes, or until browned. Makes 4 servings.

ROLL—The word is derived from the Latin *rotulus,* a diminutive of *rota,* "wheel," and its most common food usage is as a description of varieties of bread made in the form of small pointed, oval, or round cakes, and generally intended to be eaten for breakfast or dinner.

    The word roll is also used to describe other roll-shape or rolled-up foods, for example: jelly rolls, veal rolls, etc.

ROSE HIP

ROLL, TO—The phrase is used to describe several culinary processes: 1) The flattening of dough into a thin sheet with a rolling pin, as for cookies or piecrust; 2) the shaping of foods such as ground meat, cookie dough, candy, etc., into round balls; 3) the coating of foods with flour or dry crumbs, chopped nuts, parsley, paprika, etc.; 4) the shaping of foods into long tubular shapes which are then sliced, as the dough for refrigerator cookies; 5) the crushing of cookies or crackers into fine crumbs with a rolling pin.

ROMAINE—One of the principal types of lettuce, also known as Cos lettuce. Romaine has a long narrow cylindrical head with stiff leaves and a broad rib. The leaves are dark green on the outside, becoming greenish-white near the center. Romaine is a flavorful and crisp lettuce and it lends itself excellently to tossed salads of mixed greens. Properly refrigerated in a plastic bag, Romaine retains its crispness and quality longer than most lettuces.

ROOT BEER—The bottled beverage generally called root beer nowadays is a non-alcoholic drink containing carbonated water, sugar, caramel coloring, and a combination of natural and artificial flavorings.

Originally, however, root beer was a beverage made by the fermentation of an infusion of roots, barks, and such herbs as sarsaparilla, sassafras, spruce, wild cherry, spikenard, wintergreen, and ginger with sugar and yeast. The action of the yeast on the sugar produced a small percentage of alcohol and the effervescence was caused by the action of the carbon dioxide. A root-beer flavoring or extract is sold in packages in very limited areas.

Nutritive Food Value
Sweetened, 6 fluid ounces (¾ cup) = 75 to 85 calories
Low calorie, 6 fluid ounces (¾ cup) = less than 1 calorie

ROSEFISH—Also known as a redfish, this is a salt-water food fish, *Sebastes marinus,* found in the northern coastal waters of Europe and America. When mature it reaches a length of about eleven inches, weighs between three quarters and one pound, and is a bright rose-red or orange-red in color. It may be marketed as an ocean perch. The fish is fatty, with firm flesh and a bland flavor which makes it suitable for preparation with a variety of sauces.

Availability—Available year round fresh whole or filleted and as frozen fillets, plain, or breaded and fried.

Purchasing Guide—See Red Snapper.

Storage—See Red Snapper.

Nutritive Food Values
Fresh, 3½ ounces, panfried = 227 calories
Frozen, breaded and fried, 3½ ounces, reheated = 319 calories

Basic Preparation—See Red Snapper.

SESAME-BAKED ROSEFISH

2 pounds rosefish fillets, fresh or frozen
Salt
Melted butter or margarine
3 cups soft bread crumbs
¼ teaspoon pepper
¼ cup toasted sesame seed (See Note)
½ teaspoon dried thyme

If frozen fillets are used, thaw until they can be separated. Put in greased shallow baking dish. Sprinkle with salt and cover with ¼ cup melted butter. Mix 1 teaspoon salt, ⅓ cup melted butter, and remaining ingredients. Spread on fish. Bake in preheated moderate oven (375°F.) about 30 minutes. Makes 6 servings.

NOTE: Toast seed in preheated moderate oven (350°F.) 10 minutes.

ROSEFISH MARINARA

2 pounds rosefish fillets, fresh or frozen
¼ cup cooking oil
½ cup minced celery
1 garlic clove, minced
½ teaspoon each salt, sugar, and dried basil
¼ teaspoon cayenne
1 teaspoon dried oregano
¼ cup chopped parsley
1 can (29 ounces) tomatoes

If frozen fillets are used, thaw until they can be separated. Heat oil in large skillet. Add celery and cook for 2 or 3 minutes. Add remaining ingredients except fish and simmer, uncovered, about 25 minutes. Separate fillets and put in another large skillet. Add water to cover. Put lid on skillet and bring to boil. Simmer for 5 to 10 minutes, or until fish flakes easily with a fork. Serve with the hot marinara sauce, and with rice, if desired. Makes 6 servings.

ROSE HIP—The fleshy, swollen red seed capsule of any of various roses, but especially of the wild rose. The capsules are rich in vitamin C and are used commercially in making a vitamin C concentrate sold in health-food stores. They are also sold dried whole, cut, and powdered. Excellent jelly and jam can be prepared from fresh rose hips.

ROSEMARY

ROSE-HIP JAM

3 cups fully ripe rose hips
1 orange
1 lemon
1 cup water
1½ cups sugar

Remove the stiff hairs from calyx end of rose hips, split open, and scrape out the seeds. Wash hips and measure 1½ cups. Cut peel from orange and lemon in thin slivers. Add to the water and boil for 5 minutes. Add sugar and stir until dissolved. Add the juice from the orange and lemon and the rose hips. Cover and simmer for 15 minutes. Uncover and cook until hips are clear and transparent and syrup is thick. Pour into hot sterilized jars; seal. Makes about two ½-pint jars.

ROSEMARY [*Rosemarinus officinalis*]—

A perennial evergreen shrub which grows wild in southern Europe and is cultivated throughout the rest of Europe and the United States. It reaches a height of from four to five feet, and has branching stems which bear long thin dark-green leaves with grayish undersides and a strongly aromatic smell. The leaves, fresh or dried, are used as an herb seasoning.

Rosemary can flavor many dishes. It may be added to fruit cups and various soups, almost any hearty meat or poultry, fish stuffings and creamed seafood dishes, cheese sauces and eggs, herb breads and stuffings, many sauces and marinades, fruit salads, and vegetables such as lentils, mushrooms, peas, potatoes, spinach, and squash.

Rosemary is not limited to culinary endeavors, however. Its sweet smell adds to toilet water and potpourri. It can be used in making wines and cordials, too.

Rosemary, like all herbs, is at its best when fresh. If bought dried, it should be crumbled before using to release the rosemary's full flavor.

FLORENTINE PORK ROAST ARISTA

1 loin of pork (3 to 4 pounds)
3 garlic cloves, halved
1 tablespoon dried rosemary, crushed or 2 tablespoons fresh rosemary leaves
3 whole cloves
Salt and pepper to taste
Water
Red or white dry wine

Trim pork of excess fat. Wet garlic and roll in rosemary. Cut 3 pockets in meat by inserting pointed knife and making each hole large enough to hold a garlic clove. Insert garlic cloves and whole cloves into these pockets; rub meat with salt and pepper. Place on rack in roasting pan with a mixture of equal parts of water and wine, about 2 inches deep. Cook in open pan in preheated slow oven (300°F.). Baste occasionally. Allow 45 minutes of roasting time per pound. Cool in its own juice. The meat should be moist. Serve with cold, not chilled, green beans or broccoli, dressed with a simple French dressing. Makes 6 to 8 servings.

NOTE: This dish can be made successfully with other roasting cuts of pork, with leg of veal, boned rump of veal, and with leg of lamb. Traditionally, Pork Arista is served cold, but it is also good hot.

BROILED FRESH ALBACORE

¼ cup olive oil
¼ cup salad oil
1 bay leaf
Pepper to taste
½ teaspoon salt
½ teaspoon dried rosemary, crushed
Juice of 1 lemon
6 albacore steaks (½ pound each), cut 1 inch thick
Lemon wedges or Hollandaise Sauce

Combine all ingredients except fish and lemon wedges, and blend thoroughly. Marinate albacore steaks in mixture, turning occasionally, for 1 to 3 hours. Grill fish over charcoal or in preheated broiler. Baste with remaining marinade. Cook for 8 to 10 minutes, turning once with spatula. Remove to hot dish and serve with lemon wedges. Makes 6 servings.

ROSEMARY CHICKEN IN CREAM

1 large frying chicken, cut into pieces
¼ cup all-purpose flour
1 teaspoon salt
¼ teaspoon pepper
1 teaspoon rosemary leaves, crushed
2 cups light cream (about)
Hot milk
Chopped parsley

Coat chicken pieces with next 4 ingredients, mixed together. Put in greased shallow baking dish. Almost cover chicken with cream. Bake, uncovered, in preheated slow oven (325°F.) about 2 hours. Turn the chicken pieces after the first hour. If the gravy is too thick, add a little more light cream. At serving time, put chicken pieces on a heated serving dish and keep warm. Stir enough hot milk into gravy to make it desired consistency; pour over chicken. Sprinkle with parsley. Makes 4 servings.

VEAL ROSEMARY

2 tablespoons cooking oil
2 tablespoons butter or margarine
1½ pounds boned veal shoulder, cut into 1-inch cubes
1 onion, chopped
2 tablespoons all-purpose flour
1 teaspoon rosemary leaves, crushed
1 can (1 pound) tomatoes
½ cup dry white wine
1 cup chicken bouillon
Salt and pepper
¼ pound mushrooms, sliced

Heat oil and butter in heavy skillet. Add veal and onion and cook until browned. Stir in flour and rosemary. Add tomatoes, wine, and bouillon. Bring to boil, stirring constantly. Season with salt and pepper to taste. Add mushrooms and pour into greased 2-quart casserole. Cover and bake in preheated moderate oven (350°F.) for 1 hour, or until veal is tender. Good with rice or mashed potatoes. Makes 4 to 6 servings.

ROSETTE—A type of waffle or fried cake made of a thin batter of milk, eggs, and flour, fried in deep fat. Rosettes may be made in a skillet, but preferably they are prepared by dipping a specially shaped rosette iron into the batter and then immersing the iron in the hot fat. As it becomes crisp, the rosette is lifted from the iron and allowed to fry until crisp and brown. A rosette iron consists of a long handle onto which various shapes, such as butterflies, flowers, and rings, are screwed. It may also be a timbale-shape iron. Rosettes can be prepared ahead of time and, after draining on absorbent paper, can be stored in an airtight container. After frying they can be sprinkled with confectioners' sugar or granulated sugar mixed with ground cinnamon. They can also be served as a nonsweet appetizer and can be sprinkled with garlic or celery salt.

To achieve thin crusty rosettes, chill the batter at least two hours before frying. While the fat is heating, let the rosette iron heat too. In this way the rosettes will not stick to the iron and will come off easily.

ROSETTES

- 2 eggs, well beaten
- ¼ teaspoon salt
- 1 cup sifted all-purpose flour
- 1 cup milk
- 2 tablespoons cooking oil
- Fat or oil for deep frying

Beat together all ingredients except fat with a rotary egg beater until smooth and well blended. Chill for 2 hours. Heat fat until 375°F. registers on a frying thermometer. Dip rosette iron into batter until the mold is about three-fourths covered. Do not allow the batter to come above the top of the iron or it will be difficult to remove the rosette. Dip the covered mold into the hot fat. Fry for 25 to 30 seconds. With a fork loosen the rosette and let it float in the fat and fry until brown on both sides. Drain on absorbent paper. Dip rosette iron again into batter and continue frying. Makes about 36 rosettes.

NOTE: For a sweet rosette add 1 tablespoon sugar to the batter.

ROSEWATER—This is an essence distilled from rose petals, and it carries the delicious scent and flavor of the flower.

Rosewater has been known for thousands of years to the countries of the East. It was used for religious ceremonies, such as the purification of temples and mosques, and even for Christian baptism. It also had extensive cosmetic uses.

In the kitchen, rosewater makes an admirable flavoring, used instead of vanilla, almond, and other extracts, or sometimes in conjunction with these. Oriental cookery has always relied on rosewater, and many of the poetic desserts and confections of India, Iran, and Turkey are flavored with it. Victorian cookery made much use of it, and the French do so to this day.

Rosewater can be bought, imported from France or Near Eastern countries like Lebanon, in specialty food stores and shops where Arab groceries are sold.

TURKISH DREAMS

- ⅓ cup melted butter or margarine
- 4 round shredded-wheat biscuits
- ½ cup honey
- ¼ cup sugar
- ¼ cup water
- ⅛ teaspoon salt
- ⅔ cup chopped nuts
- 2 teaspoons rosewater

Pour melted butter over biscuits in shallow baking dish. Bake in preheated hot oven (425°F.) about 20 minutes. Bring remaining ingredients except flavoring to boil. Add flavoring and spoon over biscuits. Serve warm or cool. Makes 4 servings.

INDIAN RAVO

- ½ pound almonds
- Butter
- ¼ pound seedless raisins
- 4 cups milk
- 1 cup sugar
- ¾ cup cream of wheat
- 2 tablespoons rosewater
- ½ teaspoon each ground nutmeg and cardamom

Blanch almonds and slice; fry in butter until golden. Fry raisins lightly, leaving them soft. Drain. Heat milk with sugar, add cream of wheat, and cook until thickened; add rosewater. Mix in thoroughly nutmeg and cardamom without letting the mixture boil and remove from heat at once. Pour into a flat serving dish and sprinkle top with reserved almonds and raisins. Serve hot. Makes 6 servings.

EAST INDIAN ROSE PUDDING

- 1 cup blanched almonds
- 2 tablespoons butter or margarine
- ¾ cup seedless raisins
- 4 cups milk
- 1 cup sugar
- ¾ cup quick-cooking farina
- 2 tablespoons rosewater
- ½ teaspoon each ground nutmeg and cardamom

Slice almonds and brown in butter. Add raisins and sauté lightly. Heat milk with sugar in saucepan. Stir in farina and cook until thickened. stirring frequently. Remove from heat and add flavoring and spices. Pour into serving dish and top with reserved almonds and raisins. Serve warm. Makes 6 servings.

ROTISSERIE

RUSSIAN CREAM

1 cup light cream
¾ cup sugar
1½ teaspoons unflavored gelatin
1 tablespoon cold water
2 tablespoons rosewater
1 cup dairy sour cream
Frozen fruit

Heat light cream and sugar in top part of double boiler until lukewarm. Add gelatin softened in water; stir until dissolved. Remove from heat and cool. Add rosewater. Fold in sour cream beaten to a smooth fluffy consistency. Pour into individual molds. Refrigerate for 3 to 4 hours. Unmold and serve with partially thawed frozen fruit. Makes 4 servings.

SOUR-CREAM DEVONSHIRE PEARS

1 can (1 pound, 13 ounces) pear halves
Juice of 1 orange
Juice of ½ lemon
¼ teaspoon ground ginger
1 cinnamon stick
3 whole cloves
1 cup currant jelly
Red food coloring
1 cup heavy cream
½ cup dairy sour cream
2 tablespoons sugar
2 tablespoons rosewater

Drain pears, reserving syrup. In saucepan mix syrup with orange and lemon juices and spices. Let stand for 1½ hours. Add pears and simmer until thoroughly heated. Cool; chill. Beat jelly until smooth. Add small amount of red coloring and 3 tablespoons liquid from chilled pears. Remove pears to serving dish and cover with jelly mixture. Whip heavy cream until stiff. Fold in remaining ingredients and spoon in a circle on pears. Makes 8 servings.

OLD-FASHIONED ROSEWATER SUGAR COOKIES

1 cup butter or margarine
1¾ cups sugar (about)
2 eggs
4½ cups sifted all-purpose flour
1 teaspoon each baking soda, baking powder, and salt
1 cup dairy sour cream
1 tablespoon rosewater

Cream butter with 1½ cups sugar until fluffy. Add eggs, one at a time, beating well after each addition. Add sifted dry ingredients alternately with sour cream, mixing after each addition until smooth. Blend in rosewater. Wrap in wax paper and chill overnight, or until firm enough to roll. Roll on floured board about ¼ inch thick and cut with 3-inch cookie cutter; put on ungreased cookie sheets. Sprinkle with sugar; bake in preheated moderate oven (375°F.) for 12 minutes, or until browned. Makes about 5 dozen cookies.

ROTISSERIE—There are several meanings for this French word which implies both roasting and rotating. It may be a stationary or portable appliance used to cook foods by rotating them in front of or over a source of heat. Or it may be a shop where meats are roasted and sold. Or again, it may be that part of a restaurant kitchen where the roasting is done by *rôtisseurs*, chefs especially trained in the art of roasting, broiling, and even frying.

Any turning spit that was ever used by primitive man to cook the day's hunt over a campfire was a rotisserie. So were the spits that stood near or in the fireplaces of castles and inns from the Middle Ages on, where flesh and fowl were roasted for the lord and his household, and for travelers. Before electricity, the turning of the spit was done either by the patient hands of apprentices or women.

Rotisserie roasting allows air to circulate around the food as it cooks, and it subjects the food to direct heat. Both factors make for a deliciousness of flavor that cannot be duplicated. This unique flavor is the reason for the popularity of the modern rotisserie.

Skewer or truss any meat, poultry or fish that is to be cooked on the rotisserie, so that no part sticks out to be overcooked or charred. If you are spit-roasting chickens, it may be easier to cut off the wings and use for another recipe as they are not easy to tie to a compact shape. Also important is to insert the spit rod so that the meat is balanced. If your meat is a pork loin with bones, the rod needs to be inserted closer to the bone side rather than centered. Lopsided roasts cause the turning mechanism to falter and can result in uneven cooking.

Even though the rod is square in cross section, it is important to fasten the roast with prongs at both ends to keep it from moving on the spit during roasting.

Before using any rotisserie, the manufacturer's instructions for use should be carefully read.

BARBECUED BOLOGNA ROLL

1 piece (3 pounds) whole bologna roll
2 tablespoons prepared mustard
1 cup orange marmalade
Cooked whole potatoes
Butter or margarine, softened
Whole zucchini
Salt and pepper

Remove casing from bologna. Score bologna and center on spit, making sure meat is well centered and held firmly in place by skewers. Put on second notch or according to manufacturer's directions. Cook, brushing occasionally with mixture of mustard and marmalade, 1 to 1½ hours, depending on thickness and temperature of meat when starting to cook. Shorly before serving, brush potatoes with butter and put on rack to heat. Cook zucchini in small amount of boiling salted water until nearly tender. Split, season with salt and pepper and brush with butter. Put on rack to brown. Makes 10 to 12 servings.

Barbecued Bologna Roll

ROUX—A French culinary term for a mixture of flour and fat cooked together and used to thicken soups and sauces. The flour and fat are cooked before the liquid is added to them in order to give them a certain color and taste and, above all, to avoid the raw, pasty taste of insufficiently cooked flour.

There are three kinds of *roux:* brown, blond, and white.

Brown roux is used to thicken rich brown sauces for red meats. Flour and such fats as butter, pork, drippings, etc., are cooked together until the mixture turns an even light-brown color. The cooking must be done very slowly and gently and the mixture has to be stirred frequently, for if the flour burns, it will not thicken properly. Brown *roux* can be refrigerated and frozen.

Blond roux is a pale gold color, and is made with butter only. It is cooked for less time than the brown variety, and it is used to thicken the sauces used in lighter dishes, such as fish, chicken, veal, etc. It too can be refrigerated and frozen.

White roux is also only made with butter, but it is cooked for a shorter time than the blond and must be stirred constantly. It is used for cream and other white sauces.

All *roux* should be made in a heavy-bottomed saucepan that will hold the heat well and evenly, to allow slow cooking. Aluminum tends to discolor a white sauce, so it is better to use an enamelware, copper-bottomed, stainless steel, heatproof glass, or copper pan for a white *roux*.

Purists of French cooking make their *roux* from clarified fats, that is fats that have been melted down and strained to remove any gritty particles, or in the case of

51

RUE

butter, the milk casein. These particles burn easily during cooking and taste bitter, whereas a clarified fat gives a suave, satin-smooth *roux*.

RUE [*Ruta graveolens*]

The leaves of this small perennial plant have limited use as a culinary herb because they are very bitter. Great care should be taken in picking rue, for the grayish-green leaves are thick and covered with a nonhairy bloom which rubs off when touched. It sometimes caused a severe rash. The plant itself grows up to two feet, is evergreen, and has pretty four-petaled bright yellow flowers.

Rue can be used in the kitchen in small amounts. Chicken broth takes its flavor well, as do minced chicken or mushroom canapés. The Europeans make sandwiches of rue leaves, either minced or whole, and buttered brown bread.

Rue's bitterness is an addition to beef, lamb, kidney, or chicken stews, and it may be mixed sparingly with cottage or cream cheese. Rue can be included in salad dressings, or it can be sprinkled over boiled potatoes. Discretion, and always discretion, is the key word in the use of rue.

RUM

Rum is an alcoholic beverage distilled from the fermented products of sugar cane. Rum was an important part of early American commerce: in the famous triangle trade of colonial days, slaves were brought from Africa to the West Indies and sold for molasses which was then carried to New England where distilleries produced the rum which was in its turn the medium of exchange for more slaves in Africa.

There are three chief kinds of rum. The oldest type is Jamaican rum. This was the rum known to our ancestors, heavy, dark, full-bodied, and usually aged in wood. Cuban rum is a relatively modern refinement of this. Dry and lightbodied, Cuban-type rum has only been produced since the last part of the 19th century. It is also distilled in Puerto Rico and the Virgin Islands. More aromatic rums than either the Jamaican and Cuban are produced throughout the Caribbean area.

Historically, rum has been popular in the United States. In the early days it was sometimes mixed with molasses and called blackstrap, or mixed with cider and called stonewall. Rum was equally popular in England, where **in the British Navy a tot of rum was issued to sailors at sea.**

Rum is used in many mixed drinks and as a flavoring in many foods. In cooked foods the alcoholic content evaporates and the flavor alone remains.

ITALIAN RUM CAKE

3 eggs
1 cup sugar
3 tablespoons cold water
2 teaspoons vanilla extract
1 cup sifted all-purpose flour
2 teaspoons baking powder
Topping
Garnishes

Beat eggs until light. Gradually beat in sugar. Keep on beating until mixture is thick and pale in color. If possible, use an electric beater at high speed for 6 minutes. Stir in water and vanilla. Sift flour with baking powder. Fold into batter. Bake in greased and floured 9-inch springform pan in preheated moderate oven (350°F.) for 30 minutes, or until cake tests clean. Cool in pan while making the Topping. Pour topping over cooled cake in pan and chill until serving time. Remove cake from pan and garnish with orange segments, glacé cherries, and rosettes of whipped cream. Makes 8 to 12 servings.

Topping

1 envelope unflavored gelatin
¼ cup cold water
2 cups hot milk
¾ cup sugar
4 egg yolks, lightly beaten
⅓ cup dark rum
1 large seedless orange
1 cup heavy cream

Soften gelatin in cold water. Stir in hot milk and sugar. Cook over low heat until mixture is hot and gelatin dissolved. Mixture must *not* boil. Gradually pour over egg yolks, stirring constantly. Stir in rum. Set in bowl of cracked ice and stir constantly until mixture cools and begins to set. Peel orange and separate into segments. Fold orange segments and cream into custard.

NORWEGIAN RUM CREAM

2 eggs, separated
6 tablespoons sugar
1½ tablespoons unflavored gelatin
3 tablespoons cold water
2 cups heavy cream, whipped
¼ cup rum

Beat egg yolks and sugar together over very low heat until smooth and slightly thickened. Cool. Soak gelatin in cold water for 5 minutes. Put gelatin over very low heat and stir until dissolved. Add to egg-yolk mixture. Cool. Fold in whipped cream, rum, and egg whites beaten until stiff but not dry. Pour mixture into lightly oiled 1½-quart mold. Chill until firm. Unmold and serve with sweetened berries or with small nut cookies. Makes 6 to 8 servings.

SPARKLING RUM PUNCH

½ fresh pineapple, sliced
½ cup sugar
¼ cup water
1 cup lemon juice
2 cups pineapple juice
5½ cups light rum
2 cups sliced fresh strawberries
2 quarts chilled club soda

Cover pineapple with sugar and water. Let stand until sugar is dissolved. Add lemon juice, pineapple juice, and rum. Chill for several hours. Pour mixture into a large bowl. Add strawberries and soda. Add a small block of ice. Makes 20 servings.

DAIQUIRI

Combine 1 tablespoon fresh lime juice with 1 teaspoon sugar and 2 ounces white rum in a cocktail shaker with cracked ice. Shake until well blended. Strain and pour into cocktail glass. Makes 1 serving.
NOTE: Can be shaken with 1 raw egg white for a smooth drink with a foamy topping.

Frozen Daiquiri

Prepare the same mixture as above, shaking the mixture with shaved ice. Serve unstrained with short straws. This mixture can also be whirled in a blender with shaved ice. Pour mixture into a cocktail glass filled with shaved ice and serve immediately.

RUSSIAN COOKERY

by PRINCESS ALEXANDRA KROPOTKIN

Russia is an immense country that stretches over the European and Asiatic continents. It is about 7,000 miles from the Russian western frontier with Poland to the eastern one at the end of Siberia, on the Pacific Ocean. From north to south the distances in Russia range up to 3,000 miles. A country so vast offers not only an enormous variety of landscapes, climates, and foodstuffs, but also of populations. The USSR, or Union of Soviet Socialist Republics, has some seventy major nationalities within her borders. These have any number of subdivisions, each in its turn with different ways of preparing this or that dish.

Besides these purely Russian variations, the French influence, which imprinted itself under Catherine the Great (r. 1762-1796), is very apparent. Catherine was a **great Francophile, a friend of Voltaire with whom she** corresponded regularly. She imported French chefs and followed French recipes with true gastronomical fervor. Most of the sauces so popular with the Russians are of French origin.

Catherine the Great also brought with her some German methods of food preparation. The word *forshmak,* "a warm appetizer," is one of the remainders of this influence. The word has become a permanent part of the Russian language. Roast goose, such a tremendous favorite with Russians at all times, probably can also be attributed to German influence. Of course Russians have a silly joke about a goose; they say it is "too much for one and not enough for two." But they love the bird, stuffed with *kasha* (cooked buckwheat groats) and served with some kind of salad on the side. A favorite is cabbage cut into eighths, put up like sauerkraut, with whole apples fermented in the barrel with the cabbage. These are called *marinovony e iabloki,* that is, "pickled apples." Some Russian delicatessens in this country carry them.

Earlier Russian rulers were also responsible for bringing foreign influences to bear upon Russian food. One of the first to do so was Ivan the Terrible (r. 1533-1584), who sent for Italian architects to build additions within the Kremlin. With them came a sizeable contingent of Italian workmen. It is to the Italians of those distant days that the Russians owe the sherbets, ice creams, and fancy pastries of which they are so inordinately fond to this day.

Besides the French, German, and Italian influences, still a fourth was introduced during the reign of Peter the Great (r. 1682-1725) whose eyes turned to the west and who was the founder of Russian naval power. He lived surrounded by Dutchmen, whom he regarded as the greatest of ship builders, and many of the vegetable dishes and spiced honeycakes found in Russian cookery go back to his days.

Persian and Turkish accents have percolated into Russia through the Caucasus. Hence, the *shashlik* and its variations (skewered broiled mutton, or lamb, served at times with mushroom caps alternating, or tomato slices); also the pilafs. These dishes have become so familar in Russian menus that the average Russian just considers them part of his own food tradition, without a thought of where they originated.

Poland was part of Imperial Russia for so long that any number of Polish recipes have become incorporated in the Russian food pattern; the famous soup, *borsch,* is said to be of Polish origin. Besides whatever German dishes came in with Catherine the Great, certain German ways of preparing food infiltrated through the Baltic provinces which were part of Russia.

The habit of *zakuska,* or cocktail appetizer, is said to have arrived with Rurik, the Scandinavian prince who became the first Czar of Russia. In 862 A.D. he was invited to "rule and make laws." With him came many fellow Scandinavians. Actually *zakuska* in Russian means the "Bite-down." You take your tiny glassful of vodka, drink it, no sipping ever, then "bit it down" with a bit of herring, or whatever appetizer you may fancy.

The usual *zakuska* in a private home consists of just one dish, herring. That is standard. Perhaps there may be a second dish, probably a few slices of sausage, or maybe pickled mushrooms, or a small salad of some kind. Black bread invariably accompanies *zakuski* and, in fact, is part of any dinner. A dish of sweet (unsalted) butter goes along with the *zakuski.*

After the *zakuska* course comes a large tureen of soup. Nearly always the soup has a chunk of meat in it and any vegetables that are available; carrots, cabbage, and turnip are the most usual; minced dill for sprinkling. The meat will be taken from the soup and placed on a separate dish. Sauerkraut, with freshly grated carrot and

RUSSIAN COOKERY

a few drops of olive or cooking oil, often accompanies the meat. This is the cheapest and easiest of so-called salads, and on winter days one sees it on every table.

The most usual complement to the soup is a big pot of baked *kasha*. This may be varied by a dish of pearl barley, possibly a *pirog,* a nonsweet pastry filled with fish, eggs, or cabbage. *Pirozhki,* little pastries with fillings similar to those of *pirogi,* are reserved, in homes, for meals when guests are present.

After the soup, the dessert, for an everyday home dinner, is very simple. It is probably *kissel,* a fruit purée thickened with cornstarch, or maybe a fruit compote, or possibly some store-prepared pastry.

Generally speaking, pastries are more likely to be eaten with the inevitable tea with the *samovar* which comes later, when homemade jam also appears. The jam is added to the cup of tea (with no milk), or taken from a tiny saucer which is placed to the left of each person, next to the cup of tea. The saucer measures about two and a half inches across and the name for it is *bliudechko.* You put some jam on it, not much, then take tiny half teaspoonfuls, put them in your mouth, and then take a sip of tea.

Russians, all Russians, have a real complex about jam. Only homemade jam, the way Russians make it, is right. Every berry must remain whole and be quite separate in the heavy syrup. No such thing as a mixed-up mass of fruit, however tasty, can be tolerated.

Russian jam is delicious; it is taken with tea and is not for spreading. A great number of Russians living in exile in this country make their own jam. They grumble, however, at the quality of various fruits, at the strawberries in particular, for Russian strawberries are far more aromatic than those grown here. Raspberries, and gooseberries as well, are excellent and very popular and easy to get in Russia.

Tea is the most universal beverage, morning, noon, and night. Coffee was only for the sophisticated in the days before the Czar was ousted. Today coffee is far more widely known and it is drunk in many private homes. But tea is still the more usual drink. The Navy quaffs tea, laced with rum.

Kvass, a slightly fermented drink made from either white or dark rye bread, accompanies many meals. Foreigners rarely take to *kvass*. There is, however, a perfectly delightful fruit *kvass,* which should be imitated in this country. This is made from cranberries or lingonberries, which are very common in Russia, with sometimes a small amount of raspberries. The beverage is very slightly fermented. Served well chilled, it is delightfully refreshing.

Breakfast in Russia, called *utrennii chai,* morning tea, isn't much of a meal. Bread, usually white, small sweet rolls, sweet butter, and maybe a couple of soft-boiled eggs, make the meal. Lunch is *zavtrak.* For a home lunch, or even in a cafeteria, unless this is your main meal, one dish of fish, or pot-cheese cakes, maybe a small salad, perhaps some *kasha,* or new potatoes in the spring, make up the menu. Many people drink milk with lunch, especially if the meal is eaten at home.

Obed, dinner, is the main meal, at whatever hour it is consumed; this, today, varies according to work schedules. With or without guests, if no salad is served with the meat course, a separate vegetable course follows the meat. This may be meat taken from the soup, or maybe a lighter soup will be served, with chicken in some form or other to follow, or perhaps the delicious little hazel hens, *riabchiki,* quickly roasted, with a salad, may follow the soup.

Riabchiki, infinitely tastier and more succulent than American Rock Cornish hens, abound in Russia. They are quite small and have a very slight gamy flavor. They are never stuffed, just roasted quickly and served at once.

Very young small spring chickens, either steamed or quick-roasted, served with a gooseberry sauce, always rate high acclaim. They are truly delicious, if you can get the chickens young enough. Game of all kinds has always been extremely popular in Russia, particularly woodcock. With woodcock, or wild duck which is also very popular, go pickled cherries or preserved lingonberries. Also a chestnut purée, when available, made from fresh or dried chestnuts.

There are certain rules to be followed when a guest at a party dinner. Russians are incredibly hospitable and someone will drink your health during the outset of the *zakuska* period, saying *Za vashe zdorove* (your health). The person toasted must down his, or her, drink, then get another one and respond with *Za vashe* (your). Bottoms up, always. The prolonged toasting may make people quite intoxicated. To counteract this, thoughtful hostesses provide a platter of sliced Swiss cheese, for a good bite of this cheese is the old cavalry receipt for staying sober. Take the cheese after every drink and hope there are not too many toasts.

If the host is fairly affluent, there will be caviar in some form or another with the *zakuski.* Caviar always was a luxury. Nowadays in Soviet territory caviar seems to be less expensive. The top kinds are still in the luxury class, the *Malossol,* lightly salted, large grained, and very slightly smoked; next come several grades of smaller-grained caviar, smokier, and saltier than the *Malossol.* There is also pressed caviar, black, excellent on open-face sandwiches. This is very popular in present-day Russia. Comparatively inexpensive, it appears at the buffets which are usual in all large theaters and hotels.

All caviars must be served in a bowl, surrounded with ice and lemon wedges. Most plebian of all caviars is the red one, made of salmon roe. If it is large grained and not too salty, quite a few people in the United States like it. Very few Russians do. To serve this caviar to its best advantage, a little sour cream with finely snipped chives should accompany the caviar in a separate bowl. Like other kinds of caviar this too must be served ice cold. It makes a good cocktail snack, with split, lightly toasted English muffins. In fact, these should accompany all types of caviar. They are best left unbuttered.

Besides the usual vodka, a party spread requires two other vodkas, to be drunk from the same kind of thimble-size glasses. These vodkas are *Zubrovka,* a yellowish, herb-infused vodka, very aromatic, and just as strong as ordinary vodka; and *Riabinovka,* a distillate of mountain-ash berries, slightly pinkish in color and a great favorite with the ladies. They think it less dangerous than ordinary vodka, which it certainly is not.

RUSSIAN COOKBOOK

ZAKUSKI
[Appetizers]

SALAT OLIVIER
[Olivier Salad]

A very popular zakuska *dish with quite a tradition behind it. It was created by the Czar's French chef and first served to his royal master; the Czar was so delighted that he ordered the salad to be named for his ingenious chef.*

- 1 whole breast of chicken, cooked*
- 3 medium-size potatoes, boiled and peeled
- 2 small dill pickles, peeled and cut into thin slices
- 1 teaspoon Worcestershire
- 3 tablespoons mayonnaise
- 2 hard-cooked eggs, cut into 6 wedges
- 6 large olives
- 1 tomato, cut into 6 slices

Trim off all skin and fat from the chicken. Slice meat into very thin strips. The potatoes should be firm enough to be sliced into even ¼-inch slices. Add pickles. Mix Worcestershire into mayonnaise. Combine it very carefully with the chicken, potatoes, and dill pickles, lifting with a fork to avoid breaking. Pile the salad onto an oval *zakuska* dish. Decorate with 6 egg wedges, 6 olives, and 6 slices of tomato. Makes 6 servings.
*This is best made with breast of cold boiled chicken, although roast chicken can be used. Some gourmets prefer cold duck.

IKRA IZ BAKLAZHANOV
[Eggplant Caviar]

- 1 large eggplant
- 2 small onions, minced
- ¼ cup olive or cooking oil
- ¼ cup tomato purée or 1 cup (about) tomato sauce
- 2 teaspoons lemon juice
- 2 teaspoons salt
- Pepper
- Dash of garlic salt (optional)

Drop whole eggplant into a pot of boiling water. Cook about 20 minutes. Drain and cool sufficiently to handle. Cut off stem end and remove skin. Cut into halves lengthwise and chop very fine. Simmer onion in a little oil in a large heavy skillet for 10 minutes without browning. Add chopped eggplant, tomato purée, and remaining oil. Cook slowly for 10 minutes, stirring constantly. Cook very slowly, covered about 30 minutes longer, stirring occasionally. Some eggplants are drier than others and may require a little more oil or even a teaspoon of water. When the eggplant has the required thick and moist consistency, add lemon juice, salt, a dash of pepper, and garlic salt, if desired. Serve well chilled. Makes 6 servings.

SALAT IZ TELIATINI S OGURTSAMU
[Veal and Cucumber Salad]

- ½ cup mayonnaise
- ½ cup dairy sour cream
- 1 teaspoon Worcestershire
- 2 cups diced cold cooked veal
- 1 cup diced peeled cucumbers
- ½ cup diced dill pickles
- 1 cup diced peeled tart apples
- 2 cups diced cold cooked potatoes

Mix mayonnaise, sour cream, and Worcestershire. Add remaining ingredients and toss very carefully with fork. Serve very cold. Makes 6 servings.

ANCHOVIES ON EGG SLICES

This is the simplest of all Russian appetizers.

Cut rounds of pumpernickel bread the size of a slice of hard-cooked egg. Spread the bread lightly with unsalted butter. Cover each round with a slice of egg. Lay 2 thin strips of anchovy crosswise across the egg. Russians like the Norwegian anchovies that come in small wooden casks. They are difficult to clean and bone. Ordinary anchovy fillets taken from a can, drained of the oil, and cut down the middle, serve just as well.

SELYODKA
[Herrings]

- 2 large or 3 small herring fillets (see note)
- Mustard Dressing
- Vegetable Garnish

Cover herring with Mustard Dressing and decorate with Vegetable Garnish. Makes 4 to 6 servings.
NOTE: Scandinavian Matjes herring can be used; it is skinned and boned, and sold in fillets. Schmaltz herring is favored in Russia, but preparing it is plenty of trouble; it must be soaked first in cold water for a couple of hours, and then in cold tea or milk for another 3 hours. After this the fish is skinned, boned, and filleted. If using large herrings, split each into 2 pieces.

Mustard Dressing

- 2 tablespoons olive oil
- 1 tablespoon sharp prepared mustard
- 1 teaspoon sugar, diluted in 1 teaspoon water

Stir oil into mustard, drop by drop. Add sugar and water. Mix well. Let stand for 15 minutes. Pour over fillets.

RUSSIAN

Vegetable Garnish

This is simply slices of cold boiled potato, sliced cooked beet, and a peeled and sliced dill pickle. Arrange around the herring fillets.

SOUPS

UKRAINSKI BORSCH
[Ukrainian Borsch]

This soup is a complete meal in itself.

- 2 pounds soup meat
- ½ pound lean smoked pork
- Water
- 1 bay leaf
- 6 peppercorns
- 1 garlic clove
- 1 bunch of soup greens
- 8 medium-size beets
- 1 cup shredded cabbage
- 2 large onions, chopped
- 3 raw large potatoes, peeled and halved
- 6 tomatoes, peeled, seeded, and chopped
- 1 cup cooked navy beans
- 1 tablespoon cider vinegar
- 1 teaspoon sugar
- 5 frankfurters, sliced
- 1 tablespoon all-purpose flour
- 1 tablespoon butter
- Dairy sour cream

Put soup meat and pork in deep kettle. Cover with 2½ quarts of water. Bring to boil and cook for about 15 minutes. Skim; add bay leaf, peppercorns, garlic, and soup greens which should include a carrot, celery, a leek, some parsley, and a parsley root. Simmer, covered, for 2 hours. Cook 7 beets, unpeeled, in the soup separately. Peel remaining beet and grate. Mix with 3 tablespoons water. This is for coloring, to be added at the last moment. When the beets are tender, peel and dice. Add beets to soup with cabbage, onions, and potatoes. Discard soup greens or cut them up and return to kettle. Add tomatoes, navy beans, vinegar, and sugar. Cook for another hour. Add frankfurters 20 minutes before serving. Skim off excess fat. Cut meat into serving pieces. Thicken soup with flour browned in butter; bring to a boil. Add beet juice drained from raw beet for red color. Serve very hot in large soup plates, with side plates for meat. A bowl of dairy sour cream accompanies the soup. Makes 3 quarts.

IABLOCHNII SUP
[Apple Soup]

- 6 large tart apples
- 3 cups water
- 1 cup sugar
- 1 cup dairy sour cream
- 2 cups light red wine (claret or rosé)
- 1 tablespoon lemon juice
- Ground cinnamon (optional)

Peel and core apples. Reserve peels. Stew apples in 2 cups water until soft. Put stewed apples through sieve. In another pan cook peels in remaining 1 cup water, strain, and add to apple purée. Add sugar and sour cream at room temperature, and mix well until quite smooth. Slowly add wine and lemon juice. Serve chilled. If desired, dust very lightly with ground cinnamon. Makes about 2 quarts.

RASSOLNIK S YACHMENEM
[Soup with Pickles]

- 2 tablespoons medium barley
- 3 cups water
- 3 cans (10½ ounces) condensed consommé
- 1 can (13¾) condensed chicken broth
- 2 cups diced raw potatoes
- 1 large onion, minced
- 3 tablespoons butter or margarine
- 1 veal kidney or 5 lamb kidneys, trimmed and sliced
- 1 tablespoon all-purpose flour
- 2 small dill pickles, thinly sliced
- ½ cup dairy sour cream, at room temperature
- 2 tablespoons minced parsley
- Pepper to taste

Cook barley in water about 1 hour. Drain and reserve. In deep kettle combine consommé and chicken broth. Add potatoes and cook until half tender. Cook onion in hot butter until soft but not brown. Add kidney and cook, stirring constantly, for 3 minutes. Stir in flour and cook for 3 minutes. Add pickles, barley, and kidneys to soup mixture. Bring to boil. Lower heat and simmer, covered, for 15 minutes. Pour sour cream into large soup tureen. Add a few teaspoons of soup and beat vigorously to prevent curdling. Pour remaining soup over mixture. Sprinkle with parsley and pepper. Makes 2 quarts.

SOLDATSKIE SHCHI
[Soldiers' Sauerkraut Soup]

- 2 pounds beef flank
- Water
- 1 bay leaf
- 2 tablespoons each minced dill and parsley
- 2 carrots, sliced
- 1 turnip, diced
- 2 celery stalks, diced
- 3 raw large potatoes, peeled and diced
- 2 onions, chopped
- 2 tablespoons bacon fat
- 1½ pounds sauerkraut, rinsed and drained
- 1 tablespoon all-purpose flour
- ½ pound Polish sausage (kielbasa) or 4 frankfurters

Put beef in deep kettle. Cover with 2 quarts of water; add bay leaf, dill, and parsley. Bring to a boil. Simmer, covered, for 1 hour, skimming as needed. Add next 4 vegetables. Continue simmering for 1 more hour. Sauté onions in hot bacon fat for 5 minutes; add sauerkraut. Cook slowly, covered, for 20 minutes. Add to soup. Mix flour with a little cold water until smooth and stir into soup. Cook sausage and cut into 1-inch pieces. Add to soup and simmer for 15 minutes. Skim off excess fat before serving. Garnish with additional minced parsley and dill, or dill alone. Serve with sour cream and plenty of rye bread on the side. Makes about 2 quarts.

CABBAGE PIROZHKI

- 5 cups chopped green cabbage (about 1¼ pounds)
- 2 tablespoons salt
- 2 onions, chopped
- ¼ cup butter or margarine
- 2 hard-cooked eggs, chopped
- 1 tablespoon minced dill or parsley
- Pastry (2 cup flour recipe) or Raised Dough for Pirozhki

Mix cabbage with salt and let stand for 15 minutes. Squeeze juice out of cabbage. Put cabbage into a colander and pour boiling water over it. Let drain for 30 minutes. Sauté onions in butter. Add cabbage and cook slowly for 30 minutes. Do not brown mixture. Add eggs and dill. Cool. Roll pastry ⅛ inch thick into rectangle about 15 x 16 inches; cut into 12 pieces, each 4 x 5 inches. Put filling on half of each piece. Moisten edges with water and fold other half of dough over filling; seal edges. Bake on greased and floured cookie sheet in preheated moderate oven (375°F.) for 25 to 30 minutes, or until **pirozhki** are brown. Makes 12 **pirozhki**.

MEAT AND ANCHOVY PIROZHKI

- 1 onion, chopped
- 2 tablespoons butter or margarine
- 1½ cups ground cooked beef
- ¼ cup thick gravy
- 2 anchovy fillets, minced
- 1½ teaspoons minced parsley
- 1 teaspoon minced dill
- 1 hard-cooked egg, chopped
- Pastry (2-cup flour recipe) or Raised Dough for Pirozhki

Sauté onion in butter until golden. Add meat and cook for 5 minutes. Add next 5 ingredients. Cool. Roll, cut, fill, and bake pastry as directed in Cabbage **Pirozhki** (above). Makes 12 **pirozhki**.

LIVER PIROZHKI

- 1 pound calf's liver, cut into thin slices
- 1 slice of salt pork
- 1 large onion, chopped
- 1 thick slice of day-old bread, crust removed
- Water
- 1 tablespoon mixed grated nutmeg and pepper
- 1 tablespoon butter
- 3 tablespoons Madeira wine
- 1 tablespoon rum
- Pastry (2-cup flour recipe) or Raised Dough for Pirozhki

Have liver at room temperature. Cut salt pork into into 1-inch cubes. Put pork, liver, and onion in heavy pan, cover, and cook over high heat. Stir frequently with a spoon. Cook until liver is brown. Chop liver and discard salt pork. Put liver through the meat grinder twice. Soak bread in a little water. Squeeze dry and add to liver. Add nutmeg and pepper, butter, wine, and rum. Mix until very smooth. Chill. Roll, cut, and fill pastry pieces as directed in Cabbage *Pirozhki*. Bake on greased and floured cookie sheet in preheated hot oven (425°F.) for 15 minutes. Lower heat to moderate (350°F.) and bake for another 15 to 20 minutes. Makes 12 *pirozhki*.

RAISED DOUGH FOR PIROGI OR PIROZHKI

- ¼ cup water*
- 1 envelope active dry yeast or 1 cake compressed yeast
- ½ cup butter or margarine
- 1 cup lukewarm milk
- 1 teaspoon salt
- 2 teaspoons sugar
- 4½ to 5 cups sifted all-purpose flour
- 3 eggs, slightly beaten

*Use very warm water (105°F. to 115°F.) for dry yeast; use lukewarm water (80°F. to 90°F.) for compressed. Sprinkle dry yeast or crumble cake yeast into water. Let stand for a few minutes, then stir until dissolved. Add butter to milk and stir until butter is melted. Add dissolved yeast, salt, and sugar. Beat in 1 cup flour. Beat in eggs and then beat in remaining flour until a soft dough is formed. Knead dough on a lightly floured board until smooth and elastic. Put dough into a greased bowl. Grease the top and let rise in a warm place until doubled in bulk. Punch down and roll into **a pirog** 14 x 18 inches, or into 12 **pirozhki**, each 4 x 5 inches. Bake as directed in each recipe.

FISH

SYOMGA S SOUSOM IZ IKRI
[Salmon Steaks with Caviar Sauce]

- 2 salmon steaks, 1 inch thick
- Salt and pepper
- Cooking oil
- ¼ cup butter or margarine
- ¼ cup all-purpose flour
- 1½ cups light cream
- 2 egg yolks
- 1 teaspoon lemon juice
- 2 tablespoons caviar (see note)

Rub salmon steaks with a little salt and plenty of pepper; brush with oil. Broil for 8 minutes. Turn steaks and brush unbroiled side with oil and broil 8 minutes longer. Make cream sauce with butter, flour, and cream; do not season. Beat hot sauce into egg yolks mixed with lemon juice. When fish steaks are broiled, add caviar to the sauce; season to taste with salt. Pour over salmon steaks. Serve at once. Makes 2 servings.

NOTE: The caviar in this recipe can perfectly well be good red caviar, large grained and not too salty.

RUSSIAN

FILE KAMBALI SO SLIVKAMI I LUKOM
[Fillets of Flounder with Sweet Cream and Scallions]

- 2 pounds flounder fillets
- Salt
- ¼ cup fresh bread crumbs
- 1½ tablespoons butter
- 1½ cups light cream
- ¼ cup minced scallions
- Pepper

Sprinkle fillets with salt; let stand for 1 hour. Dry thoroughly with absorbent paper. Cut each fillet across into 3 or 4 pieces, depending on size of fillet. Sauté bread crumbs in hot butter for 5 minutes, add cream, and cook for 5 more minutes. Put fillets in cream and bread-crumb sauce. Add scallions and a little pepper and simmer gently for 10 to 15 minutes. Makes 6 servings.
NOTE: Use a saucepan or casserole that can go to the table. Serve small new potatoes and a plain cucumber salad with this dish, which is a luncheon favorite in Russia.

MEAT, AND CHEESE

BIF STROGONOV
[Beef Stroganoff]

- 1½ pounds top sirloin of beef
- 1 teaspoon salt
- 1 teaspoon pepper
- 3 tablespoons butter or margarine
- 1 tablespoon all-purpose flour
- 1 cup beef bouillon
- ¾ teaspoon hot prepared mustard
- 2 small onions, sliced
- 3 tablespoons dairy sour cream, at room temperature

Remove all fat and gristle from meat. Cut into narrow strips 2 inches long and ½ inch thick. Sprinkle meat strips with salt and pepper. Melt 1½ tablespoons butter; blend in flour. Stir in bouillon and bring to boil; stir in mustard. Cook, stirring constantly, until thick and smooth. Heat remaining 1½ tablespoons butter in another saucepan. The butter must be very hot. Brown meat and onions quickly on all sides. Add sour cream to mustard sauce. Bring to boil. Add meat and onions to sauce. Cover saucepan and keep hot for 20 minutes, either over pilot light or on asbestos plate set over lowest possible heat. The mixture must be kept hot, but must not simmer. Before serving, heat through over high heat for about 3 minutes. Makes 3 or 4 servings.

SVINYE KOTLETY S SOUSOM IZ CHERNOSLIV ILI KISLYKH VISHEN
[Breaded Pork Chops with Prune or Sour-Cherry Sauce]

- 6 pork chops, trimmed of fat
- All-purpose flour mixed with a little salt
- Fine dry bread crumbs
- 2 tablespoons butter
- 1 cup puréed prunes or cherries
- 1 teaspoon grated lemon rind
- ½ teaspoon ground cinnamon
- ¼ teaspoon ground cloves
- ½ cup water (about)
- ½ cup port

Drop chops into boiling salted water. Reduce heat and simmer for 15 minutes. Drain chops and dry. Cool. Dust with lightly salted flour and roll in bread crumbs. Sauté chops in hot butter for 5 minutes on each side. Cook gently for 20 minutes, turning once. If using prunes, they should be soaked, well cooked, pitted, and put through a coarse sieve. Canned pitted sour cherries are also good. They should be stewed, finely chopped, and sweetened with 2 tablespoons sugar. Add lemon rind, spices, and water to purée if it seems too thick. Heat and add wine. Bring to boil. Pour over chops and serve very hot. Makes 6 servings.

SYRNIKI
[Fried Cheese Cakes]

Skim-milk cottage cheese and farmer's cheese are also suited to this recipe; the latter does not need to be sieved.

- 1 pound very dry pot cheese
- ½ teaspoon salt
- 2 eggs, lightly beaten
- ½ cup all-purpose flour
- Butter
- Dairy sour cream
- Fresh dill, minced

Put cheese through food mill or sieve, or pound smooth. Beat in salt, eggs, and flour until thoroughly mixed and very smooth. Chill for 2 hours. To shape, use a little dough at a time, keeping remainder in refrigerator. With floured hands, shape dough into flat round 2-inch cakes. Fry over medium heat in hot butter for 10 minutes. Lower heat and cook for another 10 to 15 minutes. Turn cakes once during each frying time to brown on both sides. Serve with sour cream and dill. Makes 10 to 12 cakes, depending on size.
Variation—Add 1 more tablespoon all-purpose flour to basic mixture. Pat mixture into greased shallow baking dish. Sprinkle with fine bread crumbs and dot with butter. Bake in preheated moderate oven (375°F.) for 20 to 30 minutes, or until browned. Serve with a creamed vegetable or as a dessert with a fruit compote.

VEGETABLES

Vegetables are served chiefly as a separate course or as special salads accompanying boiled or roast meat. They also come to table as part of the zakuski course, the appetizers. Northern districts of Russia rely on root vegetables during the cold months, and the first fresh lettuce, dressed with sour cream, is greeted as a veritable praznik, a real holiday treat.

SALAT IZ MORKOVI I KISLOI KAPUSTY
[Carrot and Sauerkraut Salad]

In Russia this is a favorite winter salad to serve with meat or fish.

Drain 2 cups sauerkraut thoroughly, and chill. Shred raw carrots fine or grate them on a coarse grater until you have 1 cup. Mix the carrots with sauerkraut and 2 tablespoons of olive or salad oil. Makes 4 servings.

KARTOFEL'S ANCHOUSAMI
[Scalloped Potatoes with Anchovies]

- 2 onions, chopped
  Butter
- 8 anchovy fillets, drained and finely minced (or more to taste)
- 6 cups sliced cooked potatoes
- 1½ cups dairy sour cream
  Salt and pepper
  Fine dry bread crumbs

Sauté onions in 2 tablespoons butter. Add anchovies and cook for 2 minutes. Butter an ovenproof dish. Spread with a layer of potatoes, moisten with a little sour cream, then add a layer of anchovies and onions. Sprinkle lightly with salt and pepper. Repeat until dish is full. Top with bread crumbs and 1 tablespoon melted butter. Brown in preheated medium oven (350°F.) for 30 minutes. Serve with a bland green salad. Makes 6 servings.

SVEZHIYE PODZHARENYYE OGURTZY
[Braised Cucumbers]

- 4 small cucumbers (see note)
  Salt
- 2 tablespoons butter
- 1 small onion, chopped
- 2 tablespoons all-purpose flour
- ¼ cup dairy sour cream
  Pepper and grated nutmeg

Peel cucumbers and cut each one lengthwise into 4 slices. Remove some of the seeds. Sprinkle cucumbers lightly with salt and let stand for 20 minutes. Dry well with a towel. Heat 1 tablespoon butter; add cucumbers and sauté for 15 to 20 minutes. Sauté onion in remaining 1 tablespoon butter until golden brown. Add flour to onion and cook for 5 minutes; then add cucumbers. Stir in sour cream. Boil up once. Season with freshly ground pepper to taste and a dash of nutmeg. Simmer for 5 minutes. Serve with roast lamb. Makes 4 to 6 servings.
NOTE: The cucumbers should be young and firm, with small seeds.

SPARZHA ZAPECHENNAYA S SUKHARYAMI I SLIVKAMI
[Asparagus Baked with Bread Crumbs and Cream]

- 2 pounds asparagus
  Sugar and salt to taste
- 1 cup soft bread crumbs
  Butter
- 1 tablespoon lemon juice
  Pepper
- 1 cup light cream

Cook asparagus until just soft, adding a little sugar as well as salt to the water in which you cook the asparagus. Drain for 1 hour. Cut off stalks, leaving only the really soft parts. Place these in buttered ovenproof dish. Use a dish you can serve at table. Sauté bread crumbs in 3 tablespoons butter. Sprinkle lemon juice on asparagus; dust with pepper and cover with half the bread crumbs. Add cream; cover with rest of bread crumbs. Bake in preheated hot oven (400°F.) for 15 minutes. Makes 6 servings.

PERTZY FARSHIROVANNYE TIORTOI MORKOV'YU
[Green Peppers Stuffed with Grated Carrots]

This is a favorite dish from the Caucasus.

- 4 green peppers
- 2½ cups grated carrots (see note)
- 2 tablespoons grated onion
- 4 tablespoons butter
- 3 tablespoons fine dry bread crumbs
  Salt and pepper
- 2 tablespoons grated cheese

Scald peppers about 10 minutes; cut off tops, scoop out seeds and white membrane. Mix grated carrots and onion with 2 tablespoons softened butter and 1 tablespoon bread crumbs. Season with salt and pepper to taste. Stuff peppers with this mixture and top stuffing with remaining 2 tablespoons bread crumbs and cheese. Dot with remaining 2 tablespoons butter. Put in well-buttered baking dish and bake in preheated moderate oven (350°F.) for 30 to 40 minutes. Serve from dish in which baked. Makes 4 servings.
NOTE: Corn, freshly grated or canned, may be substituted for the carrots. In this case add a little water to moisten the corn.

RUSSIAN

OLAD'I S LUKOM
[Baked Onion Dumplings]

I consider this one of the finest Russian contributions to vegetable cookery. They are absolutely wonderful with roast lamb.

- 6 large onions
- 1 tablespoon butter
- 2 cups consommé
- Salt and pepper
- Pastry (2 cup-flour recipe)

With a thin skewer pierce onions carefully in 3 or 4 places. Put in cold salted water and bring to a boil. Drain onions and put them in a pot with butter and sonsommé. Bring to a boil and simmer until tender. The onions must remain whole. When they are done, drain them thoroughly for 1 hour. Dry in a towel and dust them with salt and pepper to taste. Wrap onions in pastry squares rolled ⅛ inch thick as you would wrap an apple for apple dumplings. Refrigerate for 30 minutes. Bake in preheated hot oven (425°F.) for 20 minutes. Serve very hot. Makes 6 servings.

GRECHNEVAIA KASHA
[Buckwheat Porridge]

The basic Russian cereal. Since in America buckwheat groats are usually sold packaged, package directions may be followed for cooking.

- 1 cup large-grained buckwheat groats (see note)
- 1 tablespoon butter
- 5 cups boiling water (about)
- Salt to taste

In skillet cook groats in hot butter over medium heat for 10 minutes, stirring constantly. Transfer groats to 2-quart casserole. Add boiling water to cover, and salt. Bake, covered, in preheated hot oven (400°F.) for 15 minutes. Lower heat to moderate (350°F.) and stir. Replace cover and continue to cook for 45 minutes, or until groats are tender, adding a little more water if necessary. Makes 6 to 8 servings.
NOTE: If large-grained groats are not available, use medium groats.

SAUCE

SOUS IZ KHRENA
[Horseradish Sauce]

This is a very popular sauce for boiled or braised meat or fish.

- 1 tablespoon mayonnaise
- 1½ cups dairy sour cream
- ½ cup freshly grated horseradish (see note)
- 1 teaspoon salt
- 2 teaspoons sugar
- 1 tablespoon cider vinegar

Mix all ingredients until smooth. Put into serving bowl and chill for at least 6 hours. Makes about 1½ cups.
NOTE: If using bottled horseradish omit vinegar.

SPETSIALNI RUSSKI SOUS DLIA ZHARENOI GOVIADINI
[Special Russian Sauce for American Pot Roast]

Brown pot roast well and prepare as usual. When there is plenty of dark gravy in kettle, skim off fat and thicken with a flour-and-water paste.

Add 2 tablespoons minced pitted green olives and 2 tablespoons juice from any spiced fruit such as peaches, pears, or plums to gravy. Bring to boil. Just before serving, add dark rum to taste. Don't let gravy boil after rum is added.

DESSERTS

KISSEL

The best known Russian dessert, which is a fruit purée thickened with cornstarch or potato flour, chilled, and served with cream. The consistency of kissel should be thinner and softer than that of a gelatin dessert. This form of fruit porridge is not exclusive to Russia, but is also popular in all of Scandinavia. Kissel *is an excellent dessert, especially when made with cranberries or other tart berries. Any ripe berries, frozen berries, or canned berries can be used for* kissel. *Frozen or canned berries need not be sweetened.*

Defrost frozen berries. Or cook any ripe berries with water to cover until fruit is tender. Sweeten to taste. Strain berries through food mill or sieve. The purée should be the consistency of heavy cream. Measure purée. For each cup purée, allow 2 to 3 teaspoons cornstarch or potato flour, depending on thickness desired. Blend cornstarch with a little water to make a smooth paste. Reheat purée. Stir in starch. Cook over medium heat, stirring constantly, until purée is thickened and clear. Pour into glass serving dish and chill thoroughly. Serve with heavy cream. Allow ½ to ¾ cup *kissel* for each serving.

KOMPOT IZ NAREZANYKH POPOLAM GRUSH I VISHEN
[Pear Halves and Cherry Compote]

Use cooked fresh or canned pear halves and cooked fresh or canned pitted sweet cherries in equal quantities. Combine fruit syrups. Add ¼ teaspoon vanilla extract and 2 drops of almond extract for each 1 to 1½ cups syrup. Pile cherries in middle of a glass serving dish. Arrange pear halves around them. Pour over just enough syrup to cover fruits. Chill thoroughly. Serve with plain heavy cream and thin plain cookies.

RUSSIAN

KHVOROST
[Twigs]

   3 eggs
3½ cups sifted all-purpose flour
  ½ cup water
   3 tablespoons gin, rye whisky, or rum
     Sugar
  ½ teaspoon salt
     Fat for deep frying
     Ground cinnamon or nutmeg

Beat eggs into flour, one at a time. Add water, gin, ¼ cup sugar, and salt. Knead dough on floured board until blended. Let stand for 15 minutes. Roll out very thin on lightly floured board. Cut into strips 7 x 1½ inches. Cut a small lengthwise slit 1 inch from one end of each strip. Twist the other end of strip through this slit, so you have a loop. Heat fat until you see a faint bluish smoke (375°F. on a frying thermometer). Drop 8 or 10 loops into oil together. Cook about 2 minutes, or until slightly browned. Remove *khvorost* with slotted spoon and drain well on paper towels. Serve piled on a hot platter. Sprinkle generously with sugar and cinnamon. Makes 18 to 20.

GUREEVSKAIA KASHA
[Guriev Pudding]

A very old traditional Russian dessert

  2 cups shelled walnuts
  3 cups milk
  3 cups light cream
  ½ teaspoon salt
  ¾ cup semolina or farina
  ½ cup sugar
  ½ cup seedless raisins, chopped
  ½ teaspoon almond extract
  1 cup mixed candied fruits, coarsely chopped
    Apricot jam
    Fine bread crumbs
    Sugar

Put walnuts through a nut grinder, pound in a mortar, or whirl in a blender. Combine milk, cream and salt in shallow saucepan. Bring mixture to a boil and sprinkle in semolina. Cook for 7 minutes, stirring constantly with a wooden spoon. Remove from heat and add sugar, nuts, raisins, and almond extract. Put a layer of the cooked semolina in a bowl and top it with a little apricot jam, then some of the chopped fruit. Repeat until there are 6 layers, with candied fruit on top. (The jam is a substitute for the milk skins which is the authentic Russian ingredient for this dessert. The milk is cooked very slowly and as soon as a skin forms it is taken off and laid on a plate. This classic way of making Guriev Pudding is definitely not to the American taste.) Sprinkle with bread crumbs and sugar. Serve warm. Makes 8 servings.
NOTE: Glacé fruits, apricots, cherries, peaches, pears, etc., are even better than plain sugared candied fruit.

RUSSKII IABLOCHNII PIROG
[Apple Pie]

  8 large apples, peeled, cored, and thinly sliced
  ½ cup seedless raisins
  ½ cup (or more) sugar
  3 tablespoons dry wine
1½ teaspoons grated orange rind
  ¼ cup finely ground blanched almonds
  ½ teaspoon almond extract
  2 tablespoons currant jelly
    Pastry for 2-crust 9-inch pie

Combine apples, raisins, sugar, wine, orange rind, almonds, and almond extract. Cook over low heat for 15 minutes, stirring constantly. If apples are dry add a couple of tablespoons of water. Stir in jelly when mixture is thick and apples are done; cool. Fill pastry-lined pie pan with mixture and cover with top crust. Cut two small slits in top crust. Bake in preheated moderate oven (375°F.) for 45 to 60 minutes. Serve warm. Makes 6 to 8 servings.

IABLOCHNII KREM
[Cream of Apples]

This is usually a company dessert. It should be made in a mold of fancy shape.

2½ pounds cooking apples, cored
    Water
  2 egg whites
  2 envelopes unflavored gelatin
  1 tablespoon grated lemon rind
  ½ cup sugar
  1 teaspoon vanilla extract
  2 tablespoons rum
  1 cup heavy cream

Cook apples in ½ cup water until tender. Add more water if apples are dry, but liquid should be almost absorbed when apples are done. Put apples through food mill or coarse sieve. There should be 3 cups thick apple sauce. Cool. Beat egg whites until stiff. Fold into cooled apple pulp and beat again until quite stiff. Soften gelatin in ½ cup cold water. Let stand for a few minutes. Add ½ cup boiling water and lemon rind. Chill until mixture begins to set. Combine with apple mixture; add sugar, vanilla, and rum. Whip cream until it holds soft peaks. Fold cream into apple mixture. Pour into a well-chilled 2-quart mold. Chill at least 4 hours. Unmold and serve with a rum-flavored thin custard sauce. Makes 8 servings.

KOMPOT IZ APELSIN I CHERNOSLIV
[Prune-Orange Compote]

In glass serving dish combine cooked pitted prunes and fresh orange sections. Sprinkle with grated orange peel. Moisten with a little fresh orange juice or water in which the prunes were cooked. Sweeten to taste. Chill before serving.

RUTABAGA

RUTABAGA

RUTABAGA—A root vegetable which belongs to the mustard family and is closely related to cabbage, cauliflower, Brussels sprouts, kale, kohlrabi, mustard, and turnips. Rutabaga is larger than the turnip, has smooth yellowish skin and flesh, and smooth leaves. The flesh has a typical sweet flavor. There are white varieties of rutabaga, but the yellow is the best known.

Rutabagas are also known as Swedish turnips or swedes, and the name comes from a Swedish word. It is a cold-weather vegetable and one of the staple crops of northern Europe, where it has nourished countries through wars and famines. As recently as World War II, many would not have survived without rutabagas.

Rutabagas are admittedly not one of the more delicate vegetables. But well cooked, they add nourishment and robustness to winter meals. They can be cooked in any way turnips are cooked.

Availability and Purchasing Guide—In season from July to April. Look for smooth, firm roots that are heavy for their size. Some may be coated with a thin layer of paraffin to prevent spoilage.

Storage—Store in a dry, well-ventilated place, about 55°F., or refrigerate. Rutabagas will keep for about 1 month.

Nutritive Food Values—Some vitamin A and a small amount of vitamin C.
½ cup (3 ounces) boiled and drained = 30 calories.

Basic Preparation—Wash and pare; slice or dice.
To Boil—Cook, covered, in 1 inch of boiling salted water for 25 to 40 minutes, or until tender. Drain; add butter or margarine; season with salt and pepper.

A teaspoon of sugar added to cooking water improves the flavor. Rutabagas are good creamed with minced onion or chives and a dash of Worcestershire.
To Freeze—Cook rutabagas as above; mash. Cool, and spoon into freezer containers, allowing ½-inch headspace.

Can also be cut raw into cubes or slices. Scald in boiling water for 3 minutes. Chill in ice water. Drain; pack in freezer containers with ½-inch headspace. Seal.

RUTABAGA-POTATO SOUP

1 small rutabaga (about 1 pound)
1 teaspoon salt
1½ cups water
3 raw medium potatoes, peeled and thinly sliced
2 cups milk
¾ teaspoon sugar
1 cup chicken broth or bouillon
2 tablespoons butter or margarine
Seasoned salt and seasoned pepper to taste

Peel rutabaga and cut in small pieces. Add salt and water. Cook, covered, 15 to 20 minutes. Add potatoes and cook about 10 minutes (do not drain). Mash, add milk and remaining ingredients and heat. (Or add 1 cup milk and whirl in blender until smooth—add more milk if necessary. Add any remaining milk and other ingredients and heat.) Makes about 1½ quarts, or 6 servings.

RUTABAGA WITH SALT PORK

4 cups cubed rutabaga
¼ pound salt pork, finely chopped
1 onion, minced
Salt and pepper to taste

Cook rutabaga in boiling water until tender; drain. Fry pork until brown and crisp; add onion and cook for a few minutes longer. Add drained rutabaga. Cook for 5 minutes, stirring often to brown cubes slightly. Season with salt and pepper. Makes 4 to 6 servings.

RUTABAGA AU GRATIN

6 tablespoons butter or margarine
¼ cup all-purpose flour
2 cups milk
1 cup shredded sharp Cheddar cheese
Salt and pepper to taste
4 cups diced cooked rutabaga
½ cup soft bread crumbs

Melt ¼ cup butter and stir in flour. Gradually stir in milk. Cook over low heat, stirring constantly, until smooth and thick. Add cheese and stir until melted. Season with salt and pepper. Pour sauce over rutabaga in greased 1½-quart shallow baking dish. Mix crumbs with remaining 2 tablespoons butter and sprinkle over top. Bake in preheated hot oven (400°F.) about 15 minutes. Makes 6 servings.

SCALLOPED RUTABAGA AND APPLES

1 large rutabaga (3 to 3½ pounds), peeled and diced
Salt
3 tablespoons butter or margarine
2 cups sliced peeled apples
Brown sugar
⅛ teaspoon ground cinnamon
⅓ cup all-purpose flour

Cook rutabaga in small amount of boiling salted water, drain and mash with 1 tablespoon butter. Toss apples with ¼ cup firmly packed brown sugar and cinnamon. Arrange alternate layers of rutabaga and apples in greased 2-quart casserole, beginning and ending with rutabaga. Mix remaining 2 tablespoons butter, flour and ⅓ cup firmly packed brown sugar until crumbly. Sprinkle on casserole, cover and bake in preheated moderate oven (350°F.) 45 minutes. Uncover and bake 15 minutes longer. Makes 6 to 8 servings.
NOTE: Sliced peeled fresh pears can be substituted for the apples.

RUTABAGA-MACARONI SALAD

1 cup elbow macaroni
 Salt
¾ cup shredded rutabaga
¼ cup chopped green pepper
2 green onions, sliced
1 cup diced celery
 Mayonnaise
 Seasoned salt
 Lemon-pepper seasoning
 Salad greens
1 tomato, finely diced or cut in wedges

Cook macaroni in boiling salted water. Drain and rinse in cold water. Mix with next 4 ingredients and add mayonnaise to moisten. Add seasonings to taste. Line salad bowl with greens. Add salad and garnish with tomato. Makes 4 servings.
NOTE: Seashell or other shape macaroni can be used, if preferred.

MASHED RUTABAGA WITH ONION

1 medium rutabaga
2 onions
2 tablespoons butter or margarine
½ teaspoon salt
¼ teaspoon pepper

Cook rutabaga and onions in small amount of boiling salted water until tender. Drain. Mash; add butter and seasonings and beat well. Makes 4 to 6 servings.

RYE—A hardy annual cereal grass, *Secale cereale*, closely allied to wheat. It grows from four to six feet high and looks very much like wheat growing in the fields. Rye is the fifth most important cereal crop in the United States. The seeds are used to make flour, malt liquors, whisky, Holland gin, and a Russian drink, *kvass*.

Rye is also used as an animal fodder. Rye flour is usually mixed with wheat flour to make rye breads. These are especially popular with people of central and northern European and Slavic origin, countries where rye bread is a basic food. Pumpernickel bread, the heavy dark loaf, is made of all rye flour.

Rye can be grown in colder and damper climates than can wheat. It is thought that rye may have grown as a weed in parts of Asia where wheat was cultivated thousands of years ago. Ancient civilizations in warm climates, such as the Egyptian, did not seem to grow rye, but there are early traces of the grain in cold northern Europe. During Roman times it flourished in central Europe. Countries that could grow wheat easily looked down on its harsher cousin, rye. Theoprastus, a Roman naturalist who probably lived in the 3rd or 4th century B.C., thought that if wheat was planted on poor soils it would turn into rye.

This feeling by wheat eaters that rye was somehow inferior carried over into England. Part of the reason may be that rye flour was traditionally a part of the bread that was eaten by the poor.

The early Americans who came to New England found rye to be a more successful crop than wheat. Corn, grown first by the Indians, was the most important food of these early settlers, and the staple bread, known as rye'n'Injun, was made from rye flour and cornmeal. The Puritans, according to an 18th-century writer, were fond of saying: "Brown bread and the Gospel is good fare."

Rye flour can be used alone or combined with wheat flour. The rye flour makes a stickier and less-elastic dough than wheat. It is used to make breads, rolls, muffins, crackers.

Availability—Rye flour is available in food stores and health-food stores. It is sold as dark, light, medium, or unspecified rye flour. Rye grits and cream of rye are also available, as are rye wafers.

Storage—Whole rye flours or any other whole-rye products which contain the rye germ should be refrigerated. Refrigerator shelf: 6 months

Nutritive Food Values—A source of energy with small amounts of protein, potassium, and B vitamins.
Whole-grain, 3½ ounces = 334 calories
Light flour, 3½ ounces = 357 calories
Medium flour, 3½ ounces = 350 calories
Dark flour, 3½ ounces = 327 calories

FINNISH BREAD

1½ cups hot water
1 tablespoon sugar
1 tablespoon salt
2 tablespoons margarine
½ cup water*
1 package active dry yeast or 1 cake compressed yeast
3 cups rye flour
2½ cups all-purpose flour (about)

Measure hot water into a large mixing bowl. Stir in sugar, salt, and margarine. Cool to lukewarm. Measure ½ cup water into small warm bowl. *Use very warm water (105°F. to 115°F.) for dry yeast; use lukewarm (80°F. to 90°F.) for compressed. Sprinkle or crumple yeast into water. Let stand for a few minutes, then stir until dissolved. Add yeast mixture and rye flour to first mixture. Beat until smooth. Add 2 cups all-purpose flour and mix well. Add enough additional flour to make a soft dough. Turn out onto lightly floured board and knead until smooth and elastic, 8 to 10 minutes. Place in greased bowl, turning to grease all sides. Cover; let rise in warm place, free from draft, until doubled in bulk, about 45 minutes. Punch dough down; divide into halves. Shape into 2 loaves. Place in greased loaf pans 9 x 5 x 3 inches. Cover; let rise in warm place, free from draft, until doubled in bulk, about 40 minutes. Bake in preheated hot oven (400°F.) about 30 minutes, or until done. Serve warm with honey. Makes 2 loaves.

RYE

ONION RYE BREAD

A home baker can save up to two thirds the cost of variety breads.

    1 cup milk
    3 tablespoons sugar
    1 teaspoon salt
    3 tablespoons butter or margarine
    1 package active dry yeast
    ½ cup warm water (105° to 115°F.)
    2 tablespoons caraway seed
    ½ cup minced onion
    3 cups all-purpose flour
    1½ cups rye flour
    Cornmeal

Scald milk. Add sugar, salt and butter and stir until melted. Put in large bowl and cool to lukewarm. Dissolve yeast in water. Add yeast, caraway seed and onion to first mixture. Mix flours together and gradually stir into yeast mixture. Turn out on floured board and knead until smooth and elastic. Put in greased bowl and turn to grease top. Let rise in warm place free from drafts 2 hours, or until doubled in bulk. Punch down and roll out on floured board to form rectangle about 15 x 10 inches. Roll up starting from longer side. Pinch to seal edges. Taper ends by rolling back and forth on board. Put on greased baking sheet sprinkled with cornmeal. Let rise in warm place free from drafts 1 hour 15 minutes, or until doubled in bulk. Cut several shallow diagonal slashes in top. Bake in preheated moderate oven (350°) 25 minutes, or until golden brown. Cool on wire rack. Makes 1 large loaf.

CARAWAY RYE LOAVES

    3 cups rye flour
    1 package active dry yeast
    Vegetable oil
    2 cups milk
    ½ cup firmly packed light-brown sugar
    2 teaspoons salt
    2 teaspoons caraway seed
    2½ to 3½ cups all-purpose flour
    Yellow cornmeal

In large bowl of electric mixer, stir together rye flour and yeast. Put 2 tablespoons oil and next 4 ingredients in saucepan over low heat, stirring to blend, until very warm (120°F. to 130°F.). Add to flour mixture and beat at medium speed of electric mixer 2 minutes, or until smooth. Stir in enough all-purpose flour to make a moderately stiff dough. Turn out on lightly floured board and knead 10 minutes, or until smooth and elastic. Shape in ball and put in greased bowl, turning to grease top. Cover and let rise in warm place 1¼ hours, or until doubled in bulk. Punch down and divide in half. Shape in 2 balls and let rest on board 10 minutes. Roll each in a 14 x 9 inch rectangle. Starting at 9 inch end; roll up jelly-roll fashion. Seal seam, then, with side of hand, press ends to seal. Roll back and forth, tapering ends to elongate slightly. Put on greased baking sheet sprinkled with cornmeal. Cut 3 gashes diagonally ¼ inch deep across top of each loaf. Let rise in warm place 30 minutes, or until doubled in bulk. Bake in preheated hot oven (400°F.) 20 minutes. Reduce heat to 350°F. and bake 15 minutes longer, or until done. Brush with oil and cool on wire racks. Makes 2 loaves.

RYE-HONEY COOKIES

    2 cups honey
    1 cup rye flour
    1 cup cake flour
    1 teaspoon ground ginger

Heat honey until liquid. Sift together rye flour, cake flour, and ginger. Place flour in skillet and heat gently. The flour must not change color in any way. Gradually stir flour into hot honey. Beat vigorously with a large spoon until the dough clears the spoon. Cool until stiff enough to roll. Roll dough paper-thin on floured board and cut into 2-inch rounds. Bake on greased cookie sheets in preheated moderate oven (350°F.) for 10 to 12 minutes, or until well browned. Makes about 8 dozen cookies.
NOTE: This is a hard, chewy, flat cookie.

SWEDISH RYE COOKIES

    1 cup sifted all-purpose flour
    1 cup sifted rye flour
    ½ teaspoon salt
    ¾ cup soft butter
    ½ cup sugar
    2 teaspoons grated orange rind

Sift together flours and salt. Cream butter and sugar thoroughly with orange rind. Mix in flour until smooth dough forms. Wrap in wax paper or aluminum foil and chill until easy to handle, 2 hours in refrigerator or 30 minutes in freezing compartment. Divide dough into **halves; roll out ⅛ inch thick between sheets of wax paper or aluminum foil. Cut with floured 2½ inch doughnut cutter. Put on ungreased cookie sheet and prick with fork several times. Bake in preheated slow oven (325°F.) for 8 to 10 minutes. Watch carefully; these burn easily. Makes 4 dozen.**

S

SABAYON—A dessert sauce or simple dessert made of sugar, beaten eggs or egg yolks, and wine or liqueur or orange and lemon juice and grated rind. A variation containing whipped cream is also made. Sabayon is actually the French name for the Italian zabaglione or Austrian weinschaum. For a Sabayon recipe see section The Sauce Cook Book, dessert sauces.

SABLEFISH—A saltwater fish found in Pacific waters, also called black cod or skil, but unrelated to the cod. The oyster-white meat has a delicate flavor, but is very oily so it is best prepared by broiling or barbecuing. It is also commercially smoked and marketed as Alaskan or Canadian smoked black cod, a delicious preparation. Serve smoked sablefish like smoked salmon, and cook in the ways smoked salmon is prepared.

Availability and Purchasing Guide—Available fresh on West Coast only, whole and in steaks and fillets. Smoked sablefish may be found more generally. Sablefish are large, up to 40 pounds; buy steaks or fillets unless cooking on a large outdoor barbecue.

Storage—Wrap fresh or smoked fish in moistureproof paper and refrigerate.
Fresh, refrigerator shelf, raw: 1 to 2 days
Smoked, refrigerator shelf: 1 to 2 weeks
Fresh or smoked, prepared for freezing, freezer: 3 to 4 months

Nutritive Food Values—Good source of protein and fat.
Fresh, 3½ ounces, raw = 190 calories

Basic Preparation—Brush steaks or fillets with lemon or lime juice and sprinkle with lemon or lime rind before broiling, barbecuing or baking. Smoked sablefish can be broiled; or flake and use for fish cakes and casseroles.

BAKED SABLEFISH CREOLE

1 piece (2 pounds) of fresh sablefish
Salt and pepper
½ cup red wine
1 medium onion, chopped
1 garlic clove, minced
¼ cup butter or margarine
1 can (1 pound) tomatoes
Chopped parsley

Put fish in buttered shallow baking dish and sprinkle with salt and pepper. Add wine. Bake in preheated hot oven (400°F.) about 25 minutes, basting several times with wine in the bottom of the dish. Cook onion and garlic in butter for 2 or 3 minutes. Add tomatoes and simmer for 15 to 20 minutes. Season to taste and serve poured around fish. Top with parsley. Makes 4 to 6 servings.

SACCHARIN—A crystalline chemical used alone or in combination with other chemicals to add sweetners to foods without the addition of sugar. Believed to be the first of the artificial sweetners, it is very sweet, 250 to 300 times as sweet as sugar. It has a slight aftertaste of bitter almond and sometimes leaves a dryness in the throat. Since it has no food value, it is useful in both diabetic and low-calorie diets.

Saccharin has been found to be a carcinogen in some animal tests, and as a result is under review by the FDA. For a time saccharin was removed from the GRAS list (ingredients generally recognized as safe), and is being subjected to further tests.

SADDLE—In culinary usage the word is applied to a meat cut, most often of venison, mutton, or lamb, taken

SAFFLOWER

from below the last ribs to the legs on both sides and including the loins. It is a luxurious cut and may be roasted either bone-in or boned.

The term "saddle of hare," found in English literature, refers to a cut extending from the base of the hare's shoulder to the tail.

SAFFLOWER or BASTARD SAFFRON

—An Old World herb, *Carthamus tinctorius*, resembling a thistle, with large vivid red or orange flowers. Native to the East Indies, it is cultivated in southern Europe and in Egypt. The flowers are used as the basis of a dye widely used in the Orient for dyeing silks and cottons.

An edible oil it is cold-pressed from the white seeds which remain when the blossoms fade. Safflower oil is light, flavorless, and colorless. It does not solidify under refrigeration as do many other oils so it is good for salad dressings and marinades, as well as for frying and other recipes in which oil is an ingredient. It is also the basis for a palatable margarine, favored for its low cholesterol count, butter-like flavor and easy spreadability. Safflower oil is available in food stores.

SAFFRON

—A small crocus, *Crocus satirus*, with purple flowers. There are three deep orange-yellow stigmas, or filaments, in the center of each tiny blossom. These are aromatic when dried, with a pungent taste, and they are used to add flavor and color in cooking. The stigmas are so tiny they must be picked by hand, and it takes at least 4,000 of them to produce one ounce of saffron, which accounts for its high price. They are dried in a kiln, either loosely or between paper-covered boards. As a cooking spice, saffron, comes either in the shape of the dried filament shreds or it is ground. Saffron colors any food a bright yellow.

Saffron appears to have come from the Near East. Its name would bear this out, for it is an adaptation of the Arabic word *za'faran,* "yellow."

Since antiquity, the deep-yellow color of saffron and its aromatic properties have been used for dyeing, for flavoring foods, and for medicinal purposes. As early as 4,000 B.C., the Assyrians used it as a medicine, and so did the Egyptians, who also anointed their royalty with saffron-tinted oil. In the Song of Solomon (4:14) in the Bible, saffron is mentioned as one of the chief spices. The gods and goddesses of the ancient Greeks were dressed in saffron-colored robes. Greeks and Romans made saffron into a fragrant essence which was sprinkled in streets and theaters to sweeten the air, and also used as a personal cosmetic.

The Roman legions introduced saffron into England. It became tremendously popular there both as a dyestuff and as a food flavoring. A 14th-century cook book lists saffron as an ingredient in more than half its recipes. At first saffron was grown in monastery and manor gardens, but by the 16th century it had become a commercial crop for export.

The different varieties of saffron have varying degrees of pungency: Italian saffron, for instance, is stronger than the Spanish saffron which is imported into the United States.

Either whole or ground, saffron should be used with discretion, not because of its price, but because a little saffron goes a very long way. It gives a distinctive color to breads and cakes, and is much in favor with rice dishes, especially those of Spain, Italy, the Near East, and India, where saffron is much used. Saffron also enhances cream soups, sauces, potatoes, and veal and chicken dishes.

Availability—Whole or ground Spanish saffron is available in some food stores, in gourmet stores, and in stores catering to people of Mediterranean descent. Most drugstores also carry it.

SAFFRON VEAL

- 1/8 to 1/4 teaspoon whole or ground saffron (amount depends on taste)
- 1 tablespoon hot water
- 2 pounds veal steak, cut into 1/2-inch strips
- 1/4 cup butter or margarine
- 1/2 teaspoon salt
- 1/4 teaspoon pepper
- 1 tablespoon instant minced onion
- 1/4 cup hot bouillon
- 2 cups light cream
- 1 tablespoon cornstarch
- 1 tablespoon cold water

Soak saffron in hot water. Trim all fat and gristle off meat. Melt butter in skillet; add veal strips and cook for about 2 minutes, or until browned on all sides. If whole saffron is used, strain and use liquid. Add saffron, salt, pepper, and minced onion to veal. Stir in bouillon. Cook, covered, over lowest possible heat for 35 minutes, or until veal is tender. Stir frequently and check for moisture; add a little more bouillon if necessary to prevent scorching; add cream. Mix together cornstarch and cold water to make a smooth paste. Stir into meat. Cook, stirring constantly, until sauce is thickened and smooth. Serve very hot with buttered noodles or rice. Makes 6 servings.

SAFFRON TEA BREAD

- 2 cups sifted all-purpose flour
- 2 teaspoons baking powder
- 1 teaspoon salt
- 1/2 cup shortening
- 1/4 teaspoon baking soda
- 1/8 teaspoon ground saffron
- 2 teaspoons grated lemon rind
- 3/4 cup sugar
- 2 large eggs
- 3/4 cup water
- 2 tablespoons lemon juice

Sift first 3 ingredients together and set aside. Mix shortening with next 3 ingredients, gradually blend in sugar. Beat in eggs, one at a time. Mix water and lemon juice and add to mixture alternately with sifted dry ingredients. Beat for 30 seconds. Pour into well greased, lightly floured loaf pan 9 x 5 x 3 inches. Bake in preheated moderate oven (350°F.) for 1 hour, or until done. Cool in pan for 10 minutes. Turn out onto a rack to finish cooling. Let stand overnight before slicing. Good with cream cheese.

SAFFRON RICE

- ¼ teaspoon ground saffron
- 2 tablespoons boiling water
- ⅛ teaspoon garlic powder
- ¼ teaspoon white pepper
- 1 teaspoon salt
- 3 tablespoons cooking oil
- 2½ cups boiling chicken broth or bouillon
- 1 cup raw long-grain rice
- ¼ cup seedless raisins
- 3 tablespoons shredded blanched almonds

Dissolve saffron in boiling water and put in saucepan with next 5 ingredients. Bring to a boil. Stir in rice and raisins. Bring again to a boil and put in greased 1-quart casserole. Cover and bake in preheated moderate oven (350°F.) for 45 minutes, or until rice is tender. Stir in almonds 10 minutes before rice is done. Makes 6 servings.
NOTE: This rice dish is good with chicken, lamb, shrimps, or other seafood.

SAGE [*Salvia officinalis*]

There are over 500 varieties of this popular herb growing in temperate zones throughout the world. The fresh or dried leaves are widely used in cooking for their aromatic bitter taste. Dalmatian sage, grown in Yugoslavia and imported in great amounts into this country, is one of the best varieties of the plant. In addition to the imported Dalmatian sage and the common garden sage *(Salvia officinalis)*, other varieties are white sage, Cyprus sage, *Salvia horminum* (another garden variety), meadow sage, pineapple sage, and clary sage. Not of culinary or medicinal value is the unrelated purple sage or sagebrush, which grows profusely on the western plains of the United States.

The garden sage, long grown in New England, is generally one to two feet high, with grayish leaves and bluish or purplish flowers. Clary sage, usually called only clary, is taller with unusually large leaves. Dalmatian and pineapple sage are especially mild, and the pineapple has a pineapple fragrance.

The name "sage" comes through French from the Latin *salvus*, meaning "safe, whole, or healthy." Since its earliest usage as a medicinal plant it has been said to lengthen and strengthen life. An Arabian proverb, also well known in England, asks "How can a man die who has Sage in his garden?" This question has been answered most eloquently by an 18th-century Englishman, Sir John Hill, who summed up the properties of sage in *Virtues of British Herbs* in 1662. "Sage," said Sir John, "will retard the rapid progress of decay that treads upon our heels so fast in the latter years of life . . . and prevent absolutely that sad depression of spirits, which age often feels and always fears." It will, in answer to the Arabian question, "make the lamp of life, so long as nature lets it burn, burn brightly."

Another of the reasons for sage's popularity and value lay in its culinary use. It was one of the most popular of medieval herbs, flavoring pottage, salads, poultry stuffings, and meat pies.

Accustomed to the many uses and the goodness of sage as a seasoning, it is no surprise that the colonists early brought the plant to this country. Its flavor went well with pork, the colonists' chief meat, as well as in stuffing for their poultry and game. The Shakers began the growing and commercial packaging of the popular herb; America's huge meat-packing industry made and still makes much use of it in sausages. Today, sage rates as the most popular of the seasoning herbs and is one of the most important ingredients in prepared poultry seasoning. Its use does not have to be limited to stuffing and pork products, however; it also adds flavor to cheese, fish, poultry, salad dressings, chowders, cream soups, and such vegetables as Brussels sprouts, carrots, eggplant, lima beans, onions, peas, and tomatoes.

Ground fresh sage is available, as are cut dried leaves and stems of sage, which are also known as sage "tea," and whole dried sage leaves. Since fresh sage has a superb flavor, it is well worth growing it or buying it fresh.

CHICKEN LIVERS WITH SAGE

Thread small skewers alternately with chicken livers, bacon slices, and dry or fresh sage leaves. Broil as usual. Season with salt and pepper when done. Allow 3 or 4 chicken livers, 2 bacon slices, and a few leaves of sage for each serving.
NOTE: This is one of the happiest flavor combinations, especially when made with fresh sage.

SAGE STUFFING

- 1 chicken bouillon cube
- ½ cup hot water
- 9 cups toasted soft bread crumbs
- 1½ teaspoons salt
- 1 tablespoon dried sage
- ½ teaspoon pepper
- ½ cup instant minced onion
- 1 cup butter or margarine, melted

Dissolve bouillon cube in hot water; add rest of ingredients. Use to stuff a 10- to 12-pound ready-to-cook turkey. Makes about 8 cups stuffing.

SAGO

A starch extracted from the pithy trunks of various tropical palms, among them the sago palm. It is basic food in the southwest Pacific where sago meal is used for making thick soups, biscuits, and puddings. In the United States it is occasionally used for thickening puddings and sauce.

To make sago, the palm trees are felled and the trunk is cut into pieces. Then the bark is taken off and the inner portion soaked in water to remove the starch. The pulpy paste that results is dried and used as sago meal. When the paste is rubbed through a sieve, pearl sago results. Sago flour is also made from the sago meal. Small and large pearl sago is available in health-food and specialty food stores.

When used for cooking, pearl sago must be soaked for 1 hour before use. Soak each ¼ cup pearl sago in ½ cup water until water is absorbed.

SAKE

The national alcoholic drink of Japan. Made by fermenting rice, its character lies somewhere between western beers and wines. It is yellowish-white and is often drunk warm.

SALAD COOKBOOK

SALAD—The first salads were edible herbs or plants dressed only with salt. The word "salad," in fact, derives from the Latin word for salt, *sal*. Salt was the universal preservative, and vegetables could be kept the year round with some sort of salt dressing. From this simple beginning, salads have expanded to include a wide variety of ingredients: fruits, vegetables, herbs, meat, cheese, and fish, cooked or uncooked. There is everything from a simple lettuce salad to a chef's salad which is a main dish full of meats and cheeses. Salads are usually eaten cold, but there are hot salads, such as hot potato salad.

Depending on their ingredients, salads may be the main course of a meal or one of its accompaniments. Regional and individual tastes dictate when an accompanying salad is served. Most often a salad is served with or after the main course. But on the West Coast, the salad is served first. This, in fact, is done in some European countries as well, where the hors-d'oeuvre often consists of a vegetable salad of some sort.

Whatever the ingredients of the salad and whenever it is served, authorities agree that it should have a moist dressing: oil and vinegar, mayonnaise, or variations of these ingredients.

SALAD GREENS

Availability—Salad greens are available in food stores all year round. Peak months are generally May through August. For further information check Endive, Lettuce, Spinach and Watercress (see index).

Nutritive Food Values
  Endive—a good source of vitamin A and a fair source of iron.
  Lettuce has small amounts of vitamins A and C, and minerals if outer leaves are to be eaten.
  Spinach—An excellent source of vitamin C and iron and a fair source of riboflavin.
  Watercress—a good source of vitamin A and C; supplies a variety of minerals and some iron.
  All salad greens are low in calories.

3½ ounces, raw = 13 to 18 calories

TO MAKE A GOOD SALAD

Storing Lettuce—Rinse under running water, drain well, wrap in foil or other moisture-proof wrap, and refrigerate.

Preparing Greens—Wash greens thoroughly, changing water frequently and having final water very cold. Shake off excess water from greens and drain well; dry completely on clean dish towel or paper towels. Put in plastic bag and store in refrigerator to crisp. Greens should not be frozen.

Salad Bowl—Use a wood, glass or china bowl. Be sure bowl is large enough to hold greens during tossing. Bowl can be rubbed with split clove of garlic before greens are added. Tear greens—one kind or a combination of several—in bite-size pieces and add to bowl with any other ingredients. Firm heads may be cut in wedges. Add dressing just before serving and toss lightly but thoroughly to coat each leaf.

Salad Dressing Variations—Any favorite oil, such as olive, safflower, peanut, corn or soy, or a combination of oils can be used. Use one fourth to one third as much vinegar as oil. Red- or white-wine, cider, herb or other vinegar can be used. Or vary dressing with lemon, lime or orange juice. Add a few chopped fresh herbs, such as thyme, marjoram, basil, oregano or dill, or a pinch of dried herbs. Dry or Dijon mustard, minced chives and/or parsley can be added to the dressing. For convenience, make a double batch of your favorite dressing and keep it on hand in the refrigerator. Bring to room temperature and shake well before using. Many bottled dressings are available. Shake well before using and refrigerate after opening.

TOSSED SALAD VARIATIONS

Vary a simple tossed salad of greens with the addition of green-pepper strips, sliced ripe or green olives, cut green onions, sliced radishes and/or cucumbers, sliced red or white onions, tomato wedges or small whole tomatoes, chopped nuts, slivered carrots, cooked peas or other vegetables, avocado slices, raisins, or tiny croutons. Or add fruits such as diced red apple, a few well-drained grapefruit or orange sections, diced melon, sliced fresh or canned pears, seedless or seeded grapes, drained fruit cocktail, or pineapple cubes.

Adding Dressing—In most cases dressing should be added just before serving. Avoid using too much or you will have a limp wilted salad, and much of a salad's visual appeal lies in its crispness.

TOSSED SALADS

BLUEBERRY-RADISH SALAD

    1   teaspoon grated orange rind
        Juice of 1 orange
    ⅓   cup oil of your choice
    2   tablespoons minced parsley
        Salt and freshly ground white pepper
    6   cups torn escarole (or mixed greens if preferred)
    1½ cups coarsely shredded radishes
    1   cup fresh blueberries

Combine and mix well first 4 ingredients. Season with salt and white pepper. Put escarole in bowl. Top with radishes, then sprinkle with blueberries. Just before serving, add dressing and toss. Good with cottage cheese. Makes 6 servings.

SALAD

DATE-ORANGE SALAD

- 1 cup pitted dates, cut in lengthwise strips
- 2 tablespoons lime or lemon juice
- 1/3 cup oil of your choice
- 1 tablespoon honey
- 2 tablespoons minced green onion
  Salt and freshly ground pepper
- 3 oranges
- 6 cups torn greens

Put first 5 ingredients in salad bowl and season lightly with salt and pepper. Mix well and marinate at least 1/2 hour. Meanwhile, peel oranges and remove all white membrane. Thinly slice oranges crosswise. Just before serving, add to first mixture with the greens and toss. Good with ham or pork. Makes 6 servings.

PRUNE AND MANDARIN-ORANGE SALAD

- 2 tablespoons lemon juice
- 1/3 cup bottled French dressing
- 1 cup cut-up pitted prunes
- 1 can (11 ounces) mandarin-orange wedges, drained
- 6 cups torn greens
- 1 small red onion, thinly sliced
- 1/4 cup salted nuts, chopped

Mix well in salad bowl first 3 ingredients. Marinate at least 1/2 hour. Just before serving, add mandarin oranges and greens. Toss, then sprinkle with onion rings and nuts. Good with chicken. Makes 6 servings.

ROQUEFORT SALAD

- 6 to 8 cups bite-size pieces of salad greens
- 1 garlic clove
  Salt to taste
- 1/4 cup olive oil
- 1 tablespoon cider vinegar
- 1 1/2 tablespoons fresh lemon juice
- 1/4 teaspoon pepper
- 1/2 cup (about 2 ounces) crumbled Roquefort cheese

Place greens in a salad bowl that has been rubbed with garlic. Add salt, oil, vinegar, lemon juice, pepper, and Roquefort. Toss lightly. Serve at once. Makes 6 to 8 servings.

CHINESE-STYLE SALAD

- 1 medium cucumber, partially peeled, then thinly sliced
- 1/3 cup finely chopped green onion
- 4 cups thinly sliced (1/8 inch) Chinese cabbage
- 1/2 cup thinly sliced radishes
- 1 cup dairy sour cream
- 1 to 1 1/2 tablespoons soy sauce
- 2 tablespoons rice vinegar
  Dash of monosodium glutamate

In salad bowl, combine and toss first 4 ingredients. Chill until serving time. Combine and mix well sour cream with remaining ingredients. Serve in separate dish as dressing. Good with pork or beef. Makes 6 servings.
NOTE: If desired, omit last 4 ingredients and toss salad ingredients with French dressing to moisten.

CAULIFLOWER-OLIVE SALAD

- 1 1/2 to 2 cups thinly sliced cauliflower florets
- 1/2 cup coarsely chopped black olives
- 1 jar (2 ounces) chopped pimiento, drained
- 1/4 cup minced green onions
  Pinch of marjoram or oregano
- 2 tablespoons red-wine vinegar
- 1/3 cup oil of your choice
  Salt
  Dash of hot pepper sauce
- 5 cups torn greens

Put first 7 ingredients in salad bowl; toss well and season with salt and pepper sauce. Just before serving, add greens and toss. Good with hamburgers. Makes 6 servings.

TOSSED ZUCCHINI GREEN SALAD

- 2 medium zucchini, thinly sliced
- 1/3 cup minced red onion
- 1 teaspoon chopped fresh dill or 1/4 teaspoon dillweed
- 6 cups torn mixed greens
  Bottled Italian, blue-cheese or Gorgonzola dressing

Put first 4 ingredients in salad bowl and chill until serving time. Pour about 1/2 cup dressing on top, toss and serve. Good with pasta. Makes 6 servings.

FRESH-MUSHROOM AND PARSLEY SALAD

- 1 clove garlic
- 6 large firm white mushrooms, thinly sliced
- 1/3 cup minced parsley
- 2 tablespoons lemon juice or white-wine vinegar
- 1/3 cup olive oil
  Pinch of dried basil
  Dash of salt and white pepper
- 6 cups mixed greens (endive and Bibb lettuce)
- 1/3 cup finely chopped radishes

Rub wooden salad bowl with split garlic clove. Add next 4 ingredients, toss and season with basil, salt and white pepper. Marinate 1/2 hour or longer. Add greens, toss, then sprinkle with radishes. Good with beef. Makes 6 servings.

BROCCOLI AND BERMUDA-ONION SALAD

- 2 cups small fresh-broccoli buds
- 1/2 small Bermuda (sweet) onion, cut in quarters and thinly sliced crosswise (about 1 cup)
- 1 dill pickle, thinly sliced
- 1/3 to 1/2 cup bottled Italian or French dressing
- 5 cups torn romaine lettuce
- 1 pimiento, chopped

Put first 4 ingredients in salad bowl and marinate at least 1/2 hour. Add lettuce, toss, then sprinkle with pimiento. Good with sausages, frankfurters or hamburgers. Makes 6 servings.

Classic Chef's Salad

GERMAN SPINACH SALAD

- 1 pound small fresh spinach leaves
- ½ cup mayonnaise
- ½ cup dairy sour cream
- 6 anchovies, minced
- 1½ tablespoons each chopped green-onion tops and minced parsley
- 1½ tablespoons each cider vinegar and lemon juice
- ½ garlic clove, minced
- Cheddar-cheese cubes or garlic croutons

Wash and dry spinach. Mix remaining ingredients except cheese and add to spinach. Mix lightly and garnish with cheese. Makes 4 servings.

MAIN-DISH SALADS: MEAT, FISH, AND POULTRY

CLASSIC CHEF'S SALAD

- Assorted greens
- Strips of ham or tongue, Swiss cheese, and turkey or chicken
- Sliced cucumbers
- Radish roses
- Hard-cooked eggs
- French Dressing
- Salt and freshly ground pepper

Have ingredients in separate dishes, and family members or guests help themselves. Other ingredients such as anchovies, artichoke hearts, small sardines, olives, red-onion rings, or cauliflowerets may be used.

BRUSSELS CHEF'S SALAD

- 1 pint fresh, or 1 package (10 ounces) frozen, Brussels sprouts, cooked
- 1½ cups cooked ham strips
- 3 cups cooked chicken strips
- 1 cup diced process Swiss cheese
- ½ cup chopped celery
- 3 cups torn lettuce
- ¼ cup cider vinegar
- ½ cup salad oil
- ¾ teaspoon paprika
- 1 teaspoon salt
- ¼ teaspoon pepper
- 2 tablespoons sugar

Combine cooked Brussels sprouts, ham, chicken, cheese, celery, and lettuce; toss lightly. Chill. Mix remaining ingredients; blend or shake well. Before serving, combine mixtures; toss lightly, but thoroughly. Makes 6 servings.

FRENCH BEEF SALAD

- Thinly sliced cold cooked beef
- Thinly sliced tomatoes
- Sliced onion
- Sliced cooked potatoes
- Pitted ripe olives
- Vinaigrette Sauce
- Hard-cooked eggs, quartered
- Chopped parsley

Arrange first 4 ingredients in alternating layers in a salad bowl. Garnish with olives and pour Vinaigrette Sauce over top. Add quartered eggs and sprinkle with parsley.

ORANGE CHEF'S SALAD

- ½ bunch watercress
- ½ head each lettuce and romaine
- 1½ cups orange sections
- 1 cup diced unpeeled apples
- 1½ cups slivered cooked chicken
- ½ cup diced sharp Cheddar cheese
- ⅔ cup French Dressing

Tear salad greens into bite-size pieces. Add remaining ingredients and toss lightly. Makes 4 to 6 servings.

HEARTY SUPPER SALAD

- ½ pound frankfurters, thinly sliced
- 2 cooked potatoes, diced
- ½ cup thinly sliced celery
- ¼ cup finely chopped onion
- ½ green pepper, cut in thin strips
- ¼ cup vegetable oil
- 2 tablespoons cider vinegar
- 1 teaspoon salt
- ¼ teaspoon pepper
- 2 cups shredded lettuce
- ¼ cup Swiss-cheese strips
- Few tomato wedges (optional)

Brown frankfurters in skillet. Add next 8 ingredients and toss lightly; chill. Just before serving, add lettuce, cheese, and tomato wedges, if used; toss gently but thoroughly. Makes 6 to 8 servings.

PERFECT CHICKEN SALAD

- 1 roasting chicken (5 to 6 pounds), quartered
- Salt
- 1 onion, sliced
- 2 whole cloves
- 1 celery stalk
- 1 parsley sprig
- Pepper
- Mayonnaise (preferably homemade)
- Bibb lettuce or romaine
- Cucumber
- Capers
- Toasted walnut halves

Cook chicken in salted water to cover, together with onion, cloves, celery, and parsley. The white meat should take ⅓ less time to cook than the dark; remove it when it is tender, leaving the dark meat for an additional period. Cool chicken and remove skin. Cut white meat into long pieces, about 1 x 2 inches, and dice dark meat. Season to taste with salt and pepper. Toss chicken with Mayonnaise. Arrange on a salad plate with bibb lettuce at one end and crisp sliced cucumber at the other. Spoon more Mayonnaise over chicken. Garnish with capers and walnuts. Serve with tiny buttered rolls, a fruit tart, and a chilled white wine. Makes 4 servings.

LAMB, CUCUMBER, AND TOMATO SALAD

- 2 cups diced cooked lamb
- 1 cucumber, thinly sliced
- 2 tomatoes, diced
- 1 apple, diced
- 4 cups broken lettuce, romaine, and chicory
- Salt and pepper to taste
- Dairy sour cream

Mix all ingredients except sour cream. Moisten with cream; toss. Makes 4 servings.

BACON-EGG SALAD

- 2 heads Boston lettuce or romaine
- 5 hard-cooked eggs, chopped
- 12 slices bacon (about 10 ounces), cooked; reserve bacon fat
- 6 green onions, minced
- 4 tablespoons cider vinegar
- ½ teaspoon salt
- Freshly ground black pepper

Break lettuce into a large bowl. Add eggs, crisp and crumbled bacon, and green onions. To the warm bacon fat in the pan add vinegar, salt and several good grindings of fresh black pepper. Pour over salad, mix well and serve. Makes 4 servings. This is good with grilled salmon.

SAUSAGE-CHEESE-POTATO SALAD

- 2 cups diced cooked potatoes
- 3 hard-cooked eggs, diced
- 1 cup diced celery
- 1 tablespoon minced onion
- ½ cup cubed salami
- ½ cup cubed liverwurst
- ½ cup cubed sharp Cheddar cheese
- 1 cup finely sliced cabbage
- ¼ cup olive oil
- Salt and pepper
- ½ cup mayonnaise
- Salad greens
- Paprika

Mix first 8 ingredients. Add olive oil, and salt and pepper to taste. Lightly mix in mayonnaise. Put on greens and sprinkle with paprika. Makes 6 to 8 servings.

GAME SALAD

Marinate neat pieces of cold cooked rabbit, venison and game birds in French dressing sharpened with lemon juice and seasoned with grated onion. Put on lettuce and cover with mayonnaise. Garnish with celery, parsley and hard-cooked-egg slices, and with either capers and thin slices of sour pickle or cubes of currant jelly.

MEAT AND VEGETABLE SALAD

1 cup diced cooked meat (beef, lamb, or pork)
1 bunch of watercress (leaves only), chopped
1 cup diced cooked potatoes
1 cup diced cooked beets
2 large unpeeled red apples, diced
1 sweet pickle, minced
¼ cup capers
   Dressing (see Salade Parisienne)
   Salt and pepper to taste

Mix all ingredients and chill thoroughly. Makes 6 servings.

MEXICAN BEEF SALAD

Slice leftover boiled or roast beef, then shred in strips. Marinate at least 1 hour in French dressing to which a good dash of hot pepper sauce has been added. Serve on bed of lettuce; sprinkle with more French dressing and garnish with slices of tomato, green pepper rings and onion slices.

MEAT-AND-RICE-AND-EVERYTHING-NICE SALAD

1 cup diced cooked pork, veal, beef or chicken
3 cups cooked white rice
   Dressing
1 cup sliced radishes
   Salt and pepper
1 cup coarsely shredded carrot
1 cup coarsely shredded white turnip
   Mayonnaise or green-goddess dressing
   Sliced scored cucumbers
2 tomatoes, sliced
   Green-pepper strips
   Finely sliced green onion
   Black and pimiento-stuffed olives
   Watercress and pimiento rose (optional)

Mix first 3 ingredients and chill until serving time. Then stir in radishes and season to taste with salt and pepper. Pile in center of serving plate and surround with individual mounds of carrot and turnip each mixed with a little mayonnaise. Garnish with next 5 ingredients, and watercress and pimiento, if desired. Makes 4 to 6 servings.

Dressing

Mix ½ teaspoon salt, 1 teaspoon paprika, ¼ teaspoon dry mustard, ½ teaspoon curry powder, ¼ teaspoon pepper, dash of cayenne, pinch of dried tarragon, 3 tablespoons vinegar and ¼ cup olive oil.

VEAL SALAD WITH MARINATED BROCCOLI

Mix 2 cups each diced cooked veal, diced apple, and sliced celery with ⅓ cup well-seasoned French Dressing. Season to taste; chill. Pour ⅓ cup dressing over 1 bunch of warm cooked broccoli; cool, then chill. Serve with veal. Makes 4 to 6 servings.

Meat-and-Rice-and-Everything-Nice Salad

SALAD

DUCK-ORANGE SALAD

Duck and orange is a classic combination, and this salad is well worth making, even if you have to cook a duck to do so.

- 2 cups diced cooked duck
- 2 cups diced peeled oranges
- ½ cup French dressing (or a little more)
- ½ teaspoon paprika
- 1 tablespoon chutney
- Lettuce

Gently mix duck and orange with French dressing; season with paprika and chutney. Let stand in refrigerator 30 minutes. Serve on lettuce leaves. Makes 4 to 6 servings.

CURRIED ROCK-LOBSTER SALAD

- Salt
- 4 frozen rock-lobster tails (about 6 ounces each)
- 1 cup thinly sliced celery
- 2 tablespoons thinly sliced blanched almonds, toasted
- ¾ cup mayonnaise (about)
- 1½ teaspoons curry powder
- Juice of 1 lemon
- Pepper
- Stuffed olives, paprika

Bring 1½ quarts of water to boil with 1 teaspoon salt. Add lobster tails and bring to boil. Simmer for 7 minutes if frozen and 5 minutes if thawed. Drain; cool. With kitchen scissors cut under membrane of lobster, leaving outer hard shell intact. Remove meat and reserve shells. Chill meat; dice; add celery and nuts. Mix ½ cup mayonnaise with curry powder and lemon juice. Combine two mixtures. Season to taste with salt and pepper. Pile into reserved shells. Garnish with remaining mayonnaise, slices of stuffed olives, and paprika. Makes 4 servings.

SALADE RUSSE

- ¼ cup dry white wine
- 1 cup sliced boiled potatoes
- 1 cup flaked cooked fish
- 2 or 3 tomatoes, sliced
- ½ cucumber, sliced
- 1 medium head lettuce, broken
- 3 or 4 sweet pickles, chopped
- ½ cup pitted black olives
- 1 tablespoon chopped fresh tarragon leaves or generous pinch of dried tarragon
- ½ cup mayonnaise
- 2 tablespoons lemon juice
- 3 tablespoons milk

Pour wine over potatoes in bowl. Combine next 7 ingredients. Toss with mixture of remaining ingredients. Add potatoes and mix lightly. Makes 6 servings.

FRESH GRAPEFRUIT SHRIMP SALAD

- 1½ cups fresh grapefruit sections
- 2 cups cooked shrimps, deveined
- 1 cup diced celery (white part only)
- 1 tablespoon fresh lemon juice
- 1 tablespoon heavy cream
- ¼ cup mayonnaise
- ¼ teaspoon each salt and white pepper
- Salad greens

Combine grapefruit, shrimps, and celery. Mix together lemon juice, cream, mayonnaise, and salt and pepper. Add to first mixture and toss. Serve on a bed of salad greens. Makes 4 servings.

AVOCADO HALVES WITH SPICED SHRIMPS

- 1 pound fresh jumbo shrimps
- 1 heaping teaspoon pickling spice
- 2 large ripe avocados
- 1 cup dairy sour cream
- ½ teaspoon salt
- 1 tablespoon lemon juice
- 1 pimiento, diced

Cook shrimps with spice in boiling water until pink and just tender. Drain shrimps, shell, and devein. Chill. Halve avocados and remove seeds. Spoon shrimps into hollows of avocados. Mix remaining ingredients and serve as dressing for shrimps and avocados. Makes 4 servings.

SALADE PARISIENNE

- 1 cup each cooked green beans, peas, and cauliflower
- 3 raw carrots, shredded
- ½ cup sliced raw mushrooms
- ½ cup diced cooked chicken livers
- ½ cup diced cooked shrimps
- Dressing

Mix vegetables, chicken livers, and shrimps. Pour Dressing over first mixture and toss well. Makes 4 servings.

Dressing

- 1 teaspoon prepared mustard
- ⅓ cup olive oil
- Salt and pepper
- Cider vinegar
- Dash of sugar
- 1 tablespoon heavy cream

Put mustard in small bowl and gradually beat in oil. Season and add vinegar to taste. Add sugar and cream.

SALAD

SALMAGUNDI SALAD WITH SALAMI AND LIVERWURST

- 2 cups diced cooked potatoes
- 3 hard-cooked eggs, diced
- 1 cup diced celery
- 1 tablespoon minced onion
- ½ cup cubed hard salami
- ½ cup cubed liverwurst
- ½ cup cubed sharp Cheddar cheese
- 1 cup shredded cabbage
- ¼ cup olive oil
- Salt and pepper
- ½ cup mayonnaise
- Salad greens
- Paprika

Mix first 8 ingredients. Add olive oil, and salt and pepper to taste. Mix lightly but well. Add mayonnaise. Serve salad on greens with a sprinkling of paprika. Makes 4 servings.

BAKED CHICKEN SALAD

- 4 cups diced cooked chicken
- ¾ cup mayonnaise
- ¾ cup canned cream of chicken soup
- 2 cups chopped celery
- 4 hard-cooked eggs, sliced
- 1 teaspoon salt
- 1 teaspoon finely minced onion
- 2 tablespoons lemon juice
- 2 pimientos, cut up
- 1 cup crushed potato chips
- ⅔ cup finely shredded sharp Cheddar
- ⅓ cup chopped almonds (optional)

Mix first 9 ingredients. Put in greased large shallow 1½-quart baking dish. Combine potato chips with cheese, and almonds, if used, and sprinkle on top. Chill several hours or overnight. Bake in preheated hot oven (400°F.) 25 minutes, or until heated. Makes 8 servings.

JAPANESE SHRIMP AND EGG SALAD

- ½ cup raw rice
- 1 tablespoon instant minced onion
- 1 cup well-seasoned French Dressing
- 1 package (10 ounces) frozen shrimps, cooked
- 4 hard-cooked eggs
- Salad greens
- 3 sweet gherkins, chopped
- 2 tablespoons catsup
- 1 tablespoon capers

Cook and drain rice. Add onion, ½ cup French Dressing, shrimps, and 2 eggs, diced. Mix lightly with fork, and chill. Put on greens in bowl. Sprinkle pickles around edge. Grate separately remaining whites and yolks of 2 eggs. Sprinkle whites next to pickles and put yolks in center. Serve with remaining ½ cup Dressing mixed with catsup and capers. Makes 4 to 6 servings.

CRAB, ARTICHOKE AND AVOCADO SALAD

Put a layer of lettuce on a platter and arrange 1 pound crab meat in center. Surround with artichoke hearts (it's nice to stuff them with a little caviar), rings of avocado and red or green pepper. Serve a side dish of mayonnaise mixed with an equal amount of whipped cream and highly seasoned with grated onion and minced parsley.

HERRING SALAD, DANISH STYLE

- 2 salt herring
- 1 cup diced cooked beef, lamb or veal
- 2 cups diced cooked potato
- 1 cup diced cooked beets
- 1 medium onion, chopped
- 1 teaspoon dry mustard
- 1 teaspoon vinegar
- 1 cup cold medium white sauce
- 1 teaspoon sugar
- Salt and pepper
- 2 hard-cooked eggs, sieved
- Parsley

Soak herring in water overnight. Drain, bone, skin and cut in ¼-inch dice. Combine herring, meat, potato, beets and onion; chill well. Mix mustard and vinegar. Add white sauce (2 tablespoons each butter and flour, 1 cup milk, salt and pepper), sugar, and salt and pepper to taste. Mix well with herring mixture and pack into lightly greased 9 x 5 x 3-inch loaf pan. Chill thoroughly. Unmold and garnish with eggs and parsley. Makes 6 servings.

SALADE NIÇOISE

- Crisp salad greens
- Hard-cooked eggs, sliced
- Anchovy fillets
- Sliced cold potatoes
- Olive oil
- Cider vinegar
- Sliced peeled tomatoes or tiny cherry tomatoes
- Thin green-pepper rings
- Tuna fish
- Tiny ripe olives
- Cold cooked green beans
- Capers
- Onion rings
- Vinaigrette Sauce
- Fresh basil (optional)

Arrange greens on a large round or oval platter. Arrange slices of egg on the greens and top slices with a curled anchovy. Add potatoes, marinated in oil and vinegar, and remaining ingredients, except last 2. Serve with Vinaigrette Sauce seasoned with basil, if desired.
NOTE: This salad can be a whole meal at lunch or a first course at a buffet supper, followed by a ragout or stew.

Mexican Beef Salad,
Herring Salad Danish Style,
Crab, Artichoke
and Avocado Salad

SALAD

TUNA-FISH SALAD

2 cans (7 ounces each) tuna, drained and flaked
1 cup diced celery or cucumber
Juice of 1 lemon
Cooked Sour-Cream Dressing or mayonnaise
Salad greens

Mix first three ingredients. Add Cooked Salad Dressing to moisten. Chill; serve on greens. Makes 4 servings.

Variations—Add one or more of the following to the above recipe: 2 chopped hard-cooked eggs; ¼ cup diced pickles or stuffed or ripe olives; 2 tablespoons pickle relish; 1 chopped pimiento; ½ cup cooked peas or cut green beans.

Salmon Salad

Use recipe for Tuna-Fish Salad, substituting 1 can (1 pound) salmon, drained and flaked, for the tuna fish. The same variations can also be used.

HOT CHEESE-POTATO SALAD

6 medium potatoes, cooked and diced
1 cup diced celery
1 small onion, minced
⅓ cup cider vinegar
2 teaspoons salt
¼ teaspoon pepper
1 teaspoon dry mustard
2 hard-cooked eggs, chopped
⅓ cup liquid bacon fat
2 cups (½ pound) grated sharp Cheddar cheese

Mix all ingredients except cheese. Put in greased shallow broilerproof baking dish and sprinkle with cheese. Broil until golden-brown and bubbly. Makes 6 servings.

EGG-SALAD BOWL

Salad greens
10 to 12 hard-cooked eggs, sliced
1 medium red onion, thinly sliced
3 tablespoons malt vinegar
⅓ cup salad oil
1½ teaspoons salt
¼ teaspoon pepper
Dash of paprika
1 teaspoon Worcestershire
¼ cup shredded sharp Cheddar
2 tablespoons chopped parsley

Break up greens and put a generous amount in bottom and around sides of fairly shallow bowl. Fill with alternate layers of egg and onion. With rotary beater, beat together next 6 ingredients and pour over salad. Sprinkle with cheese and parsley. Makes 6 generous servings.

EGG-SALAD-STUFFED TOMATOES

4 large tomatoes
6 hard-cooked eggs
Salad dressing
1 can (3 ounces) deviled ham
Salt and pepper
Lettuce
Capers

Cut a slice from stem end of each unpeeled tomato. Scoop out pulp; turn tomatoes upside down to drain. Chop eggs, add tomato pulp, and moisten with salad dressing. Add deviled ham, and salt and pepper to taste. Fill tomato shells with mixture. Serve on lettuce, with a garnish of capers. Makes 4 servings.

BEAN AND CHEESE SALAD

1 cup dried white beans
4 cups water
1 tablespoon instant minced onion
½ green pepper, chopped
1 cup sliced celery
1 cup diced sharp Cheddar cheese
½ cup mayonnaise
1 tablespoon cider vinegar
½ teaspoon prepared mustard

Cover beans with water, bring to boil, and boil for 2 minutes. Cover pan and let stand for 1 hour; then cook until tender, adding more liquid if necessary. Drain, cool, and chill. Toss beans with onion, green pepper, celery, and cheese. Blend mayonnaise with vinegar and mustard. Add to bean mixture. Mix well, and chill. Makes 4 servings.

JELLIED TOMATO-HAM SALAD

2 envelopes unflavored gelatin
½ cup cold water
2 cups sieved cooked tomatoes
1 onion, grated
1 teaspoon sugar
Salt and pepper to taste
5 blanched almonds
10 green-pepper strips
1 cup minced cooked ham
1 teaspoon prepared mustard
½ cup cold cooked rice
1 teaspoon salad dressing
2 tablespoons dairy sour cream
½ pound cream cheese
2 tablespoons chopped green pepper
2 tablespoons chopped celery

Soak gelatin in cold water for 5 minutes. Simmer tomatoes, onion, sugar, and seasonings for 5 minutes; mix with gelatin and stir until dissolved. Cool, and pour into a quart measure or pitcher, but do not allow to harden. Lightly oil 5-cup ring mold; in bottom of mold, arrange almond halves alternating with green-pepper strips. Pour a little tomato mixture over almonds and green pepper almost to cover them; chill until firm. Fill mold with remaining tomato mixture and chill again until firm. Mix remaining ingredients. Press on firm tomato layer. Chill; unmold. Makes 6 servings.

SIDE-DISH SALADS

TWO-CABBAGE AND CARROT SALAD

- 2 cups finely shredded green cabbage
- 1 cup finely shredded red cabbage
- 1 cup coarsely shredded carrot
- ¼ green pepper, cut in thin strips
  Dressing

Prepare vegetables and chill. Just before serving, mix with dressing. Makes 6 to 8 servings.

Dressing

Mix well ½ cup mayonnaise, 1 tablespoon prepared mustard, 2 tablespoons cider vinegar, ½ teaspoon onion salt, 1 teaspoon sugar, ½ teaspoon celery seed and ¼ cup milk.

CHINESE BAMBOO SHOOTS SALAD

- 2 cups canned bamboo shoots, drained and thinly sliced
- 2 tablespoons soy sauce
- 1 tablespoon sesame oil or vegetable or peanut oil
- 1 teaspoon sugar

Combine all ingredients and mix well. Allow to stand for 1 hour before serving, tossing occasionally. Serve with roast duck, chicken, or pork. Makes 4 servings.

RANCHO SALAD

- 1 can (1 pound) kidney beans
- 1 can (1 pound, 3 ounces) white beans or cannolini beans
- 1 can (1 pound) chick-peas
- 2 onions, coarsely chopped
- 2 green onions, coarsely chopped
- 3 pimientos, chopped
- 3 celery stalks, chopped
- 12 to 18 stuffed olives, sliced
- ⅓ cup chopped parsley
- 2 canned green chilies, chopped
  Rancho Salad Dressing
  Greens
  Sliced tomatoes

Drain all beans and chick-peas. Combine with remaining ingredients except last 3; toss with Dressing. Allow the salad to mellow for 1 or 2 hours in the refrigerator. Serve on a bed of greens with a garnish of sliced tomatoes. Makes 6 to 8 servings.

Rancho Salad Dressing

- 2 garlic cloves
- 1 teaspoon salt
- 3 to 4 tablespoons cider vinegar
- 1 teaspoon pepper

Combine all ingredients.

ANISE, GRAPE AND CABBAGE SLAW

- 1 cup diced unpeeled red apples
- 1 teaspoon lemon juice
- 1 cup green seedless grapes, halved
- 2 cups medium-fine shredded green cabbage
- ¼ cup finely chopped celery
- 3 tablespoons dairy sour cream
- 1 tablespoon honey
- ¼ teaspoon crushed aniseed
- ½ teaspoon salt
- ⅛ teaspoon pepper
  Romaine lettuce

Dice apples into lemon juice to prevent discoloration. Add grapes, cabbage, and celery. Combine next 5 ingredients. Add to salad. Toss lightly. Chill. Serve on romaine lettuce. Makes 6 servings.

FRESH APPLE COLESLAW

- 2 cups finely shredded cabbage
- 2 cups diced unpeeled raw apples
- ½ cup dairy sour cream
- ¾ teaspoon dillseed
- ½ teaspoon salt
- 1 teaspoon lemon juice
  Dash of pepper
- ½ teaspoon sugar
  Head lettuce
  Unpeeled apples for garnish

Combine all ingredients except last 2. Toss lightly and serve on lettuce. Garnish with slices of unpeeled apples. Makes 6 servings.

SURPRISE SALAD

- 1 cup slivered red cabbage
- 1 cup slivered green cabbage
- 3 celery stalks, diced
- ½ cup slivered cooked ham
- ½ cup mayonnaise
  Prepared mustard
  Salt and pepper
- ⅓ cup pecan halves

Mix first 5 ingredients. Add mustard, and salt and pepper to taste. Garnish with nuts. Makes 4 servings.

ALMOND COLESLAW

- 4 cups finely shredded cabbage
- ½ cup each diced celery and cucumber
- ¼ cup diced green pepper
- 1 small onion, minced
- ½ cup toasted slivered almonds
- ½ cup mayonnaise
- 2 tablespoons each light cream and cider vinegar
- ¼ teaspoon seasoned salt
  Paprika

Mix vegetables, and chill. Just before serving, add remaining ingredients except paprika and mix well. Sprinkle with paprika. Makes 4 servings.

SALAD

CURRIED CORN SALAD

- 1 tablespoon instant chicken bouillon
- Water
- 1 package (10 ounces) frozen corn
- 1 teaspoon curry powder
- 1 tablespoon lemon juice
- 1 envelope plus 1 teaspoon unflavored gelatin
- 2 tablespoons minced green onion
- 2 pimientos, well drained and chopped
- Creamy dressing

In saucepan, mix chicken bouillon and ½ cup water. Bring to boil, add corn and cook, covered, until tender. Drain well, reserving broth, and chill corn. To reserved broth, add curry powder and lemon juice. Soften gelatin in ½ cup water. Put over low heat, stirring until dissolved. Add to vegetable broth with enough water to make 2 cups. Chill until slightly thickened. Fold in corn, onion and pimiento and mix well. Pour into 4-cup mold and chill until firm. Unmold and serve with creamy dressing flavored with chutney and lemon juice, if desired. Makes 6 servings.
NOTE: Equal amounts of cooked green beans or peas can be substituted for the corn.

HOT-AND-COLD POTATO SALAD

- 6 cups diced cooked potatoes
- 1 medium green pepper, chopped
- 1 medium onion, chopped
- 1 cup diced celery
- ½ cup diced pimiento
- 1 cup chopped dill pickles
- ½ cup French Dressing
- 1½ cups mayonnaise
- Salt and pepper
- 2 cups crushed potato chips
- 1 cup shredded sharp Cheddar cheese

Combine first 6 ingredients. Mix lightly with French Dressing and refrigerate until thoroughly chilled. Stir in mayonnaise and salt and pepper to taste. Chill for several more hours. Just before serving, put in greased shallow 2-quart broilerproof baking dish. Mix potato chips and cheese and sprinkle on salad, covering completely. Put under broiler until cheese is bubbly, but salad remains chilled. Serve at once. Makes 6 to 8 servings.

SALSIFY SALAD

Cook salsify (oyster plant) and cut in pieces the size of asparagus tips. Cool and mix with cooked asparagus tips, minced onion, minced chives and parsley. Dress with French dressing, well seasoned with mustard.

MARINATED TOMATOES

Peel 6 tomatoes and cut up. Add ¼ cup French Dressing, 1 garlic clove, and 2 tablespoons minced fresh herbs. Refrigerate; remove garlic. Makes 4 servings.

TOMATOES AND BLACK-EYED PEAS

Mix 2 cups cooked and drained black-eyed peas with 1 cup each shredded celery and drained diced tomatoes, and French dressing to moisten. Arrange on a bed of watercress and garnish with slices of Bermuda onions.

INDIVIDUAL TOMATO-ASPIC SALADS

- 2 envelopes unflavored gelatin
- ¼ cup water
- 2 cups tomato juice
- Piece of bay leaf
- ½ teaspoon salt
- 1 tablespoon confectioners' sugar
- 3 tablespoons cider vinegar
- Dash of hot pepper sauce
- ½ teaspoon Worcestershire
- Shredded lettuce
- 2 hard-cooked eggs, sliced
- Pimiento-stuffed olives
- Green Dressing

Soften gelatin in water. In small saucepan, combine ½ cup tomato juice, bay leaf, salt and sugar. Bring to boil and simmer a few minutes. Remove bay leaf and pour hot mixture over gelatin, stirring to dissolve. Add remaining 1½ cups tomato juice, vinegar, pepper sauce and Worcestershire. Stir to blend. Pour into four 6-ounce molds rinsed in cold water and chill until firm. Unmold on shredded lettuce and garnish with egg slices and olives. Serve with Green Dressing. Makes 4 servings.

Green Dressing

In blender, combine ½ cup parsley sprigs, 2 cut-up green onions, 1 tablespoon lemon juice and ¾ cup mayonnaise. Whirl until smooth. Makes about ¾ cup.

VEGETABLE-AVOCADO SALAD WITH PAPRIKA DRESSING

- 4 medium onions, thinly sliced
- Cider vinegar
- Salt and pepper to taste
- 3 carrots, thinly sliced
- 2 or 3 bunches radishes, sliced
- 3 or 4 cucumbers, peeled and cut into 2-inch pieces
- 2 or 3 avocados
- Lemon juice
- Salad greens, shredded
- Paprika Mayonnaise Dressing

Pour boiling water over onions and let stand for 5 minutes. Drain, cover with vinegar, and season with salt and pepper. Chill for several hours. Crisp carrots, radishes, and cucumbers in ice water. Peel and slice avocados; dip into lemon juice. At serving time, cover large platter with salad greens. Drain vegetables and avocado and arrange on greens. Serve with Paprika Mayonnaise Dressing. Makes 12 servings.

SALAD

MIXED VEGETABLE SALAD

- 1 green pepper, cut into rings
- 1 cucumber, peeled and diced
- 2 large tomatoes, peeled and diced
- 1 red onion, cut into rings
- 1 package (10 ounces) frozen peas, cooked and cooled
- 1 tablespoon each chopped chives and parsley
- 1 pimiento, chopped
- 1 carrot, shredded
- 1 cup (½ pound) cottage cheese
- 3 tablespoons lemon juice
- ⅓ cup salad oil
- Seasoned salt and pepper

Mix vegetables and chill until ready to serve. Mix cottage cheese, lemon juice, and salad oil. Fold into vegetables. Season to taste. Makes 6 servings.

ITALIAN SALAD

- 3 cups parsley (leaves only), chopped
- 1 cup diced boiled potatoes
- 3 hard-cooked eggs, chopped
- ½ cup French Dressing

Mix all ingredients, and chill. Makes 4 servings.

VEGETABLE SALAD WITH DEVILED HAM

- 6 cooked potatoes, diced
- 6 cooked beets, diced or 1 can (1 pound) diced beets, drained
- 4 carrots, diced
- 1 onion, chopped
- 1 can (2½ ounces) deviled ham
- 1 teaspoon dry mustard
- 1 cup mayonnaise
- Seasoned salt and pepper

Combine vegetables. Mix next 3 ingredients and fold into vegetables. Season to taste, and chill. Makes 6 servings.

FRUIT SALADS

Using Fruits—Fruits that become dark after being cut up (apples, bananas, pears) should be placed in a dressing or fruit juice as soon as they are cut. Others should have dressing added just before serving.

APPLE-AND-ORANGE SALAD

Alternate slices of unpeeled red apple and orange on watercress. Serve with sweetened French Dressing.

LAYERED CELERY-CRANBERRY-ORANGE SALAD

- 3 envelopes plus 1 teaspoon unflavored gelatin
- 2½ cups cranberry-juice cocktail
- ½ teaspoon celery salt
- ½ teaspoon celery seed
- 1½ cups thinly sliced celery
- 1 cup orange juice
- 1 teaspoon grated orange rind
- ½ cup mayonnaise
- ½ cup milk
- 1 cup heavy cream, whipped
- Celery tops
- Cherried Cranberries

Soften 2 envelopes gelatin in 1 cup cranberry juice, then put over low heat, stirring until dissolved. Add remaining 1½ cups cranberry juice and celery salt. Mix well and chill until slighty thickened. Fold in celery seed and celery. Mix well and pour into tall 6-cup mold. Chill until firm. Soften remaining 1 envelope and 1 teaspoon gelatin in orange juice and dissolve over low heat, stirring; cool. Add orange rind, mayonnaise and milk and beat until smooth, then fold in whipped cream. Pour over firm celery-cranberry layer and chill until firm. Unmold and garnish with celery tops and Cherried Cranberries. Makes 10 servings.

APPLE GLACÉ WITH HONEY-CREAM CHEESE

Simmer 4 peeled cored apples in syrup made by boiling 2 cups pineapple juice, ½ cup sugar, and a little red coloring, until apples are tender and red, turning often. Drain; chill. Put on greens. Stuff with cream cheese softened with honey. Top with walnut halves. Makes 4 servings.

JELLIED CINNAMON-APPLE SALAD

Dissolve ⅓ cup red cinnamon candies in 2 cups boiling water. Heat and pour over 1 box (3 ounces) red fruit-flavored gelatin dessert. Stir until dissolved. Chill until partially thickened. Fold in ¾ cup each chopped celery and apple, dash of salt, and ⅓ cup chopped nuts. Pour into molds; chill until firm. Unmold on greens. Makes 4 to 6 servings.

COTTAGE-CHEESE AND BLUEBERRY SALAD

- ¾ pound cottage cheese
- Dash of cayenne
- Salt to taste
- 1 pint fresh blueberries
- Watercress
- Sliced fresh, frozen, or canned peaches
- Mayonnaise

Mix first 4 ingredients lightly. Spoon in 6 mounds onto cress. Garnish each with peaches and serve with mayonnaise. Makes 6 servings.

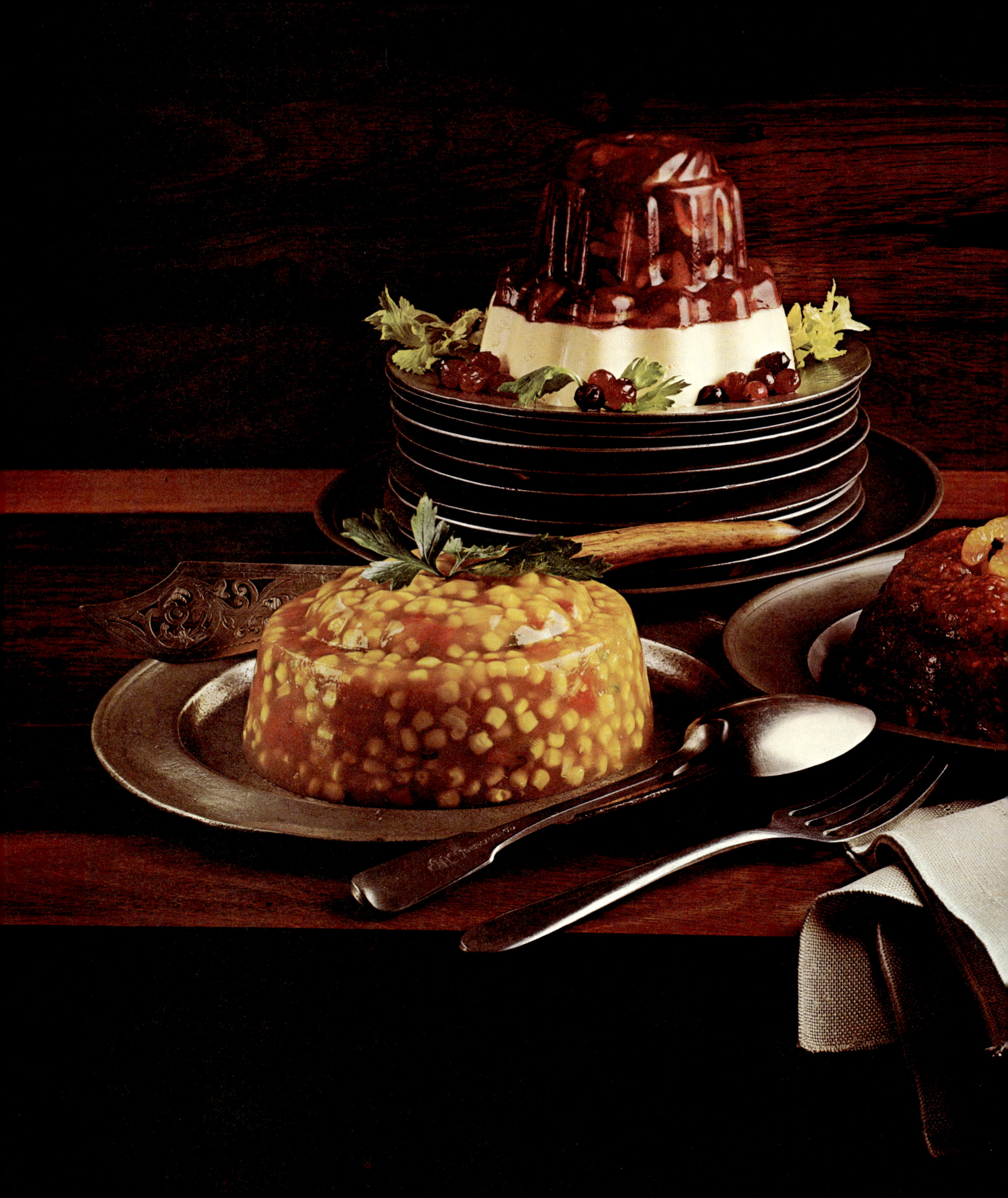

Shimmering Salad Molds — Cranberry Relish Salad; Curried Corn Salad; Layered Celery-Cranberry-Orange Salad.

SALAD

CHRISTMAS FRUIT SALAD

2 cups tangerine sections
1 cup grapefruit sections
1 cup diced pears
1 cup seedless grapes
2 tablespoons lemon juice
Sugar
Cranberry or raspberry sherbet
½ cup chopped pistachio nuts

Combine first 4 fruits. Sprinkle with lemon juice and add sugar to taste. Chill. Put in 6 individual sherbet glasses. Top each serving with a small scoop of sherbet. Sprinkle with pistachio nuts. Makes 6 servings.

CRANBERRY RELISH SALAD

1 medium thin-skinned orange
1 medium apple
2 cups fresh or frozen cranberries
1¼ cups sugar
1 package (3 ounces) orange- or lemon-flavor gelatin
2 envelopes unflavored gelatin
1 cup cold water
Grated rind and juice of 1 lemon
Mandarin-orange Wedges (optional)

Cut orange and apple in eighths and remove seeds. Force with cranberries through fine blade of food chopper. Add sugar, mix well and refrigerate a few hours, stirring occasionally to dissolve sugar. Prepare orange gelatin according to package directions. Soften unflavored gelatin in water. Put over low heat, stirring until dissolved. Add to orange gelatin with lemon rind and juice. Chill until slightly thickened. Fold in cranberry mixture, mix well and pour into 6-cup ring mold. Chill until firm. Unmold and fill center with orange wedges, if desired. Makes 10 to 12 servings.

WALDORF SALAD

Combine chunks of peeled tart apple, diced celery, and chopped walnuts with cooked salad dressing. Garnish with cranberry sauce.

OCTOBER SALAD

1 box (3 ounces) apple-flavored gelatin
2 cups hot water
⅛ teaspoon salt
⅓ cup each coarsely chopped pitted dates and nuts
1 cup diced unpeeled red apples
1 cup diced unpeeled fresh pears
Salad greens
Ginger Mayonnaise Dressing

Dissolve gelatin in hot water. Add salt and dates; chill until mixture is slightly thickened. Fold in nuts and fruit. Pour into 5-cup mold and chill until firm. Unmold on salad greens and serve with Ginger Mayonnaise Dressing. Makes 6 servings.

SALAD

SALAD DRESSINGS

NOTE: *For salad dressings based on Mayonnaise and Vinaigrette Sauce, including French Dressing, see the Sauce Cookbook.*

BUTTERMILK HORSERADISH DRESSING

Serve with potato, cabbage, or tossed green salads, or on canned or fresh fruit

- ¾ cup buttermilk
- 2 tablespoons prepared horseradish
- 1 tablespoon cider vinegar
- 1 tablespoon sugar
- ¼ teaspoon salt
- ½ teaspoon prepared mustard

Combine all ingredients. Mix thoroughly. Chill in refrigerator. Makes 1 cup.

AVOCADO DRESSING

Especially recommended for fruit salads

- ¾ cup avocado pulp
- 3 tablespoons lemon juice
- 2 tablespoons blue cheese
- 2 tablespoons heavy cream
- ½ teaspoon Worcestershire
- ¾ teaspoon salt
- 1 teaspoon prepared mustard

Sieve enough soft ripe avocado to make ¾ cup. Add lemon juice and mix well. Sieve blue cheese. Add to first mixture with remaining ingredients. Chill. Makes about 1 cup.

Ginger-Cream Dressing

Mix ½ cup mayonnaise, ½ cup dairy sour cream, ¼ cup chopped pecans and 2 tablespoons minced candied ginger.

SHERRY DRESSING

Good on fruit salads

- 1 egg, beaten
- ¼ cup sugar
- ¼ cup sherry
  Dash of salt
- 2 teaspoons butter
  Juice of ½ orange
  Juice of ½ lemon
- ¼ cup heavy cream, whipped

Combine all ingredients except cream in top part of a double boiler. Cook over boiling water until slightly thickened, stirring. Chill. Just before serving, fold in cream. Makes 1 cup.

COOKED SOUR-CREAM DRESSING

For lettuce, cabbage, egg, or vegetable salads

- 3 tablespoons sugar
- ¾ teaspoon salt
- 1 teaspoon dry mustard
- 2 teaspoons all-purpose flour
- ⅓ cup butter or margarine
- 1½ cups dairy sour cream
- 2 eggs, beaten
- ⅓ cup wine vinegar
- ⅓ teaspoon dried tarragon

Mix all ingredients. Cook, stirring constantly, until smooth and thickened. Cool; then chill. Makes 2¾ cups.

COOKED BUTTERMILK DRESSING

Serve on shredded cabbage, greens, fruit, or cooked-vegetable salads

- 2 tablespoons all-purpose flour
- 1 teaspoon dry mustard
- 1½ teaspoons salt
- ⅛ teaspoon paprika
- ½ teaspoon celery seeds
- 2 tablespoons sugar
- ⅓ cup cider vinegar
- 1 cup buttermilk

Combine dry ingredients in top part of a double boiler. Add vinegar and buttermilk. Cook over boiling water, stirring constantly, until thick. Cover and cook for 10 minutes longer. Cool, and chill. Makes 1½ cups.

COTTAGE-CHEESE DRESSING

Serve with vegetable or fruit salads

- ½ cup cottage cheese
- ⅓ cup undiluted evaporated milk
- ¾ teaspoon salt
- ½ teaspoon sugar
- 1 teaspoon paprika
  Dash of garlic or onion salt
- 2 tablespoons chopped parsley
- 1 tablespoon cider vinegar

Mix cottage cheese with milk. Add remaining ingredients. Makes 1 cup.

FLUFFY FRUIT DRESSING

Recommended for fruit salads

- ¼ cup sugar
- 1 tablespoon all-purpose flour
- ⅓ cup orange juice
- 2 tablespoons lemon juice
- ½ cup undiluted evaporated milk, chilled and whipped

Mix sugar and flour in small saucepan. Add orange and lemon juices. Cook, stirring, until thick. Chill. At serving time, fold in whipped evaporated milk. Makes 1 cup.

SOUR-CREAM DRESSING

Serve on green salads or vegetable combinations

- 1 teaspoon salt
- 1 tablespoon sugar
- 1/8 teaspoon cayenne
- 1 tablespoon lemon juice
- 2 tablespoons cider vinegar
- 1 cup dairy sour cream

Combine all ingredients and stir until thoroughly mixed. Makes 1 cup.

SALAMANDER

—In culinary language, the word denotes a kitchen tool used to brown and glaze the top of cooked foods. The original salamander is a long iron rod with an enlarged and flattened end which is heated over a fire until it is white and then waved close over the food. Other salamanders may be metal discs or plates used in the same way and yet another is a small chimneyless portable stove used for the identical browning and glazing purpose.

Salamanders take their name from the lizardlike, heat-loving animal. The rod salamander is an old kitchen tool that goes back to the Middle Ages. Salamanders today are chefs' equipment when used at all; the coming of the modern broiler has made them obsolete.

SALAMI

—One of a variety of sausages of Italian origin that can be eaten without being cooked first. There are Italian, German, Hungarian, French, and kosher salamis. The word is Italian and implies "salted," meaning that the meat is preserved. The singular of the word in Italian is *salame* and in colloquial usage this word is used for a person who is not very bright and is rather gullible.

Salamis differ from each other by their composition of meats, their spicing, their salting and curing, and their shape. Salami most often contains pork and some beef, although there are pure pork and pure beef salamis. The meat can be leaner or fatter and ground coarsely or finely. Salamis can be divided into two major groupings, hard and soft. The soft are the less chewy varieties of salami; kosher salami is an example. It is made and seasoned in the same way the hard salami is, but is softer because, after cooking, it is air-dried for only a short time or not at all. Most kosher salami comes in larger slices than the hard and is preferred by many for sandwiches because it is less chewy. Italian Genoa is a well known example of a hard salami; it is made of coarsely ground pork seasoned with garlic and sometimes wine. The salami is air-dried.

Availability—Salami in some form are available in most food stores. Kinds vary with the area.

Storage—Be sure slices of meat are flat before storage. Keep plastic-wrapped packages in wrapper. Wrap sliced meat in moisture- vapor-proof paper.

Sliced, refrigerator shelf: 2 to 3 days
Unsliced, dry and semidry varieties, kitchen shelf, casing uncut: indefinitely
Unsliced, dry and semidry varieties, refrigerator shelf, casing cut: 2 weeks

Nutritive Food Values—Excellent source of protein, good source of iron, thiamine, riboflavin, and niacin.
Hard, 3 slices, (1.2 ounces) = 123 calories
Soft, 1 ounce = 58 to 88 calories

SAILBOATS

Cut 9 thin slices of salami (any kind) into quarters. Cut thin lengthwise slices from each of 36 small sweet pickles to make a smooth base. Use tip of knife to cut out wedge-shape strip on top side of each pickle. Fill hollow with cream cheese or cheese spread. Insert a quarter slice of salami into each to form a sail. Chill. Makes 3 dozen appetizers.

SALAMI SWEET-AND-SOUR

- 1/4 pound soft salami
- 2 cups diced potatoes
- Water
- 2 cups shredded red cabbage
- 1 green pepper, minced
- 2 tablespoons cider vinegar
- 2 tablespoons sugar
- Salt and pepper

Cut salami into slivers and brown lightly in skillet. Add potatoes and boiling water to cover. Bring to boil and simmer, covered, for 10 minutes. Add cabbage, green pepper, vinegar, and sugar. Cook for 7 minutes longer, or until potatoes are tender. Season with salt and pepper to taste. Makes 4 servings.

SALAMI SKILLET

- 6 slices of bacon
- 1/4 cup diced celery
- 2 tablespoons chopped green pepper
- 2 tablespoons all-purpose flour
- 1 can (14 1/2 ounces) undiluted evaporated milk
- 1/2 teaspoon salt
- 1/4 teaspoon pepper
- 1 package (7 ounces) soft salami
- 2 hard-cooked eggs, sliced
- 1 cup wide noodles, cooked

Cook bacon until crisp. Remove from fat, drain and crumble. Pour off all but 2 tablespoons fat from skillet. In this fat, cook celery and green pepper for 2 or 3 minutes; blend in flour. Add milk, salt, and pepper and cook, stirring constantly, until thickened. Cut salami slices into quarters, reserving 4 whole slices for garnish. Add to first mixture with eggs and noodles; heat. Add bacon. Garnish with whole salami slices. Makes 4 servings.

SALLY LUNN

SALAMI OMELET

In a 10- or 12-inch skillet place 6 or 8 slices of salami (any kind), cut ¼ inch thick. Slowly brown on both sides (enough fat will be rendered for the omelet). Add 5 well-beaten eggs. With a fork distribute salami evenly. Cook until omelet takes form. Place under broiler until golden-brown. Cut as a pie to serve. Makes 3 to 4 servings.

SALAMI-CARROT SALAD

¼ pound hard salami
2 cups shredded carrots
¼ cup pickle relish
⅓ cup diced celery
½ cup mayonnaise

Cut salami into small cubes. Add other ingredients and mix well. Chill. Serve in lettuce cups, if desired. Makes 4 servings.

SALLY LUNN—A bread of English origin which has become a culinary specialty of our southern states. Traditionally, it is baked in a Turk's-head mold, however, in the south the batter is often baked in muffin pans. Although there have been so-called "quick Sally Lunns," the authentic one uses yeast as a leavening agent.

The origin of the name is obscure. It was once spelled *soleilune,* a French dialect version of "golden" or "sunshiny," which may indicate a French derivation. But the story most often told to account for the name is that the bread was invented and sold by a girl named Sally Lunn in the city of Bath, in England, around 1700. Sally Lunns are similar to Bath buns, but they do not have candied peel in them.

SALLY LUNN RING

1 package active dry yeast or 1 cake compressed yeast
¼ cup water*
3 tablespoons sugar
2 medium-size eggs at room temperature
⅔ cup milk, scalded
3½ cups sifted all-purpose flour
½ cup melted shortening
1 teaspoon salt

Sprinkle or crumble yeast into water; stir in 1 tablespoon sugar. *Use very warm water (105°F. to 115°F.) for dry yeast; use lukewarm (80°F. to 90°F.) for compressed. Let stand for a few minutes, then stir until dissolved. Add remaining 2 tablespoons sugar and beat in eggs. Cool milk to lukewarm and add. Gradually stir in half of flour and beat until the batter falls in sheets from the spoon. Cool shortening to lukewarm and add. Mix well. Combine salt with remaining flour and add gradually. Mix well. Scrape down bowl. Grease top of dough to prevent crusting. Cover bowl and let dough rise in a warm place (80°F. to 85°F.) until doubled in bulk, about 1 hour. Punch down dough, cover, and let it rest for 10 minutes. Put dough in a greased 8½-cup gelatin mold or in a Sally Lunn or Turks'-head mold. Cover and let stand in a warm place to rise again until doubled in bulk, about 45 minutes. Bake in preheated moderate oven (350°F.) for 1 hour, or until browned. Serve hot with butter. Makes one 8½-inch Sally Lunn ring.

RAISED SALLY LUNN MUFFINS

1 package active dry yeast or 1 cake compressed yeast
¼ cup water*
¾ cup milk
3 tablespoons sugar
1¼ teaspoons salt
3½ cups all-purpose flour
¼ cup soft butter or margarine
2 eggs

Sprinkle or crumble yeast into water. *Use very warm water (105°F. to 115°F.) for dry yeast; use lukewarm (80°F. to 90°F.) for compressed. Let stand for a few minutes, then stir until dissolved. Scald milk and pour over sugar and salt. Let stand until lukewarm. Stir in yeast and 2 cups flour. Beat well. Cover and let stand in a warm place until light, about 30 minutes. Beat in butter, eggs, and remaining 1½ cups flour. Break off pieces of the mixture, shape into balls, and put in greased 2½-inch muffin-pan sections. Let rise until doubled in bulk, about 45 minutes. Bake in preheated hot oven (400°F.) about 15 minutes. Makes 2 dozen.

QUICK SALLY LUNN

½ cup butter or margarine
Sugar
2 cups sifted all-purpose flour
3 teaspoons baking powder
¾ teaspoon salt
2 eggs, beaten
1 cup milk
Ground cinnamon

Cream butter; gradually add ⅓ cup sugar, creaming until **light and fluffy. Add flour sifted with baking powder and** salt alternately with eggs beaten with milk, beating until smooth. Turn into two greased pans 8 x 8 x 2 inches. Sprinkle with sugar and cinnamon. Bake in preheated hot oven (425°F.) about 20 minutes. Cut each square into 9 pieces and serve warm. Makes 18.

SALMAGUNDI—A culinary term derived from the French word *salmigondis,* "hotchpotch." It is used to describe a stew made from leftover meats, seasoned with wine, vinegar, pickles, etc., or a salad plate of diced meats, pickled vegetables, and other salad ingredients, arranged, not tossed, and served with a dressing.

SALMI or SALMIS—A sauced dish usually made with partially cooked or leftover feathered game or domestic duck or goose and often finished by cooking in a chafing dish at the table. The word is French, short for *salmigondis.*

SALMI OF DUCKLING

¼ cup butter or margarine
2 tablespoons each chopped celery and carrot
1 tablespoon minced onion
¼ cup all-purpose flour
1⅓ cups canned condensed consommé or bouillon
⅔ cup stewed fresh or canned tomatoes
4 servings cooked duckling

Heat butter in saucepan and add next 3 ingredients. Cook for 2 or 3 minutes. Blend in flour. Add liquids and tomatoes and bring to boil. Simmer for 5 minutes. Add duckling and heat well. Makes 4 servings.

SALMON *by James A. Beard*—Called the greatest of sports fish, the king of fishes, salmon has been prized as food for centuries and is probably the best known of all fish.

The origins of salmon are interesting to speculate upon. During the ice ages, it is likely that salmon were migratory Arctic fish. As glaciers advanced and retreated, the earth's surface was reshaped and bodies of water reformed or shifted. The fish that had originally been one family called the *Salmonidae* (salmon, trout, and char) were probably, during this epoch, dispersed over different parts of the world to the rivers and seas of Europe, Asia, and North America. Curiously enough, except for human transplanting of salmon, they inhabit only the waters of the Northern Hemisphere.

Pictures of salmon carved on bone have been found in France dating from about 12,000 B.C. Centuries after the cave man the Romans gave salmon its name. They were enthralled with the spectacle of hordes of leaping fish in the rivers of Gaul and so named then *salmo,* which comes from the verb "to leap." The *Salmo salar,* as the Atlantic salmon were scientifically named, eventually found its way into the literature and mythology of all Europe.

Only 300 years ago salmon flourished to such an extent in the rivers of Europe and North America that servants, being hired by new masters, accepted employment on the condition that they would be served salmon only a specified number of times a week. It had become the custom to bestow this commonplace food on the help almost daily. Salmon used to be found in the Loire, the Rhine, the Wye, the Hudson, the St. Lawrence, and the Connecticut—in nearly all the rivers of North America and Europe. Sadly enough, this is no longer true, Though salmon are hardy, they require two essentials, clean water and access to their spawning grounds. Polluted waters, dams and other by-products of civilization have severely reduced the flow of salmon on both sides of the Atlantic. Fortunately, steps are now being taken, belatedly, to preserve the waters that have not become too polluted. With care, a fraction of the once abundant Atlantic salmon will remain.

The prospects are better for the Pacific salmon, which has become such a tremendous industry that preservation is vital to local and national economies. Pacific salmon are thus flourishing from Mexico to Alaska, and along the coasts of Siberia, Japan, and China.

Whereas there is only one variety of Atlantic salmon, there are five varieties of Pacific: sockeye (*Oncorhynchus nerka*), spring (*O. tschawytscha*), coho (*O. kitsutch*), pink (*O. gorbuscha*), and chum (*O. keta*). In addition there is the steelhead, which is more closely related to the Atlantic than to the other Pacific salmon, and the blueback, which is really a coho with darker markings.

There is one important difference in the life cycles of the Atlantic and Pacific salmon. Both, to reach their spawning grounds, ascend streams and rivers sometimes for a distance of hundreds of miles, jumping rapids and rocks with astonishing strength. When the place and time for spawning are reached, male and female pair off, and the female digs a nest with a fanning motion of her tail. The male guards her while she lays her eggs and then he fertilizes them. The process is repeated a number of times over a period of several days. The feats of climbing rivers and reproducing thoroughly exhaust the fish, understandably. Pacific salmon spawn only once and then die. Atlantic salmon may live to return to the sea and spawn several times.

When the young hatch in their nests, or redds, they live for a certain length of time from food retained in the shells and then break forth as tiny alevins. They spend from three to seven years in fresh waters before migrating to salt water as young salmon. During this time they change color from a rather varistriped to the silvery skin that one usually associates with salmon.

The history of salmon as food in the Western Hemisphere predates the discovery of America. The coastal Indians used salmon as a mainstay of their diet; for winter, it was salted, smoked, kippered, dried, or beaten into pemmican. If one goes to parts of Canada and up the Columbia River when the salmon are running, it is still possible to see the Indians fishing for salmon with spears, and smoking and curing it on the spot. In the West the Indians hot-smoked salmon over a campfire, suspending the fish in forked pieces of spirea wood and surrounding it with ferns. The early settlers in both the East and West of the United Staes salted and pickled salmon for winter use. Salmon bellies, salmon tips, fillets of salmon were all preserved in brine, and delicious this preparation can be, for one still finds it in certain regions of the country.

Fresh salmon is considered one of the world's great delicacies and is served in many of the finest restaurants as a *pièce de résistance.* Such three-star French restaurants as Oustau de Baumanière, La Tour d'Argent, and **Prunier; and in London, such restaurants as Prunier's** (again), the Connaught Grill, and the Caprice serve fresh broiled salmon with Béarnaise Sauce, or poached salmon, hot or cold, with a *sauce verte.* Baumanière makes a specialty of a cold galantine of salmon, which is deftly and beautifully prepared with a stuffing, tied in a cloth, poached, and sliced in paper-thin slices for an hors d'oeuvre.

Smoked salmon is one of the most expensive foods in the world. The European variety is more heavily

SALMON

smoked, usually, than the Nova Scotia and Columbia River varieties; on the other hand, the latter are saltier. **Lox varies in its salt content and thus in its price.**

In England crimped, or cold, salmon is considered one of the prime delicacies of the social season and is featured as a buffet dish at gala balls and parties. Kippered salmon, which is a hot-smoke fish, meaning it is smoke-cooked, is also popular all through England and is served either hot or cold with various sauces and additives.

Salmon cheeks, which are just that, are one of the most prized portions of the fish. They are usually served sautéed Meunière and sometimes deep-fried, a superb treat either way.

Of course, it is canned salmon that is consumed in such astounding quantities throughout the world. Most of the canning is centered on the Pacific Coast, in Oregon, Washington, British Columbia, and Alaska. Millions of cans issue forth annually from spotless canneries, and close government inspection of the cans, the fish, and the processing make it one of the most sanitary products in the world. Canned salmon will stand any extremes of weather and temperature and remain fresh-tasting and flavorful.

The most valuable variety for canning is the sockeye. This is seldom seen fresh in the markets but is considered outstanding for canning because of its rich red flesh and firm tissue. The sockeye weighs up to fifteen pounds and is caught from southern Oregon to Alaska. Some sockeye has become landlocked and spends its life in fresh water. In this case, it bears such names as "kokanee," "kickaninny," and "redfish."

The spring or chinook, sometimes known as "the King," is another exceedingly valuable catch and is fished a great deal in the Columbia River, among other places. This species is one of the best game fish, being known for rising to a lure and giving fishermen a fine fight. The spring grows very large, sometimes reaching seventy or eighty pounds in weight, but is nevertheless as delicate to the palate as smaller species. Coho, also known as "blueback" or "silver," or even "silverside," is popular with fishermen, too. It averages about three feet in length, and its silver skin is spotted with black. In addition to its value to the canning industry the coho is much appreciated in home kitchens for cooking and freezing. Not as fatty as the preceding species, but still a popular fish, is the chum, sometimes known as "dog salmon." It is not as highly regarded for fine eating as some of the other varieties, for it is apt to be dull in flavor.

Availability and Purchasing Guide—Fresh salmon is sold whole, in steaks, fillets, and large pieces. Frozen salmon steaks are available. Salmon is also available smoked and canned. Canned salmon roe is available.

In buying salmon, allow ½ to ⅜ pound per serving, and in the case of fish as taken from the water before cleaning, allow about 1 pound.

Storage
Fresh, refrigerator shelf: 1 to 2 days
Smoked, refrigerator shelf: 2 to 3 weeks
Fresh or smoked, refrigerator frozen-food compartment, prepared for freezing: 2 to 3 weeks
Fresh or smoked, freezer, prepared for freezing: 3 to 4 months
Frozen, refrigerator frozen-food compartment: 2 months
Frozen, freezer: 1 year
Canned, unopened, kitchen shelf: 1 year
Canned or cooked, covered, refrigerator shelf: 3 to 4 days

Nutritive Food Values—Contains large amounts of phosphorus, potassium, some sodium, thiamine, riboflavin, and niacin, and some vitamin A. Canned salmon contains some calcium if the bones are eaten.
Fresh baked steak, 4.2 ounces = 218 calories
Canned, solids and liquids including bones, 4 ounces = 230 calories

Basic Preparation—Fresh salmon can be baked, broiled, deep-fried, panfried, planked, sautéed, steamed, and stewed. Canned salmon should be drained and have the skin and bones removed before using. Smoked salmon is served cold in sandwiches, salads, hors-d'oeuvre, etc.

Salmon is rather an oily fish and is best when cooked simply. It is delicious either hot or cold. As is true with all fish, there is little connective tissue in salmon; therefore, it benefits by short cooking. Frozen fish, if it is not to be stuffed, is best cooked in its frozen state. There are several ways to tell when fish is cooked to its proper point. It will flake easily when tested with a fork or toothpick; it can be easily punctured with a fork; and it will lose its translucent appearance.

To Bake—You may bake a whole fish, a piece of fish, or steaks. Season fish and place in greased baking dish on foil and brush with butter or oil. Add seasonings and some wine, broth, or tomato sauce before baking. Place in preheated very hot oven (450°F. to 475°F.). Allow 10 minutes of baking per inch of thickness, measured at the thickest point. If the fish is frozen, double the time.

To Bake in Foil—Place fish in an envelope made of aluminum foil and set on a baking sheet. Add any seasonings you choose. Pinch the edges of the foil to seal it tightly. Allow about 5 minutes at 450°F. for the heat to penetrate the foil. Then allow 10 minutes per inch of thickness for fresh fish, and double that amount of time for frozen. Serve with a tomato sauce or a mustard sauce.

To Bake Stuffed—Ask your fish dealer to remove the scales, fins, and viscera. If the fish is to be served whole, leave head and tail on. Clean and wash the fish well. Salt the interior, and then stuff with a highly seasoned bread stuffing, a shellfish stuffing, or thinly sliced vegetables, together with herbs and butter. If you have had the backbone removed, allow about 1 cup of stuffing per pound of fish; otherwise, about ¾ cup per pound. Close the opening of the fish with small skewers or with toothpicks, and lace with light string. Place on a buttered baking sheet or on a bed of finely cut leeks, carrots, onions, and celery. Oil the fish well, add a cup or two of white wine, if you wish, and bake in preheated very hot oven (450°F.) allowing 10 minutes per inch of thickness. Baste with butter or oil and fresh lemon juice or white wine. Serve with a wine sauce made with the

SALMON

pan juices; with a tomato sauce, to which you might add the pan juices; with a mushroom sauce; or with lemon butter.

To Broil—Steaks, fillets, split fish, or even whole fish, if they are fairly small ones, broil extremely well. You will find that if you broil on a generous piece of foil, you can use the margins of the foil as handles to turn the fish. Again, allow 10 minutes cooking time per inch of thickness, doubling the time for frozen (unthawed) fish. Baste with butter or with wine and butter. Broiled fish should be delicately browned on both sides. In the case of split fish, broil skin side to broiling unit first and then turn to flesh side. Serve broiled salmon with lemon butter, anchovy butter, Béarnaise sauce or sauce Maltaise. Crisp fried potatoes and a good wine are excellent accompaniments.

To Charcoal-Broil—Steaks or fillets are best for charcoal broiling. If you place the fish in a hinged grill with a handle, it will be easier to turn over the charcoal. Oil the grill well, and brush the fish with oil or butter. Broil approximately 10 minutes per inch of thickness, depending on the strength of the charcoal heat. Serve with Béarnaise sauce or with a barbecue sauce.

To Sauté—Salmon steaks or fillets are ideal for sauté meunière. For four 1-inch steaks place 3 tablespoons each butter and oil in a heavy skillet, and heat. The oil will prevent the butter from burning. Cook the fish gently over medium heat, turning once very carefully with 2 spatulas. A 1-inch steak should take 10 to 12 minutes. Add a bit of white wine to the pan as you sauté. Remove fish to a hot platter and season to taste. Add chopped parsley to the pan, together with more butter, if necessary, and heat briefly before pouring over fish. Serve with plain boiled potatoes and wedges of lemon.

As a variation, add ½ cup *red* wine to the pan just before turning the fish, and let it cook down. It will lend a delicious flavor and a pleasant color.

To Deep-Fry—Fillets, steaks, or strips of salmon may be deep-fried. The fish should be cut into even slices and rubbed with salt. Dip into batter or beaten egg and milk and then into flour, crumbs, or sesame seeds. Place carefully in a frying basket, very little at a time. Dip into hot deep fat (375°F. on a frying thermometer) and fry for 2 to 4 minutes, depending upon size of fish. Serve with lemon wedges and boiled parsley potatoes. Also try deep-fried parsley for a garnish that is unusual and delicious: Wash fresh parsley and dry well; dip for a minute into the hot fat.

To Poach—This is probably the finest preparation for salmon whether it is to be served hot or cold. It is best done in a Court Bouillon, which may later be clarified and used for a sauce or for an aspic. Cooking and handling of salmon is made simple if the fish is first placed in cheese-cloth, with ends of the cloth extending outside the fish boiler, to be used for turning or lifting the fish. Estimate 10 minutes per inch of fish measured at the thickest point, doubling the time for frozen fish.

To Freeze—Cut fish into steaks after cleaning and eviscerating. Wash thoroughly. Dip fish into an ascorbic-acid solution to prevent yellowing and development of off-flavors. Mix 1 tablespoon ascorbic acid into 4 cups water and dip fish into solution for 20 seconds. Drain fish and wrap in moisture- vapor-proof material, excluding as much air as possible. Seal.

Court Bouillon

Ingredients are based on 2 quarts liquid. If recipe is doubled, adjust seasoning accordingly.

1 to 4 cups red or white wine and an equal amount of water, depending upon the size of the fish
1 tablespoon salt, or to taste
1 celery stalk
1 onion stuck with 2 cloves
1 carrot, sliced
¼ teaspoon dried thyme
1 teaspoon dried tarragon
½ teaspoon freshly ground black pepper
1 tablespoon chopped parsley
1 bay leaf

Combine all ingredients and boil for 10 minutes before adding fish.* If it is a very large fish, you will probably want to double this recipe. You may also adjust seasonings, using dill instead of other herbs.

*Salmon may also be poached in water, or in milk; or it may be steamed over hot water, if very tightly covered and sealed. The timing is the same as for "Poached Salmon."

After fish is cooked, remove carefully to a hot platter, if it is to be served warm. Serve with hollandaise sauce and tiny boiled potatoes. Some people prefer an egg sauce, made with a cream sauce to which chopped hard-boiled eggs and, sometimes, parsley have been added. This dish, incidentally, with boiled new potatoes and fresh peas, used to be the traditional New England Fourth of July feast.

If the fish is to be served cold, it should be allowed to cool slowly. The sauce or bouillon may be strained and clarified and used as the basis for an aspic to glaze the fish. However, the fish should first be skinned very carefully and decorated with cut vegetables, truffles, olives, or whatever else may be suitable. Serve cold salmon with either a good mayonnaise or a *sauce verte*. A vegetable salad is more or less standard as an accompaniment. Cold salmon makes a festive and delicious buffet dish.

SALMON COOKBOOK

APPETIZERS

CURRIED SALMON TRIANGLES

- 1 can (1 pound) salmon
- ⅔ cup mayonnaise or salad dressing
- 1 tablespoon chili sauce
- 1 tablespoon minced pimiento
- 1 tablespoon minced green pepper
- 1 teaspoon grated onion
- ¼ teaspoon curry powder
- 16 slices of toast, cut into triangles
  Butter

Drain salmon and mash. Add remaining ingredients except toast and butter, and mix well. Butter toast triangles lightly and spread with salmon mixture. Garnish, if desired, with additional bits of pimiento and green pepper. Makes 64.

SALMON BALLS

- 1 can (7½ ounces) salmon
- 1 package (3 ounces) cream cheese, softened
- 1 tablespoon chopped pickle
- ½ teaspoon Worcestershire
  Mayonnaise to moisten
  Chopped parsley

Drain salmon and mash. Mix with remaining ingredients except parsley. Shape into ¾-inch balls and roll in parsley. Makes about 3 dozen.

SMOKED SALMON WITH CUCUMBER DIP

- 2 medium cucumbers
- ½ cup dairy sour cream
- 3 tablespoons cider vinegar
- 1 tablespoon minced chives
- ½ teaspoon crumbled fresh dill
- ¾ teaspoon salt
- ⅛ teaspoon pepper
- ¼ pound smoked salmon, very thinly sliced
  Pumpernickel bread
  Butter

Peel cucumbers and slice thin. Mix sour cream, vinegar, chives, dill, salt, and pepper. Pour over cucumbers and mix. Cover and chill for 2 to 3 hours. Put salmon on thin slices of pumpernickel, spread with butter. Serve as an appetizer, spreading cucumber mixture on top of salmon. Makes 6 servings.

Sautéed Cured Salmon

Cut salmon in thin slices and sauté quickly in a little butter or margarine. Good with creamed spinach.

SOUPS

CREAM OF SALMON SOUP

- 2 tablespoons butter or margarine
- 1 tablespoon all-purpose flour
- 3 cups milk, scalded with 1 slice of onion
- 1 can (1 pound) salmon
  Salt and pepper
  Chopped parsley

Melt butter and blend in flour. Remove onion from milk. Gradually stir milk into butter-and-flour mixture. Cook, stirring constantly, until slightly thickened. Add salmon with its liquid, breaking up fish with fork. Season with salt and pepper to taste and serve with a sprinkling of parsley. Makes about 1 quart, or 4 servings.

SALMON AND TOMATO SOUP

- 1 medium onion, chopped
- ½ green pepper, chopped
- 2 tablespoons butter or margarine
- 3 cups diced raw potatoes
- 4 cups water
- ½ teaspoon dried thyme
- 1½ teaspoons salt
- ¼ teaspoon pepper
- 2 bouillon cubes
- 1 can (1 pound) tomatoes
- 1 can (1 pound) salmon
- 2 tablespoons sherry

Cook onion and pepper in butter for 5 minutes. Add all ingredients except last 2 and simmer about 15 minutes. Add salmon, broken into chunks, and liquid from the can. Add sherry, and heat. Makes 6 servings.

SALMON-CORN CHOWDER, NEW ORLEANS STYLE

- ¼ cup butter or margarine
- ¾ cup chopped onion
- ½ cup chopped green pepper
- 1 small garlic clove, minced
- 1 can (1 pound) salmon
- 1 can (1 pound) tomatoes
- 1 can (8 ounces) whole-kernel corn
- 1 chicken bouillon cube
- 1 bay leaf
- ½ teaspoon salt
  Dash of pepper
- 1 cup water

Melt butter in 3-quart saucepan. Add next 3 ingredients and sauté, stirring frequently, 5 minutes. Drain and flake salmon, reserving liquid. Add both salmon and liquid with remaining ingredients to first mixture. Bring to boil, cover and simmer 10 to 15 minutes. Remove bay leaf. Makes about 1½ quarts, or 6 servings.

MAIN DISHES

POACHED SALMON STEAKS

4 cups boiling water
1 tablespoon white vinegar or lemon juice
1 tablespoon salt
2 onion slices
   Fresh dill or parsley sprigs
4 or 5 white peppercorns
4 small salmon steaks
   Parsley Butter, Hollandaise or Béarnaise Sauce

Put first 6 ingredients in large skillet. Bring to boil and carefully add salmon steaks in single layer (need not be thawed if frozen). Bring again to boil, cover and simmer 6 to 8 minutes, or until fish flakes easily with fork. Remove with slotted spoon to hot platter and serve with sauce. Makes 4 servings.
NOTE: To serve cold, cool fish in the broth, cover and chill. Remove to serving dish and serve with parsley butter and lemon wedges or dill sprigs and mayonnaise.

GRILL-BAKED STUFFED SALMON

1 whole salmon (5 to 7 pounds)
   Lemon juice
   Salt
½ teaspoon pepper
¾ cup each chopped green pepper, celery and onion
¼ cup minced parsley
   Pinch each dried thyme and marjoram
¼ cup vegetable oil
1 cup water
   Parsley sprigs
   Lemon Butter

Wipe fish inside and out with lemon juice and sprinkle with salt. Stuff cavity with mixture of 1 teaspoon salt, pepper and remaining ingredients, except last 4. Sew together securely to hold in stuffing. Put fish on piece of chicken wire, making a basket. Grill over medium fire, turning and basting with oil mixed with water, 1½ hours, or until done. Most of skin will remain on wire. Garnish with parsley sprigs and serve with Lemon Butter. Makes 4 to 6 servings.

DEEP-FRIED SALMON CUTLETS

2 cups flaked poached salmon steaks (about 1¼ pounds raw)
1 cup undiluted evaporated milk
1 cup soft bread crumbs
1 teaspoon vinegar
1 teaspoon salt
⅛ teaspoon paprika
1 egg, separated
1 whole egg
2 tablespoons cold water
¾ cup fine dry bread crumbs
   Fat for deep frying

Mince salmon fine. Heat evaporated milk with soft bread crumbs, vinegar, salt, and paprika until scalded. Pour over 1 slightly beaten egg yolk, add salmon, and mix well. Fold in 1 stiffly beaten egg white. Chill for several hours. Shape into 8 cutlets. Roll in crumbs and dip into remaining egg mixed with cold water. Roll again in crumbs and chill for about 1 hour longer. Then fry in hot deep fat (370° to 375°F. on a frying thermometer) until golden-brown. Serve with creamy egg sauce, chili sauce, catsup or lemon sections. Makes 4 servings.

BAKED SALMON

1 whole salmon (3 pounds)
   Salt and pepper
   All-purpose flour
¼ cup butter or margarine
1 cup tomato purée
1 small onion, minced
1 garlic clove, minced
1 tablespoon Worcestershire
½ cup light cream
   Lemon wedges

Clean and scale fish. Wash fish and wipe dry. Sprinkle inside and out with salt and pepper. Dip fish into flour and coat well. Melt butter in a shallow baking pan. Place fish in butter and bake in preheated hot oven (400°F.) for 10 to 15 minutes. Add next 4 ingredients. Bake for 30 minutes longer, basting frequently with pan juices. Using a spatula, remove fish to a serving platter. Add cream to pan drippings. Stir well to loosen all particles. Put pan over low heat and thicken sauce with a little flour mixed into a smooth paste with water. Pour sauce over fish; garnish with lemon wedges. Makes 4 to 6 servings.

COLD SALMON PLATTER

1 can (1 pound) salmon, drained
¾ cup mayonnaise
1 tablespoon lemon juice
1 tablespoon prepared mustard
1 cucumber, peeled
1 large tomato, peeled and cut in wedges
2 hard-cooked eggs, quartered
1 tablespoon chopped fresh dill or 1 teaspoon dried dillweed
   Salt and freshly ground pepper
   Paprika
   Toast (optional)

Separate salmon in chunks and put in center of platter. Mix next 3 ingredients and spread on salmon. Quarter cucumber, remove seed and cut cucumber in thin slices. Arrange with next 2 ingredients around salmon. Sprinkle with dill. Season vegetables and eggs lightly with remaining ingredients. Chill and serve with toast, if desired. Makes 4 servings.

SALMON

SALTED SALMON

- 1 fresh salmon (5 pounds)
- 5 tablespoons sugar
- 2 tablespoons salt
- 6 sprigs of fresh dill
- 2 cups coarse salt

Clean fish and remove head, tail, backbone, and fins. Mix sugar and salt and rub over fish. Cut fish into 2-inch slices. Chop leaves from 4 sprigs of dill, saving remainder for later use. In the bottom of a large bowl place a layer of coarse salt and a sprinkling of dill leaves. Put a layer of fish pieces on top of this and continue layering, ending with a layer of salt. Place a weight on top of the fish and put in the refrigerator for 3 days. Serve cold with fresh dill to decorate. Makes 6 to 8 servings.
NOTE: This recipe, of Swedish origin, makes a wonderful smorgasbord dish; it can also be served as an entrée at luncheon. It must be made of fresh, not frozen salmon.

SALMON STEAKS BROILED WITH LEMON BUTTER

- 4 salmon steaks, cut about ¾ inch thick
- 1 teaspoon salt
- Pepper to taste
- ¼ cup butter, melted
- ½ teaspoon grated lemon rind
- ¼ cup lemon juice
- Paprika
- Lemon slices
- Dill sprigs (optional)

Thaw salmon if frozen. Sprinkle both sides of steaks with salt and pepper. Put in foil-lined broiler pan. Mix next 3 ingredients and brush some on fish. Sprinkle lightly with paprika and broil 2 inches from medium heat 5 to 6 minutes, or until slightly browned. Brush again with lemon mixture, turn carefully brush and sprinkle lightly with paprika. Broil 5 to 6 minutes, or until fish flakes easily with fork. Brush with remaining mixture and garnish with lemon slices, and dill sprigs, if desired. Good with paprika-sprinkled boiled potatoes and snow peas or green peas. Makes 4 servings.

WHOLE SALMON IN ASPIC

- 1 whole salmon (6 to 8 pounds), poached and skinned
- 1 envelope unflavored gelatin
- ¼ cup cold water
- ¾ cup boiling water
- 1 can (13 ounces) ready-to-serve madrilène
- Pimiento-stuffed olives or pitted black olives
- Parsley sprigs
- Lemon slices

Put salmon carefully on large serving platter. Soften gelatin in cold water and dissolve in boiling water. Add madrilène and chill until slightly thickened. Arrange olive slices on salmon. Gently pour on gelatin mixture to coat fish. Chill until jelled and serve on same platter with a garnish of parsley and lemon slices. Makes 6 to 8 servings.

Poached Salmon Steaks with Parsley Garnish,
Salmon with Cucumber Sauce

SALMON

COLD SALMON MOUSSE

- 2 envelopes unflavored gelatin
- ½ cup water
- 2 cans (1 pound each) salmon
- 1 cup diced celery
- ½ cup minced green pepper
- ½ cup chopped pimiento
- ¼ cup lemon juice
- 3 cups mayonnaise
- 1 tablespoon grated onion
- ¼ teaspoon pepper
- Dill pickle, thinly sliced
- Hard-cooked eggs, shredded
- 3 tablespoons chopped chives or green onion

Soften gelatin in water; dissolve over hot water; cool. Mash salmon, including liquid. Add celery, green pepper, pimiento, lemon juice, 1½ cups mayonnaise, onion, and pepper; mix well. Stir in gelatin. Pack into 2-quart mold or bowl. Chill overnight. Unmold on serving plate and garnish with pickle slices and hard-cooked eggs. Serve with remaining 1½ cups mayonnaise mixed with chives. Makes 12 servings.
NOTE: Recipe may be halved, if desired.

SALMON LOAF WITH CREAMED-EGG SAUCE

- 1 can (1 pound) salmon
- 2 cups soft bread crumbs
- 2 eggs, slightly beaten
- ½ cup milk
- 2 tablespoons each chopped onion and parsley
- 1 teaspoon salt
- ⅛ teaspoon pepper
- **Creamed-Egg Sauce**

Mash salmon, including bones, skin and liquid. Add remaining ingredients, except sauce, and mix well. Put in greased 9 x 5 x 3-inch loaf pan. Bake in preheated moderate oven (350°F.) 1½ hours, or until firm. Serve with the sauce. Makes 4 servings.

Creamed-Egg Sauce

- 3 tablespoons butter or margarine
- 3 tablespoons all-purpose flour
- 1½ cups milk
- 2 hard-cooked eggs, diced
- Seasoned salt and pepper

Melt butter and blend in flour. Gradually add milk and cook, stirring, until thickened. Add eggs, and seasoned salt and pepper to taste. Makes about 2 cups.

SALMON WITH SOUFFLÉED CAPER SAUCE

Remove bones and skin from 2 cans (1 pound each) salmon. Break into large pieces in greased shallow baking dish. Bake in preheated moderate oven (350°F.) about 15 minutes. Remove from oven. Cover with a mixture of ¾ cup mayonnaise mixed with 2 tablespoons chopped parsley, 3 tablespoons capers, and dash of cayenne; fold in 2 stiffly beaten egg whites. Broil for 5 minutes, or until sauce is puffed and lightly browned. Makes 4 servings.

SCRAMBLED EGGS WITH SMOKED SALMON

- 4 thin slices of smoked salmon
- ¼ cup butter
- 9 eggs
- ½ cup light cream
- Salt and pepper
- Hot toast

Cut salmon into very thin strips. Sauté lightly in butter in large skillet. Beat eggs with cream and add to skillet. Cook over low heat, stirring occasionally, until desired doneness. Season with salt and pepper to taste and serve on or with buttered toast. Makes 4 servings.

SALMON MOUNDS WITH CURRY-MUSHROOM SAUCE

- 1 small onion, minced
- ¼ cup melted butter or margarine
- 1 can (1 pound) salmon
- Milk
- 3 cups soft bread crumbs
- 2 eggs
- ¼ teaspoon poultry seasoning
- ¼ cup minced parsley
- ¼ teaspoon salt
- Dash of ground nutmeg
- 1 can (10½ ounces) condensed cream-of-mushroom soup
- ½ teaspoon curry powder
- ½ teaspoon paprika
- 2 stuffed olives, sliced

Cook onion in butter until golden. Drain salmon, reserving liquid. Add enough milk to liquid to make ½ cup. Mix onion, salmon, liquid, crumbs, eggs, poultry seasoning, parsley, salt, and nutmeg. Shape into 6 mounds in large shallow baking dish. Combine ½ cup milk, soup, curry powder, and paprika. Pour around salmon. Top each salmon mound with a slice of olive. Bake, uncovered, in preheated moderate oven (350°F.) about 45 minutes. Makes 6 servings.

SALMON SALADS

SALMON LOUIS

- 1 can (1 pound) salmon
- 1 head lettuce
- 2 tomatoes, cut into sixths
- ½ cup mayonnaise or salad dressing
- 2 tablespoons each heavy cream and chili sauce
- 2 tablespoons each chopped green pepper and green onion
- ½ teaspoon lemon juice
- Dash each of salt and pepper
- 2 hard-cooked eggs
- 1 tablespoon chopped olives

Drain and flake salmon. Shred lettuce and put in a shallow salad bowl. Arrange salmon on lettuce. Put tomatoes around edge. Mix next 8 ingredients. Chop egg whites and add with olives, to mayonnaise mixture. Chill, and serve on salmon salad. Garnish with sieved hard-cooked egg yolks. Makes 6 servings.

SALMON-CUCUMBER SALAD

- 2 cucumbers, peeled
- 1¼ teaspoons salt
- ¼ teaspoon pepper
- 1 can (1 pound) salmon, well drained and flaked
- ¾ cup dairy sour cream
- 1 tablespoon lemon juice
- 2 tablespoons minced chives or green onions

Quarter cucumbers, remove seeds and cut cucumbers in thin slices. Sprinkle with 1 teaspoon salt and pepper and let stand 30 minutes. Drain well and mix lightly with salmon. Mix sour cream, lemon juice and remaining ¼ teaspoon salt. Pour over first mixture and sprinkle with chives. Makes 4 servings.

SALMON WITH CUCUMBER SAUCE

- 1 can (1 pound) salmon
- ½ cup dairy sour cream
- ½ teaspoon salt
- ¼ teaspoon pepper
- 1 cucumber, peeled, chopped, and drained
- Capers (optional)

Chill salmon; drain, remove skin, and break into chunks. Season sour cream with salt and pepper. Add cucumber, and mix. Serve on salmon. Garnish with capers if desired. Makes 4 to 6 servings.

SANDWICHES

CURRIED-SALMON SANDWICHES

- 1 cup flaked canned salmon
- ⅓ cup chopped celery
- ¼ cup mayonnaise
- 1 teaspoon curry powder
- 1 tablespoon pickle relish
- 12 slices of bread
- 2 eggs, beaten
- ½ cup milk
- ⅛ teaspoon salt
- Dash of pepper
- Butter or margarine

Mix salmon, celery, mayonnaise, curry powder, and relish. Spread on half of bread slices; top with remaining slices. Mix eggs, milk, salt, and pepper. Dip sandwiches into mixture and brown on both sides in hot butter in heavy skillet. Makes 6 sandwiches.

SALMON-OLIVE SANDWICHES

- 1 can (7½ ounces) salmon
- ¼ cup chopped black olives
- 2 tablespoons chili sauce
- 1 tablespoon lemon juice
- 8 slices whole-wheat bread

Mix all ingredients except bread. Spread between slices of bread. Makes 4 sandwiches.

SAUCES FOR SALMON

MUSTARD-DILL SAUCE

All ingredients should be at room temperature

- 3 tablespoons prepared mustard
- 1 tablespoon each sugar and wine vinegar
- 3 tablespoons vegetable oil
- ¼ teaspoon salt
- Dash of white pepper
- 3 tablespoons finely chopped dill

Put mustard in small mixing bowl. Add sugar and vinegar and mix well. Very gradually add oil, stirring briskly until sauce is thick and shiny. Season with salt and pepper and add dill. **To make in blender**, blend ingredients, except dill, till thick. Add dill. Makes about ½ cup.

SALSIFY

PARSLEY BUTTER

Cream ½ cup butter until soft. Beat in ½ teaspoon salt, ⅛ teaspoon pepper and 2 tablespoons minced fresh parsley. Then, drop by drop, beat in 1 tablespoon lemon juice. Makes about ½ cup.

LEMON BUTTER

Melt ½ cup butter, skim off foam and strain clear liquid into bowl, discarding milky residue in pan. Add 1 to 2 tablespoons lemon juice to clear butter. Makes about ½ cup.

SALSIFY—Another name for oyster plant, a biennial herb culitvated for its root which is used as a vegetable.

SALT—Sodium chloride (NaCl), a substance formed by the combination of one sodium atom with one atom of chlorine. It occurs abundantly in nature in the sea, in other natural brines such as the Great Salt Lake in Utah, and the Dead Sea, and in crystalline form, known as rock salt. In connection with food, salt is used as a flavoring and as a preservative.

Commercial salt, once almost solely produced by the evaporation of sea water, is nowadays largely manufactured from natural brines and rock salt. Salt is produced in different grades, the finest being table salt with the coarser grades being used for preserving and refrigeration.

Iodine is sometimes added to table salt to make iodized salt, of great importance in the prevention of goiter in regions such as the Midwest in the United States where natural iodine is scarce.

Salt, like water, is essential for man's good health. It has always played an important part in civilization. In Roman times salt was of such importance that part of every soldier's pay included an allowance for it. This *salarium* has come down to us as the word "salary." Cakes of salt were used as money and, like money, were taxed. Salt was considered to be the fitting medium for unalterable exchanges or covenants, according to the Bible, as a symbol of incorruption and purity. The Apostle, speaking of "the salt of the earth" (Matthew 5:13) can bestow no greater praise. The Devil is said to hate salt because of this purity, and in Scotland salt is thought to drive away witches.

Part of the reason that salt was considered to exemplify incorruption was its power of preserving food from spoiling. In the days when ice was available only in a natural state and had to be transported long distances, if indeed it was obtainable at all, foods had to be salted to preserve them. If there was no salt it was impossible to keep perishable foods, especially in hot weather. It is no wonder that spilling salt has long been considered unlucky.

Salt is also the world's best flavoring, bringing out the natural flavor of food. At tables today it is served in small salt shakers or dishes, often one to each person. But in the days when the substance was worth its weight in gold it was served in a huge salt cellar in the center of the table. This was often weighted at the bottom to prevent it from tipping over and spilling a grain of the precious stuff, not only because spilling salt was thought to be unlucky, but because it was so expensive. The vessel and its contents were so important that they were used to measure social rank and distinction. At the medieval table, those who sat between the host and the salt near the head of the table were "above the salt," or honored guests. Domestics and others with no social distinction were placed "below the salt." In the early days of the American Colonies, when salt was still expensive, this custom carried over to plantation homes in Virginia.

In this country salt was of the tremendous value it had been in earlier times. In the settling of the frontier in the Midwest, salt was the most expensive item required by the settlers. It was necessary, according to one merchant of prerevolutionary days to "cure their meat when they come into the buffalo country." In those days salt was as much as four times the price of beef. Not until the 19th century did the price drop as low as $2.50 a bushel.

Availability and Purchasing Guide—Salt is universally available. There are various types on the market:

Cooking or Table Salt—Fine-grained salt containing about 40 per cent sodium chloride plus such additives as sodium or magnesium carbonate to make the salt free-flowing. **Iodized** salts are table salts with potassium or sodium iodide added.

Seasoned Salt—Fine-grained cooking salt containing various combinations of sugar, monosodium glutamate, spices, starch, onion, garlic, and herbs. Among the special seasoned salts are *garlic salt, onion salt, celery salt,* and *hickory-smoked salt.*

Flake Salt (also called Dairy, Cheese, or Kosher Salt)—Coarse-grained sea salt with natural iodine and minerals. It has a far more pronounced taste than ordinary salt and is used in gourmet cooking and on breads, since it sparkles.

Pickling Salt—Fine-grained pure salt (without any additives). Since it leaves no cloudy residue, it is used especially when clear pickles are desired.

Rock Salt—Coarse-grained salt in small blocks or chunks used for baking oysters and clams and in ice-cream freezers.

Salt Substitutes—Fine-grained chloride compounds in which the sodium has been replaced by other chemicals such as calcium or potassium. They must not be used on a continuous basis without a doctor's advice.

SALT PORK—The side of a hog, cured; it is a fattier portion with less lean than bacon. The fat is cured by the dry-salt method and is not smoked. Salt pork is used for larding and barding since it does not have a smoked flavor that would change the flavor of the meat being larded. It is also used for flavoring and for adding fat to many dishes such as baked beans, clam chowder, stew, etc.

Availability—Year round, by weight and also prepackaged.

Storage—Refrigerate in original wrapper. Do not freeze. Refrigerator shelf: 2 to 3 weeks

Nutritive Food Values—Contains niacin, thiamine, and riboflavin, some calcium and potassium, and a trace of iron.
1 ounce without skin, raw = 232 calories
3½ ounces, fried = 341 calories

Basic Preparation—To release its full flavor without saltiness or rawness, salt pork should be blanched. When used as a seasoning, it should be browned before being added to other ingredients or having other ingredients added to it. The browning is not necessary for larding or barding.

To Blanch—Put salt pork, diced, in a large quantity of cold water. Bring slowly to a boil and simmer for 3 to 10 minutes, or longer depending on the amount of salt pork. Drain and plunge immediately into cold water to firm. Cut into desired shapes and brown slightly in skillet, preferably in the French manner with a little butter.

If the pork is not very salty, it may be soaked in cold water, but this is not as desirable as blanching it.

BROILED CORN WITH SALT PORK

- ¼ pound salt pork
- 1 medium onion, minced
- 3 cups cooked or canned whole-kernel corn
  Salt and pepper
- ½ cup chili sauce

Cut pork into thin slices and partially sauté. Remove from skillet and drain off all but 2 tablespoons drippings. Add onions to drippings and cook for 2 or 3 minutes. Add corn and season with salt and pepper to taste. Divide into 4 individual broilerproof baking dishes. Top with chili sauce and pork. Broil for 10 minutes. Makes 4 servings.

SALT-PORK AND BEAN CHOWDER

- 1 cup dried pea beans
  Water
- ¼ pound salt pork, diced
- 1 onion, chopped
- 1½ teaspoons salt
- ¼ teaspoon pepper
- 1 cup diced potatoes
- 1 cup diced celery and leaves
- 1 can (19 ounces) tomatoes
- 2 tablespoons all-purpose flour
- 2 cups milk, heated

Put beans and 1 quart water in large kettle. Bring to boil and boil for 2 minutes. Remove from heat and let stand for 1 hour. Cook pork and onion until lightly browned. Add with drippings to beans. Simmer, covered, for 1 hour.

Add all ingredients except last 2 and simmer for 30 minutes. Thicken with flour blended with a little cold water. Add milk. Makes about 2 quarts, or 4 to 6 servings.

BEEF WITH RED WINE

- 3 pounds beef for pot roast
- ¼ pound salt pork, blanched and diced
  Salt and pepper
- ½ cup water
- 1 cup dry red wine
- 1 onion, sliced
- 1 bay leaf, crumbled
- ½ garlic clove, minced
  All-purpose flour

Brown meat on all sides with salt pork in a heavy kettle. Sprinkle with salt and pepper. Place a rack in bottom of kettle under meat; add remaining ingredients. Cover and simmer for 3 to 3½ hours. Remove meat and thicken liquid with a flour-and-water paste. Add salt and pepper to taste. Make 4 servings.

NOTE: The salt pork is essential to the characteristic flavor of this dish.

SAMPHIRE [*Crithmum maritimum*]—A succulent-stemmed perennial which grows along the rocky coasts of northwestern Europe and Great Britain. The plant grows to a height of one to two feet and has a small white or yellowish flower. It is also known as fennel, parsley pert, and St. Peter's herb. The crisp aromatic leaves and young stems are used for salads, pickles, and a potherb.

SAND DAB—A small Pacific flounder found from California to Alaska. These dabs can reach two pounds, but the usual market size is about ten ounces. The flavor is delicate and sweet and the texture fine.

Availability—Fresh, usually sold whole, on West Coast only, year round.

Storage—Do not store unless you plan to freeze fish. Flavor is best when used at once. To freeze, scale, gut, remove fins, dip into solution of 1 tablespoon salt to 1 cup water; freeze in single layer, then wrap in moisture-vaporproof wrapping, with each dab separated by freezer paper.

Caloric Values
3½ ounces, raw = 79 calories

Basic Preparation—Scale, eviscerate, remove fins, rinse and pat dry. Panfry in mixture of oil and butter, turning once. Sprinkle with lemon juice and chopped parsley and serve at once.

Or dip fish into seasoned flour, then deep-fry in vegetable oil until golden brown and tender, a few minutes only. Serve with slices or wedges of any citrus fruit, and sautéed potato balls.

SAND DABS MEUNIÈRE

Skin fish and sprinkle with salt and pepper. Roll in all-purpose flour and brown quickly in butter. Remove to skillet and heat until golden. Add juice of 1 lemon and 1 tablespoon chopped parsley. Pour over the fish and serve at once.

SANDWICH COOKBOOK

SANDWICH—A dish made up of a filling such as sliced meat, cheese, a savory spread, etc., placed on one slice or between two or more slices of bread. In the United States and England the word is generally used to describe foods placed between slices of bread, whereas in Scandinavia and Germany, sandwiches are most often the single-slice-plus-topping variety, what we call here an "open-face" sandwich.

Sandwich sizes can vary from the long hero to the tiny bite-size tea sandwich; they can be made with all sorts of breads and rolls; and the possibilities for filling are endless: moist creamy fillings, smooth spreadable fillings, sliced meats, fish, cheese, or poultry. In fact, almost anything that spreads or slices or fits between bread or in rolls can be made into a sandwich, as nourishing or elegant as desired.

Sandwiches can be cold or hot. Among the hot sandwiches are those served with gravy and many covered with cheese and grilled under a broiler. A sandwich can be dipped into a mixture of milk and eggs and fried; or toasted in waffle irons; or cooked until crisp on a griddle. Still others can be wrapped in foil and grilled for a **barbecue, speared on skewers and toasted in special grills, or deep-fried.**

The custom of placing food between slices of bread is an old one; workers in the field have long been fed that way. But the sandwich takes its name from John Montague, fourth Earl of Sandwich (1718-1792), who, reluctant to leave the gaming tables long enough to dine, had cold beef sandwiches made for him so that he could eat as he played.

BREADS
Use breads that are firm and easily spread with butter, cheese, etc. Crusts may or may not be trimmed according to the type of sandwich being made. Always use a sharp or serrated-edge knife when slicing to prevent the tearing of the bread. Bread can be plain or toasted. If sandwiches are trimmed, save crusts from bread in a tightly covered container and use them for stuffings, croutons, and casserole toppings, as well as for making bread crumbs.

Make good use of the variety of bread available. Apart from homemade breads and rolls, these store-bought breads make good sandwiches: white, rye, cracked-wheat, pumpernickel, and oatmeal breads; frankfurter and sandwich rolls; canned orange-nut, date-nut, chocolate, and brown breads; French and Italian bread; plain and seeded hard rolls; English muffins.

For hero sandwiches, small French or Italian loaves are good. Or, if the long loaves are used, they can be cut into individual hero sandwich sizes before filling. Plain and seeded hard rolls are also good for hero-type sandwiches.

For out-of-hand sandwiches, almost any bread can be used.

For hot open-face sandwiches served with meat and gravy, white, cracked-wheat, whole-wheat, or oatmeal bread, or even sandwich rolls can be used. For cold open-face sandwiches, these same breads plus rye and pumpernickel can be used.

For tea sandwiches, canned chocolate nut, and brown breads; or crust-trimmed white, whole-wheat, cracked wheat, or oatmeal breads can be used.

SPREADING
Spread butter or margarine to the edges of the bread to prevent the filling from soaking the bread. And use soft butter for easier spreading. One pound of softened butter or margarine spreads about 96 slices if you use 1 teaspoon per slice. Mayonnaise is preferable to butter when sandwiches have to be kept for some time, as when being carried to a picnic in warm weather. It will not melt as butter or margarine does. One pint of mayonnaise spreads about 60 average slices of bread, using ½ tablespoon per slice.

FILLINGS
To prevent tearing the bread when spreading a filling, use a blunt knife or spatula. If the crusts are to be trimmed, do this before spreading the filling. Spread the filling right to the edges of the slice of bread, or else the sandwich eater will feel cheated and the sandwich may feel lumpy.

Many prepared sandwich fillings are available: deviled ham; luncheon-meat spread; liver pâté; chicken spread; sandwich spread; whipped cream cheese, cream cheese with pimientos, with olives and pimientos, with pineapple, with chives, with Roquefort, bars of date-and-nut cream cheese and clam-and-lobster cream cheese; chopped olive spread; blue-cheese spread; bacon-cheese spread; smoke-flavored cheese spread; and many others. Hot meat and poultry sandwiches can be varied by topping open-face sandwiches with sauce or gravy such as cheese sauce, meat-loaf sauce, tomato sauce, spaghetti sauce, curry sauce, brown or mushroom gravy, or à la king sauce.

GARNISHES
Add assorted pickles and olives; cucumber, carrot, and celery sticks; salad greens; tomato slices or wedges; green onions; carrot curls; radishes; onion rings; green-pepper strips. With a sweet sandwich try dates, plumped prunes, maraschino cherries, or other fruits.

SHAPES
Pinwheel Sandwiches—Cut unsliced bread into lengthwise slices and trim crusts. Flatten slices lightly with a rolling pin. Spread bread with a smooth filling and place sweet gherkins, olives, strips of pimiento or green pepper along one long side. Starting at opposite side roll up tightly and wrap closely in wax paper. Chill. When ready to serve, cut into ½-inch slices.

Rolled Sandwiches—Use slices of soft bread with the crusts trimmed. Flatten with rolling pin. Spread with watercress or parsley butter or similar filling and roll up. Cover with a damp towel and refrigerate until ready to serve. For a party look, push tiny sprigs of parsley or watercress into the sandwich ends.

SANDWICH

from soaking in. Package finished sandwiches individually wrapped and sealed in moisture- vapor-proof wrapping.

For fillings in sandwiches to be frozen use cooked egg yolk, peanut butter, cooked chicken, turkey, meat, fish, dried beef or drained crushed pineapple. Do not use very moist fillings, cooked egg white, or raw vegetables. For binders use lemon, orange, pineapple, or other fruit juice, milk, dairy sour cream, or applesauce. Avoid mayonnaise or salad dressings; they may separate when frozen.

STUPENDOUS DOUBLE-DECKER OPEN-FACED SANDWICHES

Family-pleasing, oven-hot combinations of meat, seafood, cheese and vegetables—a whole meal on two slices of bread

HAM-CHEESE SANDWICHES

- 4 slices cooked ham, ¼ inch thick and same size as bread
- 4 slices firm-type bread, lightly toasted
  Prepared mustard
- 4 slices Swiss cheese, ⅛ inch thick and same size as bread
  Parsley
  Tomato slices and wedges

Put a ham slice on each slice of bread. Spread a thin coat of mustard on ham and top with a slice of cheese. Put on baking sheet and bake in preheated very hot oven (450°F.) 10 minutes, or until cheese is melted and sandwiches are heated. Top half the slices with remaining slices to make 2 doubledecker open-faced sandwiches. Garnish with parsley and tomato slices and serve with tomato wedges. Makes 2 servings.

LIVER-PÂTÉ AND MUSHROOM SANDWICHES

- 1 can (4¾ ounces) liver pâté
- 4 slices firm-type bread, lightly toasted
- 1 can (4 ounces) sliced mushrooms, drained
- 1 tablespoon butter or margarine
- ¼ cup chopped pimiento
- 2 tablespoons chopped green pepper
  Fine dry bread crumbs
  Grated Parmesan cheese
  Pickled sweet red peppers

Spread liver pâté on bread slices, covering completely. Sauté mushrooms in butter a few minutes. Add pimiento and green pepper and distribute mixture evenly on pâté. Sprinkle lightly with crumbs and cheese. Put on baking sheet and broil under medium heat 4 to 5 minutes, or until top is well browned. Top half the slices with remaining slices to make 2 double-decker open-faced sandwiches. Serve with red peppers. Makes 2 servings.

Ham-Cheese Sandwich

Ribbon Sandwiches—Stack 2 slices of whole-wheat bread and 2 slices of white bread alternately with one or more fillings between slices. Press together and trim crusts. Wrap, and chill. Cut into ½-inch slices to serve.

Checkerboard Sandwiches—Prepare and cut ribbon sandwiches. Then stack 3 ribbon sandwiches so white and whole-wheat sections alternate. Spread filling between ribbons. Wrap; chill. To serve, cut into ½-inch slices.

Open Sandwiches—This kind of sandwich consists of one slice of bread only, spread with butter, mayonnaise, or another spread, and topped with any kind of fish, meat, or vegetable toppings, or a combination of all of these. Most open sandwiches are cold, but there are also hot ones where the topping of meat or fowl is covered with gravy.

Open sandwiches are eaten with a knife and fork. They are eaten for lunch, supper, and any-time snacks in Denmark, Sweden, Norway, Finland, and Germany, where they are standard fare. These countries excel at the art of making them as pretty as a picture by arranging the toppings not only for taste combinations, but with an eye for appearance. They use ingredients with contrasting colors such as hard-cooked egg and tomato, roast beef and chopped onion, or herring topped with dill sprigs, to name but a few of the endless combinations. Furthermore, the sandwiches are decorated with twists of lemon, cucumber, tomato, carrot curls, pickled red beets, and sprigs of parsley or dill.

To prepare handsome open sandwiches follow these rules:

Cut bread as thin as possible and use only firm breads that will not fall apart when spread with butter or mayonnaise. Crusts are generally trimmed from the bread. The filling is spread to the edges and the garnish piled on top.

FREEZING SANDWICHES

To eliminate last-minute work, many sandwiches can be frozen prior to serving. All fresh breads freeze well. Spread bread generously with soft butter to keep fillings

Avocado, Bacon and Tomato Sandwich

Cheddar-Cheese And Tomato Sandwich

Cheese, Onion and Bacon Sandwich

AVOCADO, BACON AND TOMATO SANDWICHES

- 4 slices firm-type bread, lightly toasted
  Mayonnaise
- 1 large ripe avocado, peeled and cut in ¼-inch half circles
  Thin tomato slices
  Seasoned salt and pepper
- 4 slices bacon, halved and partially cooked
  Tomato wedges and lemon slices

Spread bread slices thinly with mayonnaise. Cover with slightly overlapping avocado half circles. Garnish with tomato slices and sprinkle with seasoned salt and pepper. Top with bacon slices and bake in preheated very hot oven (450°F.) 10 minutes, or until bacon is crisp and sandwiches are heated. Top half the slices with remaining slices to make 2 double-decker open-faced sandwiches. Serve with tomato wedges and lemon slices. Makes 2 servings.

CHEDDAR-CHEESE AND TOMATO SANDWICHES

- 2 eggs, slightly beaten
- 2 cups firmly packed shredded Cheddar cheese
- ¼ cup canned tomato sauce with onions
- 4 slices firm-type bread, lightly toasted
  Stuffed green olives
  Lettuce

Mix eggs, cheese and tomato sauce and cover bread slices with mixture. Put on baking sheet and bake in preheated very hot oven (450°F.) 10 minutes, or until cheese is partially melted and sandwiches are heated. Top half the slices with remaining slices to make 2 double-decker open-faced sandwiches. Garnish with olives. Serve with additional olives and lettuce. Makes 2 servings.

CHEESE, ONION AND BACON SANDWICHES

- 1 medium onion, thinly sliced
- 4 slices firm-type bread
- 1 package (6 ounces) mozzarella or Muenster cheese, preferably sliced
  Salt and paprika
- 4 slices slab bacon, ¼ inch thick, partially cooked
  Parsley and pickles

Divide onion slices evenly on bread. Cover with cheese, sprinkle lightly with salt and paprika and put a slice of bacon on top. Put on baking sheet and bake in preheated hot oven (425°F.) 10 minutes, or until cheese melts and bacon is crisp. Top half the slices with remaining slices to make 2 double-decker open-faced sandwiches. Garnish with parsley and serve with pickles. Makes 2 servings.

SANDWICH

PIQUANT FRANKFURTER SANDWICHES

4 slices firm-type bread
 Butter or margarine
 Minced parsley
4 frankfurters
½ cup mayonnaise
1 tablespoon chili sauce
1 teaspoon prepared mustard
 Assorted pickles and olives

Spread bread slices thinly with butter and dip in parsley to cover surface completely. Cut frankfurters in half crosswise and lengthwise. Cover each slice of bread with 4 frankfurter pieces, skin side down. Mix next 3 ingredients and pour on frankfurters, leaving ends uncovered. Put on baking sheet and bake in preheated very hot oven (475°F.) 7 minutes, or until frankfurters are browned. Top half the slices with remaining slices to make 2 double-decker open-faced sandwiches. Serve with pickles and olives. Makes 2 servings.

Piquant Frankfurter Sandwich

HEARTY HOT SANDWICHES

MEXICAN-STYLE ROLLS

1 pound ground beef
1 cup coarsely chopped onion
1 tablespoon all-purpose flour
1½ teaspoons chili seasoning
½ teaspoon dried oregano
1 teaspoon salt
3 or 4 dashes hot pepper sauce
1 can (8 ounces) tomato sauce
¼ cup chili sauce
¼ cup sliced black olives
1 cup shredded sharp Cheddar cheese
8 hamburger or frankfurter rolls

Cook beef and onion until meat loses its red color, breaking up with fork. Blend in next 5 ingredients. Add tomato sauce and chili sauce and cook slowly, stirring frequently, 20 minutes, or until thick. Add olives, cool, then stir in cheese. Fill rolls with mixture and put in shallow pan (frankfurter rolls filled side up). Cover with foil and heat in preheated slow oven (325°F.) about 30 minutes. Makes 8 servings.

HAMBURGER ROLLS, ITALIAN STYLE

Cut deep slits in tops of 8 oblong hard rolls. Cook 1 pound ground beef chuck until browned, breaking up meat with fork. Add ⅔ cup tomato sauce, ¾ teaspoon salt, ¼ cup sliced stuffed olives, and 1 cup diced Muenster or Mozzarella cheese. Fill rolls and sprinkle with dried oregano. Wrap each filled roll in a piece of aluminum foil. Heat on rack over hot coals for 15 minutes, turning often. Makes 8 rolls.

SWEET-AND-SOUR HAMBURGER SANDWICHES

1 pound ground beef
¼ pound ground pork
1 teaspoon salt
¼ teaspoon pepper
6 slices of canned pineapple
1 tablespoon soy sauce
⅓ cup firmly packed brown sugar
1 tablespoon Worcestershire
½ teaspoon ground cloves
⅓ cup wine vinegar
6 green-pepper rings
6 sandwich rolls or other rolls

Mix first 4 ingredients. Shape into 6 patties and brown on both sides in greased skillet. Pour off fat. Put a pineapple slice on each patty. Mix next 5 ingredients and pour over patties. Cover and simmer for 10 minutes. Put green-pepper rings on pineapple. Cover and simmer for 5 minutes longer. Serve hamburgers with some of the sauce between split rolls. Makes 6 sandwiches.

SANDWICH

SLOPPY JOES

- 1½ pounds ground beef chuck
- 1 onion, chopped
- 1½ teaspoons salt
- ⅛ teaspoon pepper
- 3 tablespoons all-purpose flour
- ½ teaspoon Worcestershire
- 1 cup catsup
- 1¼ cups water
- 4 sandwich rolls, split and toasted

Cook beef, onion, salt, and pepper until meat loses its red color, stirring with fork. Blend in flour. Add Worcestershire, catsup, and water. Simmer, stirring frequently, for 20 minutes, or until thick. Serve between rolls. Makes 4 sandwiches.

ITALIAN SLOPPY JOES

- ¾ pound Italian-style bulk sausage
- ¾ pound ground round steak
- ¾ teaspoon each garlic powder and salt
- ¼ teaspoon pepper
- 4 cans (8 ounces each) tomato sauce
- ¾ teaspoon sweet basil
- 6 crusty French rolls
- 12 slices Mozzarella cheese (about 12 ounces)
  Paprika

Mix sausage and beef and brown in saucepan. Stir in next 4 ingredients. Bring to boil and simmer for 1½ to 2 hours. Add basil and simmer for 30 minutes longer. Skim off excess fat. Slice rolls into halves lengthwise. Cover inside top half with 2 cheese slices and sprinkle with paprika. Broil until cheese melts. Spread meat mixture on bottom half of rolls. Close sandwiches and serve hot. Makes 6.

DRIED-BEEF AND CHEESE ROLLS

- 1 jar (2½ ounces) sliced dried beef
- 1 cup diced process American cheese
- ¼ cup chopped black olives
- ⅓ cup tomato sauce
- 6 frankfurter or hamburger rolls

Cut dried beef in small pieces with scissors. Add cheese, olives and sauce and mix well. Fill rolls with mixture and put in shallow baking pan (frankfurter rolls filled side up). Heat in preheated slow oven (300°F.) about 25 minutes. Makes 6 servings.

STEAK ROLLS

- 2 tablespoons each cider vinegar and water
  Salt and pepper
- 1 cucumber, peeled and chopped
- 1 sweet onion, sliced
- 1½ pounds thinly sliced beef round steak
  All-purpose flour
- 3 tablespoons shortening
- 8 sandwich rolls, split and toasted

Mix vinegar, water, 1 teaspoon salt, and ¼ teaspoon pepper; bring to boil. Pour over cucumber and onion. Cover; refrigerate for several hours or overnight. When ready to serve, pound steak. Cut into 8 pieces. Roll in mixture of flour, salt, and pepper. Brown on both sides in hot shortening. Put a piece between halves of each roll. Serve with the sauce. Makes 8 sandwiches.

FRENCH-TOAST SANDWICHES WITH CREAMED DRIED BEEF

- Butter or margarine
- 1 jar (5 ounces) dried beef, shredded
- 3 tablespoons all-purpose flour
- 2¾ cups milk
- ½ teaspoon caraway seeds
- ¼ teaspoon dried rosemary
  Pepper
- 3 eggs
- ½ teaspoon salt
- 8 slices of white bread

Melt 3 tablespoons butter; add beef and cook for 2 or 3 minutes. Blend in flour; add 2 cups milk. Cook, stirring constantly, until thickened. Add seeds, rosemary, and pepper to taste. Keep hot. Beat eggs; add remaining ¾ cup milk and the salt. Dip bread into mixture and fry in hot butter until golden-brown on both sides. Serve beef between and over toast. Makes 4 sandwiches.

CORNED-BEEF AND CHEESE SANDWICHES, MUSTARD DRESSING

Spread 8 large slices of rye bread with prepared mustard. Cover bread with corned beef and overlapping cheese slices. Spread with Mustard Dressing to within ½ inch of edges. Put under broiler until dressing is bubbling and cheese is melted. Garnish with pimiento if desired. Makes 8 sandwiches.

Mustard Dressing

Mix thoroughly 1 cup mayonnaise, 3 tablespoons prepared mustard, 1 tablespoon prepared horseradish, 1 teaspoon Worcestershire, ½ cup well-drained pickle relish, and a dash of hot pepper sauce.

CORNED-BEEF AND PINEAPPLE ROLLS

- 1 can (12 ounces) corned beef, chopped
- 2 tablespoons prepared horseradish
- 1 can (8¼ ounces) crushed pineapple, drained
- 2 cups medium-shredded cabbage
- ⅓ cup mayonnaise
- 8 frankfurter or hamburger rolls

Mix first 5 ingredients. Fill rolls and put in shallow baking pan (frankfurter rolls filled side up). Cover with foil and heat in preheated slow oven (325°F.) about 25 minutes. Makes 8 servings.

SANDWICH

BEEF TENDERLOIN SANDWICHES

- 8 slices of bread, toasted
  Butter or margarine (about ⅔ cup)
- 1 garlic clove, minced
- 4 slices (4 ounces each) of beef tenderloin
  Salt and pepper to taste
  Sherry
- ½ pound fresh mushrooms, sliced, or 1 can (4 ounces) sliced mushrooms, drained
- ½ cup water

Spread toast with soft butter. For each sandwich cut 2 slices into triangles and put on serving plate. Melt ¼ cup butter in skillet. Add garlic and cook for 2 or 3 minutes. Add tenderloin and season with salt and pepper. Brown on both sides. Reduce heat and add ¾ cup sherry. Cover and simmer for 10 minutes, basting occasionally. Remove meat and reserve drippings. In another skillet melt ¼ cup butter. Add mushrooms and cook until lightly browned. Add ⅓ cup sherry and water. Pour into first skillet and simmer for 5 minutes. Arrange meat on toast and spoon hot sauce over. Makes 4 sandwiches.

CHEESE-AND-EGG BARBECUE SANDWICHES

- ½ pound sharp Cheddar cheese
- 2 tablespoons minced green pepper
- 1 medium onion, chopped
- 1 tablespoons catsup
- 1 egg, hard-cooked and chopped
- 2 stuffed olives, chopped
- 2 tablespoons butter or margarine, melted
- 6 sandwich rolls

Combine all ingredients except rolls and mix thoroughly. Spread on split rolls and put under broiler until cheese is melted. Makes 6 servings.

MONTE CRISTO SANDWICHES

For each sandwich use 3 slices of bread. Butter one slice first, then cover with a slice each baked ham and cooked chicken. Butter both sides of second bread slice, put on top, and cover with a generous slice of Swiss cheese. Butter third slice, and put on top; press slightly, and secure with a toothpick. Trim off crusts, and cut into haves diagonally. Mix 3 slightly beaten eggs, ⅓ cup milk, and ⅛ teaspoon salt (makes enough for 4 servings or 12 triangles). Dip sandwich halves into egg mixture. Fry in butter or margarine in skillet until golden-brown on all sides, adding more butter when necessary. Remove toothpicks. Three triangles make a generous serving.

ITALIAN GRINDERS

Split small loaves of Italian bread, or cut 10-inch pieces from long loaves, and split. Brush inside generously with **garlic flavored olive oil. Put together, sandwich fashion,** with layers of sliced salami, Mozzarella cheese, and flat anchovy fillets. Wrap in foil and heat in preheated moderate oven (350°F.).

HOT TURKEY SANDWICHES WITH MUSHROOM SAUCE

- 8 slices white bread, toasted
  Sliced cooked turkey
- 2 cans (10½ ounces each) consensed cream-of-mushroom soup
- ½ cup water
- ½ cup shredded sharp Cheddar cheese
- 8 slices bacon, partially cooked
  Hot mashed potato (optional)

Cut 4 slices of toast into halves diagonally. For each sandwich put 1 whole slice of toast plus a half on each side in baking dish or individual ovenware plate. Cover toast with turkey. Mix soup and water. Heat, stirring, until smooth. Spoon sauce over turkey and sprinkle with cheese. Top with bacon. Make a border of mashed potato around each sandwich. Put under broiler until cheese is melted and potato is lightly browned. Makes 4 sandwiches.

CHICKEN-CHEESE SANDWICHES

- 6 slices cooked chicken
- 6 slices toast
- 6 slices tomato
- ½ cup finely crumbled blue cheese
- 1 egg, beaten
- ½ cup minced canned mushrooms
- 3 bacon strips, halved

Put a slice of chicken on each toast slice. Top with a slice of tomato. Mix cheese, egg, and mushrooms. Spread on tomato and top each with a half strip of bacon. Broil until bacon is crisp. Makes 6 sandwiches.

HAWAIIAN OMELET SANDWICHES

- 8 slices toast
  Butter
- 8 eggs, beaten
- 2 teaspoons soy sauce
- ½ teaspoon salt
- ½ teaspoon monosodium glutamate
- 2 green onions, chopped
- ½ green pepper, chopped
- 1 can (8¼ ounces) pineapple tidbits, drained
- 1 medium tomato, chopped
- 1 package (6 ounces) frozen king crabmeat, thawed and drained
- 4 slices of baked ham

Spread toast with butter. Cut 4 slices diagonally into halves. Arrange 1 whole slice on each plate with a toast triangle on either side. Mix eggs and seasonings. Heat ⅓ cup butter in large skillet; add onions and green pepper; cook for 5 minutes. Add eggs and cook until set around edge. Sprinkle with next 3 ingredients. When egg is completely firm, fold omelet and cook for 5 minutes longer. Put slice of ham on each whole toast slice; cut omelet into 4 portions and put one on each ham slice. Makes 4 sandwiches.

SANDWICH

PEANUT-BUTTER, BACON AND CHEESE ROLLS

Spread tops of hamburger rolls generously with softened cream cheese, bottom halves with peanut butter. Top peanut butter wirh crisp bacon, crumbled. Put halves together and put in shallow baking pan. Cover with foil and heat in preheated slow oven (300°F.) about 25 minutes.

CRUNCHY CHEESE ROLLS

- 2 cups shredded sharp Cheddar cheese
- 1 cup chopped celery
- ½ cup chopped black olives
- ½ cup chopped almonds
- 3 tablespoons mayonnaise
- 1 teaspoon prepared mustard
- 2 teaspoons prepared horseradish
- 8 frankfurter rolls

Combine all ingredients, except rolls, and mix well. Fill rolls with mixture and put in shallow baking pan, filled side up. Cover with foil and heat in preheated slow oven (325°F.) about 25 minutes. Makes 8 sandwiches.

DENVER CHEESE SANDWICHES

- ¼ cup butter or margarine
- 1 small onion, minced
- ½ green pepper, minced
- 6 eggs, beaten
- ⅓ cup milk
- ½ teaspoon salt
- ⅛ teaspoon pepper
- 6 slices of process Swiss cheese
- 12 slices of hot toast, buttered

Melt butter in large skillet. Add onion and green pepper; cook for 5 minutes. Add next 4 ingredients, mixed. Cover and cook over very low heat until firm. Top with cheese, cover, and cook for a few minutes longer. Cut into 6 servings and serve between slices of toast. Makes 6 sandwiches.

PIZZA, WESTERN STYLE

- 1½ cups canned tomatoes, drained and chopped
- ½ teaspoon dried oregano
- 2 tablespoons olive oil
- Salt and pepper
- 1 loaf Italian bread
- Slices of Mozzarella, or Cheddar cheese (or cooked Italian-sausage slices, or anchovies)
- Grated Parmesan cheese

Put tomatoes, oregano, and olive oil in saucepan. Season with salt and pepper to taste. Bring to boil and simmer for 10 minutes. Split bread lengthwise and spread with tomato mixture. Arrange cheese slices on top and sprinkle with grated cheese. Put under preheated broiler until bubbly. Cut diagonally into 2-inch pieces. Makes 4 servings.

FRENCH-TOASTED MOZZARELLA SANDWICHES

Cut ½ pound Mozzarella cheese into 6 slices. Put between ½-inch slices of Italian bread. Dip into milk, into flour, then into well-beaten egg. Fry in hot olive oil until sandwich is golden-brown on both sides and cheese is slightly melted. Makes 6 small sandwiches.

HEARTY COLD SANDWICHES

HERO SANDWICH I

Split hero loaves of bread lengthwise and brush inside and out with olive oil. On bottom half lay slices of Swiss cheese. Top with tomato slices, hard salami, pickled red pepper, ripe and pimiento-stuffed olives, flat anchovy fillets, and Italian parsley. Add top half of bread and cut sandwich into 3 crosswise pieces.

HERO SANDWICH II

Split hero loaves of bread lengthwise and brush inside and out with olive or salad oil. On bottom half lay slices of salami or bologna, a layer of salad greens, a layer of thinly sliced roast pork or turkey, a layer each of sliced tomatoes, sliced sweet onion. Garnish with pieces of Mozzarella, olives, and crisp bacon slices. Serve open-face.

ROAST-BEEF AND BLUE-CHEESE SANDWICH

Spread white or whole-wheat bread with equal parts of blue cheese and soft butter, blended together. Top with slices of cold roast beef and sprinkle with chopped chives.

CHEF'S CLUB SANDWICH

Toast and butter large oval slices of white bread. On bottom slice put baked or broiled ham and Swiss cheese. Add second slice of toast and top with lettuce, tomato slices, and crisp bacon. Add mayonnaise if desired. Add third slice of toast and top with sliced cooked chicken and lettuce. Add fourth slice of toast. Insert toothpick in center and top with a large green or stuffed olive.

Chef's Club Sandwich

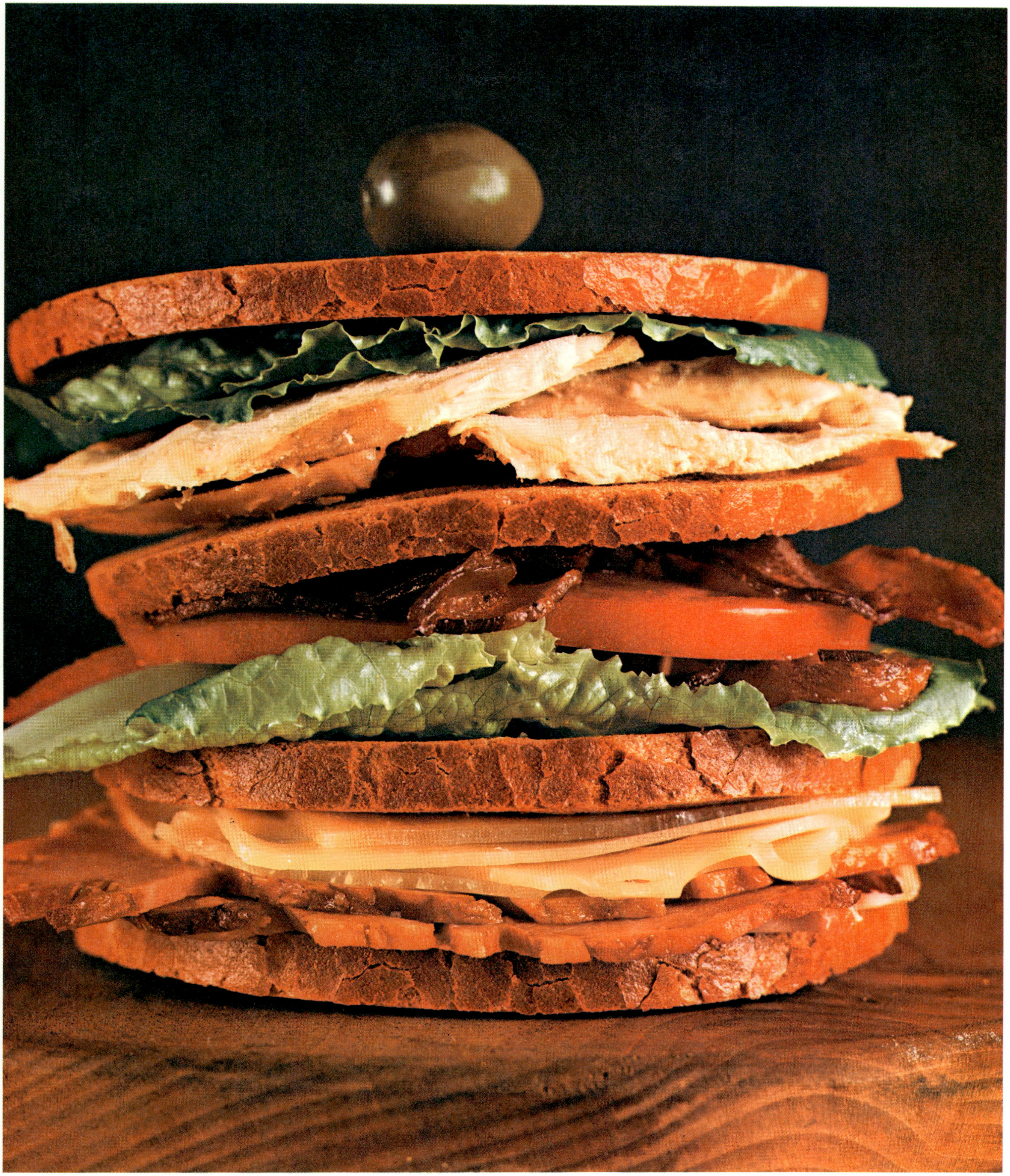

SANDWICH

HAM SALAD ROLLS

- 2 cups finely diced cooked ham
- 2 cups finely shredded cabbage
- ½ cup diced celery
- ½ green pepper, minced
- 1 hard-cooked egg, chopped
- 2 tablespoons prepared mustard
- Dash of onion salt
- 8 frankfurter rolls
- Salad dressing
- Sweet-pickle slices

Mix first 7 ingredients. Open rolls; remove some crumbs from center and add to first mixture. Moisten salad with salad dressing and fill each roll. Garnish with pickle. Makes 8 sandwiches.

DOWN-EAST SANDWICHES

Mash 1 can (1 pound) Boston-style baked beans. Spread on 4 slices of buttered toast. Add drained coleslaw, salt and pepper to taste, and a little catsup. Top each with 2 browned sausage links and a second slice of buttered toast. Serve with pickles or olives. Makes 4 sandwiches.

TUNA-EGG THREE-DECKERS

- 18 slices white toast
- Butter or margarine
- 1 can (7 ounces) tuna, flaked
- ½ cup diced celery
- ⅔ cup mayonnaise or salad dressing (about)
- ¼ cup chili sauce
- 2 tablespoons pickle relish
- 6 hard-cooked eggs, sliced
- ⅓ cup sliced stuffed olives
- 12 tomato slices
- Lettuce or other salad greens

Spread 6 slices toast with butter. Mix tuna, celery, and 2 tablespoons mayonnaise. Spread on buttered toast. Top with 6 slices of toast. Spread with mixture of ½ cup mayonnaise, chili sauce, and pickle relish. Cover with egg slices, olives, tomato, and lettuce. Top with remaining toast. Makes 6 sandwiches.

EGGPLANT, MOZZARELLA, AND PIMIENTO LONG BOYS

Split four 6-inch lengths of French bread. Brush with olive oil and sprinkle with garlic salt. Slice 1 pound Mozzarrella cheese and cover half of each length of bread. Add some pimiento slices. Peel and slice 1 medium eggplant ½ inch thick. Roll slices in flour and brown on both sides in hot fat. Season and put in overlapping slices on remaining halves of bread. Serve open. Makes 4 sandwiches.

EGG-SALAD AND TONGUE SANDWICHES

Chop 6 hard-cooked eggs. Add 1 cup finely diced celery, 1 teaspoon instant minced onion, ½ teaspoon dry mustard, ½ cup mayonnaise, and seasoned salt and pepper to taste. Toast and butter 12 slices of cheese bread. Other bread can be used, but cheese is especially good. Spread 6 slices with egg salad and put lettuce and sliced cold tongue on remaining toast. Put together, and serve with pickle relish. Makes 6 sandwiches.

SARDINE SWISS-CHEESE SANDWICHES

- 2 cans (3¾ ounces each) sardines
- 12 slices of buttered rye bread
- 6 slices of Swiss or Muenster cheese
- 6 tomato slices

Arrange sardines on 6 slices of bread. Top with a cheese slice and a slice of tomato. Cover with remaining bread. Makes 6 sandwiches.

BLUE-CHEESE AND EGG SANDWICHES

Chop 3 hard-cooked eggs. Add 1 teaspoon instant minced onion, ¼ cup crumbled blue cheese, and ¼ cup mayonnaise or salad dressing. Mix well and season to taste with salt and pepper. Spread between slices of white or rye bread. Makes 4 sandwiches.

POTATO, EGG, AND CHEESE SANDWICHES

- 2 raw medium potatoes, peeled
- Salt
- Boiling water
- 2 hard-cooked eggs
- 6 ounces sharp Cheddar cheese
- 1 medium sweet red or green pepper
- ½ small onion
- Mayonnaise or salad dressing
- Pepper
- Prepared mustard and Worcestershire

Cook potatoes in boiling salted water until tender. Drain; using medium blade, put through food chopper with eggs, cheese, pepper, and onion. Moisten mixture with mayonnaise. Season to taste with salt, pepper, mustard, and Worcestershire. Spread between slices of whole-wheat or pumpernickel bread. Makes 4 sandwiches.

SKYSCRAPER SANDWICHES

Ingredients are listed starting with the bottom layer. To build these sandwiches assemble from the bottom.

Barbecue Bonanza—White toast, buttered; fried onion rings mixed with half-melted Cheddar cheese; rye toast, buttered; pork-roll slices, fried; hot-dog relish; white toast, buttered; shredded lettuce; hard-cooked egg, sliced; white toast, spread with mayonnaise; parsley.

SANDWICH

Broadway Special

Broadway Special—Rye or pumpernickel bread, buttered; chopped liver; Vienna bread, spread with mustard; Swiss-cheese slices; green-pepper strips; rye bread, buttered; salami or bologna; dill pickle, sliced; radish rose.

Cold-Cuts Pyramid—Pumpernickel bread, buttered; corned beef spead with mustard; white bread, buttered; shredded cabbage and green pepper with salad dressing; rye bread, buttered; Muenster cheese; wafer, buttered; smoked salmon; slice of red onion; fresh dill.

Country-Club Luncheon—Pumpernickel bread, buttered; cottage cheese and red caviar; Vienna bread, buttered; shrimp-and-celery salad; chicory; white bread, buttered; crisp bacon slices; tomato slices; wheat oval, buttered; watercress.

Curry Surprise—Whole-wheat bread, buttered; ham and chicken slices; wholewheat bread spread with mayonnaise; hard-cooked egg and cucumber slices; white bread, buttered; shredded lettuce; tuna-fish salad; raisin bread; cream cheese, seasoned with curry powder; cashews, chopped; cut gingerroot.

Roman Holiday—Italian bread, buttered; hot eggplant, sliced and fried; Mozzarella cheese, sprinkled with oregano; Italian bread, spread with garlic-flavored olive oil; romaine and pimiento strips; Italian bread, buttered; anchovy fillets; olives and capers.

Seafood Delight—White bread, buttered; salmon- or tuna-and-celery salad; rye bread, spread with mayonnaise; cream cheese and olives; white bread with sandwich spread; crabmeat mixed with fresh lemon juice and green onion; rye bread; radish slices.

Sunday-Night Supper—White bread, spread with butter, seasoned with chopped mint; cold lamb, sliced; rye bread, buttered; salad of chopped cucumbers, onions, and radishes; white bread, buttered; watercress; deviled egg; gherkins.

West-Coast Extravaganza—Round of brown bread, buttered; cream-cheese pineapple spread; white bread, spread with mayonnaise; peanut butter and bacon strips; brown bread, buttered; shredded carrot with mayonnaise; white bread, buttered; stuffed olives.

SANDWICH

SANDWICH FILLINGS

Cheese

Cheddar-cheese slices, fried ham, prepared mustard

Cottage cheese, chopped dill pickle, chopped stuffed olives, chopped nuts, salad dressing.

Cottage cheese, chopped dill pickle, crumbled cooked bacon, a little mayonnaise, salt and pepper.

Cottage cheese minced green pepper and onion, on whole-wheat bread.

Cream cheese, chopped almonds, and ripe olives or soy sauce.

Cream cheese and pickled beets.

Cream cheese, chopped dates, a few drops of fresh lemon juice.

Cream cheese, chopped preserved gingerroot, a little milk.

Cream cheese, prepared horseradish, onion, finely shredded dried beef, a little cream.

Cream cheese-onion-bacon spread made with 1 package (8 ounces) cream cheese; 4 teaspoons instant minced onion; 2 tablespoons mayonnaise; ¼ teaspoon salt; ⅛ teaspoon pepper; ¼ teaspoon fresh lemon juice; 2 crisp bacon strips, crumbled.

Soften cream cheese. Add onion to mayonnaise and add to cream cheese with remaining ingredients. Makes 1 cup.

Whipped cream cheese, orange marmalade, shredded lettuce.

Cream cheese and raspberry jam.

Pimiento-cheese spread and sliced pineapple on round slices of bread.

Process American cheese, prepared mustard, sliced pineapple, bacon. Broil until bacon is crisp.

Swiss cheese and mustard on rye bread with lettuce.

Eggs

Fried or scrambled eggs on whole-wheat bread with catsup.

Chopped hard-cooked egg, pickle relish, pimiento, salad dressing.

Chopped hard-cooked egg, ripe olives, mayonnaise.

Chopped hard-cooked egg, chopped ham, minced onion and green pepper, salad dressing.

Chopped hard-cooked egg, green onion, raw spinach. Add mayonnaise and salt and pepper to taste.

Chopped hard-cooked egg and watercress with mayonnaise and a few drops of fresh lemon juice.

Chopped hard-cooked egg, sardines, mayonnaise, a little prepared mustard.

Egg salad made with 3 hard-cooked eggs, chopped; 1 tablespoon pickle relish; 4 stuffed olives, chopped; ¼ cup finely diced celery; 1 teaspoon each of chili sauce and minced green pepper; ¼ cup mayonnaise. Mix all ingredients thoroughly. Makes about 1 cup of filling.

Sliced hard-cooked egg, sliced tomato, mayonnaise.

Fish and Shellfish

Anchovy fillets dipped into lemon juice on hot buttered toast.

Heated frozen fried clams on hot buttered toast, tartar sauce.

Heated fish sticks in toasted frankfurter rolls with tartar sauce, chili sauce, catsup, or coleslaw.

Salmon, minced celery, mayonnaise, curry powder.

Sardine, sliced Swiss cheese, sliced tomato, and cucumber.

Chopped cooked shrimps and canned chopped mushrooms, prepared mustard, softened cream cheese.

Tuna, mayonnaise, very thin slices of peeled lemon.

Meat and Poultry

Crisp bacon, mashed or sliced banana with fresh lime juice, plain or curry mayonnaise.

Chopped canned corned beef or tongue, sour-pickle relish, mayonnaise.

Ground roast beef, chopped pickle and celery, prepared mustard, mayonnaise.

Ground cooked steak and prepared mustard on toasted sandwich rolls.

Mock-chicken made with 1 medium onion, minced; 1 tablespoon butter; ½ pound ground beef; ½ cup water; ½ teaspoon poultry seasoning; 2 tablespoons all-purpose flour; ½ cup undiluted evaporated milk; salt and pepper to taste; mayonnaise.

Cook onion in butter until golden-brown. Add beef, water, and poultry seasoning; simmer for a few minutes. Mix flour and milk; stir into meat mixture and cook until thickened. Add salt and pepper to taste. Cool, then chill. When ready to use, add enough mayonnaise to make mixture of spreading consistency. Makes about 1½ cups.

Hamburger salad made with 1 cup crumbled leftover meat loaf or beef patties; ½ cup shredded raw carrot; 2 tablespoons diced celery; 1 tablespoon chopped green-onion tops; 2 parsley sprigs, chopped; ⅓ cup mayonnaise; salt and pepper to taste.

Combine all ingredients and mix well. Makes about 1½ cups.

Ground beef cooked with chopped celery and onion, mixed with a little horseradish and salad dressing.

Ground beef cooked with a little chopped onion, mixed with chili sauce and mayonnaise.

Panbroiled thin steaks, butter mixed with chopped chives, in sandwich rolls.

Ground bologna, carrot, and almonds; mayonnaise, cream, Worcestershire, salt.

Ground cooked chicken or turkey with the skin, almonds, mayonnaise.

Chopped cooked chicken or turkey, grated process American cheese, pickle relish, mayonnaise.

Ground cooked ham or luncheon meat, cheese, sweet pickle, mayonnaise.

Ground cooked lamb, chopped fresh mint, minced onion, mayonnaise, salt and pepper.

Liverwurst, sliced tomato, lettuce, mayonnaise.

Thinly sliced cooked meat, spread with mustard or chopped mustard pickle, pickle relish, catsup, chili sauce, or tartare sauce.

Sliced meat loaf, pickle relish, sliced hard-cooked egg, and salad dressing.

Sliced meat loaf, tomato, and cheese, spread with prepared mustard.

Cold slivered roast pork or other meat on toasted sandwich rolls with hot barbecue sauce.

SARDINE—The name used to describe various small salt-water food fish with weak bones which can be preserved in oil. These include the pilchard, alewife, herring, and sprat. It is probably the French sardine, found in abundance around the island of Sardinia, from which the over-all name is derived. Fresh, sardines have an excellent flavor; canned, they are a mainstay of sandwich fixings.

Sardines are fatty fish. They differ according to kind, depending on locality. The North Atlantic coast around Maine and the Pacific coast in this country, as well as waters off the coasts of the United Kingdom, Norway, Denmark, Sweden, Finland, Portugal, Spain, South Africa, and Iceland provide various kinds of sardines.

In Europe sardines are important food fish. The silvery little fish are iridescent, silver below, and green or blue above. Sometimes they have small black spots. They travel quickly through the water, usually near or on the surface. They are usually fished with nets at night when they come to the surface to feed on the plankton. The moonlight shining on their silvery splashing has made them known as the "silver harvest."

Availability—Pilchards, weighing from 1½ to 2 ounces, are available fresh year round. Alewives and other types of sea herring used as sardines are available fresh, weighing 2 to 8 ounces, during the summer months. Sardines are also available salted and smoked. Larger sardines are sold as "smoked boneless herring." Canned sardines packed in oil as is or skinless and boneless are widely available. Sometimes tomato sauce forms the packing liquid. In Europe, Portuguese and French sardines are especially highly prized. Those from Portugal are usually packed in a high grade of pure olive oil; the French variety often have herb and spice mixtures added.

Storage
Fresh, refrigerator shelf: 1 to 2 days
Canned, kitchen shelf, unopened: 1 year
Canned, refrigerator shelf, opened and covered: 4 to 5 days

Nutritive Food Values—Excellent source of protein and good source of calcium, iron, and niacin.
Atlantic, canned in oil, 3 ounces, drained solids = 173 calories
Norwegian canned in oil, 3 ounces, drained solids = 167 calories
Canned in tomato sauce, 3 ounces solids, 1 ounce sauce = 200 calories

Basic Preparation—Fresh sardines are usually deep-fried, like any small fish. Drain canned sardines well on absorbent paper before using.
To Deep-Fry Fresh Sardines—Wash and clean the sardines. Dip in all-purpose flour, then in beaten egg. Roll in cornmeal or fine dry bread crumbs. Fry in hot deep fat (375°F. on a frying thermometer) until brown and crisp. Drain on absorbent paper and season with salt and pepper. Serve with Sauce Tartar or Italian Tomato Sauce.

SARDINE

BROILED SARDINES ON TOAST

¼ cup butter or margarine
¼ cup soft bread crumbs
2 hard-cooked eggs, chopped
1 cup half-and-half (half milk, half light cream)
   Salt and pepper
1 can (4 ounces) sardines in oil, drained
   Buttered toast
   Paprika

Melt butter in saucepan. Add crumbs, eggs, and half-and-half. Heat, and season to taste with salt and pepper. Broil sardines about 5 minutes. Arrange on toast and cover with egg mixture. Sprinkle with paprika. Makes 2 servings.

SARDINE-TOMATO RABBIT

1 onion, sliced
1 can (15 ounces) sardines in oil
2 teaspoons dry mustard
1 can (10½ ounces) condensed tomato soup
¼ pound Cheddar cheese, shredded
   Salt and pepper
8 slices toast

Cook onion until golden in oil drained from sardines. Add mustard, soup and sardines; heat. Add cheese and heat until melted. Season with salt and pepper and serve on toast. Makes 4 servings.

SARDINE COCKTAIL

Drain 1 can (15 ounces) large sardines. Cut into bite-size pieces and chill. When ready to serve place sardine pieces on lettuce. Cover with chilled cocktail sauce. Pass horseradish and hot pepper sauce. Makes 4 servings.

DEVILED SARDINES

1 can (4 ounces) sardines in oil
2 garlic cloves, crushed
1 tablespoon each minced onion and green pepper
1 tablespoon prepared mustard
1 teaspoon prepared horseradish
1 tablespoon water
2 tablespoons salad oil
½ teaspoon each salt, celery salt, paprika, and pepper
⅛ teaspoon cayenne
   Juice of ½ lemon
   Lemon and tomato wedges, pickles (optional)

Drain sardines and arrange on serving plate. Mix garlic, onion, and green pepper. Add mustard, horseradish mixed with water, and salad oil. Mix thoroughly. Add seasonings and lemon juice. Mix well and pour over sardines. If desired, garnish with lemon and tomato wedges, and pickles. Serve as an appetizer or hors-d'oeuvre, with crackers, celery hearts, or potato chips, if desired. Makes 4 servings.

SARSAPARILLA

SARDINE AND CHEESE SALAD

    Lettuce or other salad greens
¼ pound Cheddar cheese, slivered
2 cans (4 ounces each) sardines in oil, drained
    French Dressing

Line salad bowl with lettuce. Arrange cheese and sardines in bowl. Pour dressing over top. Makes 4 servings.

SARDINES WITH SPINACH AND CHEESE

3 tablespoons butter or margarine
3 tablespoons all-purpose flour
1 teaspoon salt
¼ teaspoon white pepper
¾ cup undiluted evaporated milk
¾ cup water
1 teaspoon Worcestershire
¾ cup shredded sharp process cheese
1 can (15 ounces) sardines
1 package (10 ounces) frozen spinach
    Paprika

Melt butter in top part of double boiler; blend in flour, salt, and pepper. Add milk diluted with water and Worcestershire; cook over boiling water, stirring constantly, until thickened. Add ½ cup cheese and continue cooking until cheese melts. Heat sardines in skillet in their liquid. Cook spinach according to directions on package; drain well. Put hot spinach in greased shallow baking dish; top with drained sardines. Pour cheese sauce over sardines. Sprinkle with paprika and remaining cheese. Put in hot oven (400°F.) for 10 minutes, or until topping melts. Makes 4 servings.

SARDINE SANDWICHES

1 can (4 ounces) sardines in oil, drained
1 hard-cooked egg, mashed
6 stuffed olives, mashed
    Salt, paprika, and lemon juice
    Mayonnaise
8 slices of light rye bread

Mash sardines. Mix with egg and olives. Season to taste with salt, paprika, and lemon juice. Add mayonnaise to moisten. Spread between bread slices. Makes 4 sandwiches.

BROILED SARDINE OPEN-FACE SANDWICHES

Toast 4 slices of bread. Spread toast with mayonnaise or salad dressing. Arrange thin tomato slices and 1 or 2 cans sardines, drained, over toast. Top with 4 slices American cheese. Broil 2 minutes, or until cheese is bubbling hot. Serve at once. Makes 4 sandwiches.

CREAMED SARDINES AND PEAS ON ROLLS

1 can (15 ounces) sardines
1 can (10½ ounces) condensed cream of mushroom soup
1 cup milk
2 tablespoons all-purpose flour
1 cup cooked peas
    Salt and pepper
6 sandwich rolls
    Paprika

Drain sardines and flake in small pieces. Mix soup and ¾ cup milk. Blend flour with remaining ¼ cup milk. Add to soup; cook, stirring constantly, until thickened. Add sardines, peas, and salt and pepper to taste; heat thoroughly. Toast rolls and top with sardine mixture. Sprinkle with paprika. Makes 6 servings.

SARDINE SUMMER SALAD

Mix salad greens, tomato wedges, onion rings, bits of cucumber, radish slices and strips of green pepper and cheese. Toss with French dressing and spoon into salad bowls. Top with well-chilled and drained canned sardines.

SARDINE-EGG SALAD

Arrange drained canned sardines, hard-cooked egg slices and oinion rings on shredded lettuce. Top with mayonnaise or salad dressing blended with a little curry powder. Garnish with strips of pimiento or sliced olives.

SARDINE-EGG DOUBLE-DECKER SANDWICH

First deck: Make your favorite egg salad and spread on bread. Add second slice of bread, and butter top. **Second deck:** Arrange drained sardines on buttered bread and sprinkle with chopped green onion. Spread a bread slice with mayonnaise and prepared mustard and put on onion, spread side down. Insert picks to hold sandwich together, and cut diagonally in fourths.

SARSAPARILLA—At one time sarsaparilla products were made with the flavoring extracted from the dried roots of several tropical smilax vines indigenous to Central and South America. The name is from the

Spanish, a combination of *zarza,* "bramble or brier," and *parrilla,* "little vine."

The "wild sarsaparilla" early settlers of New England were so pleased to find was a different plant, a perennial herb of the genus *Arolia,* but its aromatic roots were treated as the tropical variety was.

Nowadays, all sarsaparilla products, the best known of which is a soft drink, are made from artificial flavoring.

SASSAFRAS—A handsome tree of the laurel family, one variety of which, *Sassafras albidum* or *variifolium,* is a native of North America. Its height ranges from thirty to sixty feet, although occasionally one may grow as high as ninety feet. The bark is rough and gray, and the bright green leaves are of three shapes, all on the same tree. These leaves, when dried and ground, are the prime ingredient of filé, a thickening and seasoning agent which forms the base of gumbo.

SAUCE, BASIC—How To Cook Superbly: The Basic Sauces, Brown And White

by HELEN EVANS BROWN

Some of the most useful bits of knowledge a cook can have are how to make good basic brown and white sauces. With the recipe I will give you for a basic brown sauce, what the French call *"Sauce espagnole,"* you can make all kinds of marvelous sauces for meat, poultry, game, and leftovers, merely by adding a little of this and that. I will also give you two basic white sauces: Béchamel and Velouté. Béchamel is simply milk thickened with a *roux* of flour and butter, while Velouté is made with white stock from veal or chicken broth. One or the other of these two sauces can be used to make hundreds of good-tasting dishes from Sauce Mornay (the classic cheese sauce) to cream soups, scalloped and gratin dishes, *crêpes farçis* (stuffed pancakes), all creamed dishes, and main-dish soufflés.

BASIC BROWN SAUCE, SAUCE ESPAGNOLE

Some authorities claim that this sauce originated in Spain, hence its name. Others prefer the story that it is called "Spanish sauce" because Spaniards are dark-complexioned, just as the famous white sauce Allemande is named after the fair-skinned Germans. Either way, it's the Frenchiest of sauces.

Equipment

If you have the ordinary kitchen measures and a stock pot (a big pot or kettle that will hold at least 8 quarts) you're all set, although I do hope you have enough freezer room so that you can keep this sauce on hand. You'll use only a little each time, usually 1 cup, and if you freeze it in ½-pint containers you will have it when you need it.

- ½ cup each diced carrot, onion, and celery
- ¼ cup diced ham
- ⅔ cup butter (about)
- 2 quarts Brown Stock
- 2 tablespoons minced parsley
- ½ teaspoon each dried thyme and marjoram
- ¼ teaspoon whole allspice
- 1 small garlic clove
- ½ bay leaf
- ½ cup all-purpose flour
- ½ cup each tomato purée and white wine
- Salt

First you make a *mirepoix*: Cook, diced carrot, onion, celery, and ham in ¼ cup butter until vegetables are very tender. Drain off butter and save. Add *mirepoix* to Brown Stock (or use 6 cans (10½ ounces each) condensed beef bouillon). Add parsley, thyme, marjoram, allspice, garlic, and bay leaf, tied together in cheesecloth; simmer for 2 hours, skimming when necessary. Remove bag of herbs and strain, pressing to extract juices from vegetables. To reserved butter add more butter to make ½ cup. Put in a large saucepan and stir in flour. Cook, stirring, until it browns slightly (this is a brown *roux*); cool a minute, then stir in strained liquid. Add tomato purée and white wine, simmer for another 2 hours, skimming when necessary. This will give your sauce brilliance. It should be thick enough to lightly coat a metal spoon. Cook, pack in 1-cup jars, and freeze until needed. Add salt to taste at that time.

BROWN STOCK

As you may have noticed in the instructions above, you can use canned beef bouillon in the place of this stock, but the superior product and the satisfaction you get from starting from scratch are worth the extra time it will take to make the real thing. If you are the thrifty type, you may have saved bones from beef as well as scraps of meat, and perhaps carcasses of chicken or turkey, or chicken gizzards and necks, and bits of veal. If so, you're ahead of the game as you can use these for your stock, making up the amount with some uncooked beef shanks. If you haven't, start saving now; you can collect bits that might otherwise be thrown away and freeze them until needed. You will want at least half meat and the rest bones. Beef is best and some should be raw. Some veal and poultry may be added, and even a small amount of pork—not ham, although you will need scraps of that for your sauce, and not lamb as the flavor is too definite.

SAUCE

- 5 pounds meat and bones
- 1 cup sliced carrots
- 1 cup sliced onions
- 1 cup sliced celery (outside stalk and leaves)
- 1 teaspoon salt
- Bouquet garni of 4 parsley branches, 1 bay leaf, 1 thyme sprig or ¼ teaspoon ground thyme, and 2 whole cloves
- Water

If you buy your meat and bones, have the butcher chop them into chunks. If they are leftovers and you have a cleaver, do it yourself. Brown the bones in preheated very hot oven (450°F.), then transfer to a large pot; add the vegetables, salt, and *bouquet garni*. (To make this, wrap the parsley around the bay leaf, cloves, and thyme, and tie with a white thread; or tie all the herbs and spices together in a piece of cheesecloth.) Cover with 2½ quarts cold water (if this doesn't cover the meat and bones completely, add more until it does), and put over high heat. As it comes to a boil, skim off the brown scum that rises to the top. Do this carefully until all the scum has been removed, then turn heat to very low, so that the liquid stops bubbling, and the surface seems barely to move, or "smile." Let it cook this way, really under a simmer, for anywhere from 5 hours to however long it takes for the meat to fall from the bones and have absolutely no taste; all the flavor has gone into the stock. Now strain, making sure that every drop is saved. Discard the well-drained meat and bones. You should have 2 quarts of stock. If there is more, continue cooking until it has reduced to that amount. If you have less than 2 quarts, make up the amount with water. Cool stock uncovered, then refrigerate overnight. Next day, remove and discard the cake of fat that has formed on top. You now have 2 quarts of fine beef stock, rich enough so that it is lightly jellied.

BASIC WHITE SAUCES, BÉCHAMEL AND VELOUTÉ

Equipment

You'll need no extra equipment for Sauce Béchamel, although I hope by now you have invested in a French whip, *fouet*, or similar wire whip, so useful for smoothing sauces and batters and for whipping. For Sauce Velouté, you'll need a stock pot or some large kettle or pot that will hold 8 quarts. Standard measuring cups and spoons are also in order.

SAUCE BÉCHAMEL

- 3 tablespoons butter
- 3 tablespoons all-purpose flour
- 2½ cups milk
- Salt and pepper
- ⅓ cup light cream (optional)

Make a white or "blond" *roux* with butter and flour. Melt butter, add flour, and cook, stirring with a whip, for 2 minutes. Do not allow it to brown, even slightly. Now add milk, whipping as you add. Some authorities say that the sauce will lump unless the milk is heated, but I have never found this to be so. Bring just to the boil, then turn heat very low, and simmer for at least 10 minutes, or until the sauce has been reduced to 2 cups. Add salt to taste, about ½ teaspoon, and a little pepper, preferably white for the sake of appearance. Makes 2 cups.

NOTE: Béchamel sauce is very often finished with about ⅓ cup cream for extra richness. Carême, a famous French chef, also added 2 egg yolks and 1 tablespoon butter plus a little grated nutmeg. This is as good a time as any to take up the problem of the addition of egg yolks to a hot sauce. Put the egg yolks in a small bowl and beat them slightly; then slowly beat in about ½ cup hot sauce. When mixed, pour this mixture into the remaining sauce, beating it as you add. Do not boil after the addition of egg yolks.

SAUCE VELOUTÉ

This sauce isn't quite as simple to make, as you need white stock as the base. However, a large batch can be made at one time and frozen in 1-cup jars.

- ¾ cup butter
- ¾ cup all-purpose flour
- 2 quarts White Stock
- 1 small onion
- 2 whole cloves
- ½ bay leaf

Make a *roux* with butter and flour, as in Sauce Béchamel. Add White Stock, onion stuck with cloves, and bay leaf. Bring to a boil, turn heat low, and simmer for 1 hour, skimming if necessary. Cool, and use as directed; or freeze for future use. Sauce Velouté may be made with fish stock when it is to be used for seafood. Makes 2 quarts.

WHITE STOCK

- 6 pounds veal bones and meat or 6 pounds chicken backs, necks, and gizzards or 6 pounds (altogether) veal and chicken bones and meat
- 2½ quarts water
- ½ cup each sliced carrot, onion, and celery
- 1 chopped leek (optional)
- 1 teaspoon salt
- Bouquet garni: 1 bay leaf, 4 parsley branches, 1 thyme sprig or ¼ teaspoon ground thyme, and 1 whole clove, tied together

Have meat and bones chopped into pieces. Put them in a large pot with vegetables, salt, and herbs. Cover with water; add enough more to cover meat and bones. Bring to a boil and skim off all the scum that rises to the top. Turn heat very low so that the liquid barely moves and cook about 5 hours, or until all the meat has fallen from the bones and the flavor has gone into the stock. Skim occasionally during the cooking. Strain, cool, then refrigerate. Next day, lift off and discard the fat that has hardened on top. You should have 2 quarts, partially jellied.

SAUCE COOKBOOK

BROWN SAUCES BASED ON SAUCE ESPAGNOLE

SAUCE DEMI-GLACE

For filet mignon or other fine cuts of beef or for ham

- 3 cups Sauce Espagnole
- 1 cup White Stock
- 1 tablespoon glace-de-viande or meat extract

Simmer all ingredients until reduced one-half. Makes about 2 cups.

SAUCE BORDELAISE

For all steaks and for beef tenderloin. It is also very good on broiled mushrooms or broiled mutton chops.

You need marrow for this. Ask your butcher for 3 or 4 marrow bones and have him split them. Remove marrow and slice. Bring salted water to the boil, add marrow, and remove from heat. Let stand while preparing rest of sauce. Mince 1 small garlic clove and 1 shallot or green onion and sauté in 1 tablespoon butter until soft. Add ½ cup red wine (preferably, of course, a red Bordeaux, as this is how the sauce acquired its name, but a Cabernet or a Beaujolais will do), 1 cup Sauce Espagnole, and a dash of hot pepper sauce. Simmer until thickened, then add salt to taste, the drained marrow, 1 tablespoon fresh lemon juice, and 1 teaspoon minced parsley. Makes about 1¾ cups.

SAUCE CHASSEUR

For red meat, game, and poultry

- ½ pound mushrooms, stems only, sliced
- 1 shallot, minced
- 2 tablespoons butter or margarine
- ¼ teaspoon salt
- Pepper to taste
- ¼ cup dry white wine
- ½ cup Sauce Espagnole
- 1 tablespoon tomato sauce
- ¼ teaspoon each minced parsley and fresh tarragon

Reserve mushroom caps for other use. Sauté mushroom stems and shallot in butter. Add salt and pepper. Cook until golden-brown. Add wine and cook until liquid is reduced to half of its original volume. Add remaining ingredients and simmer until slightly thickened. Makes about 1 cup.

SAUCE DIABLE

For deviled beef ribs, deviled turkey breast, or any meat that is grilled, where a hot sauce is desired.

Combine 1 cup Sauce Espagnole, 1 tablespoon prepared mustard, 1 tablespoon Worcestershire, a dash of hot pepper sauce, 1 tablespoon cider vinegar, and ¼ cup white wine. Simmer for 10 minutes and strain; then add salt to taste and 2 teaspoons minced parsley. Makes about 1¼ cups.

DUXELLES SAUCE

For eggs, fish, and chicken

- 6 fresh mushrooms, chopped
- 2 tablespoons butter
- ¼ cup white wine
- ¼ cup Sauce Espagnole
- 1 tablespoon tomato purée
- 1 tablespoon minced parsley
- Salt and pepper

Sauté mushrooms in butter until moisture has evaporated. Add wine and simmer for a few minutes. Add remaining ingredients and stir until well blended. Reheat and season to taste with salt and pepper. Makes about ¾ cup.

SAUCE ITALIENNE

For kidneys, liver, pork chops, roast veal, chicken, and leftover cooked meats.

- 1 teaspoon chopped shallot
- 2 tomatoes, peeled, seeded, and chopped
- **¾ cup Marsala wine**
- ½ cup Sauce Espagnole
- 1 tablespoon tomato paste
- ¼ cup chopped mushrooms
- 2 tablespoons finely diced cooked ham
- ½ teaspoon glace-de-viande or meat extract
- Few parsley sprigs, chopped

Put shallot, tomatoes, and wine in a saucepan and cook until tomatoes are soft and volume's reduced by half. Add Sauce Espagnole, tomato paste, mushrooms, and ham. Bring to a boil and cook about 5 minutes. Add *glace-de-viande* and parsley. Makes about 1 cup.

SAUCE MADÈRE

For sweetbreads, ham, smoked tongue, veal, and beef tenderloin.

To 1 cup Sauce Espagnole add ½ cup canned tomatoes and ¼ cup Madeira or mellow sherry. Simmer until the volume is reduced by half. Strain, add a few grains of cayenne, salt to taste, and a good dash of sugar. Makes about 1⅔ cups.

SAUCE

WHITE SAUCES BASED ON SAUCE BÉCHAMEL AND VELOUTÉ

Ravigote Sauce—see Ravigote entry.

SAUCE AURORE

For poached eggs, chicken, sweetbreads, and seafood

To 1 cup Sauce Béchamel add ¼ cup tomato purée and 1 teaspoon paprika. Makes about 1¼ cups.

SAUCE ALLEMANDE

For poached fish, poultry, hot hors-d'oeuvre, and dishes which are to be topped with crumbs.

- 1½ cups Sauce Velouté
- 2 egg yolks
- ½ cup heavy cream
  Salt, white pepper, and lemon juice

Heat Sauce Velouté until just simmering. Beat egg yolks and cream until blended. Gradually beat in, a few drops at a time, ½ cup hot sauce. Add remaining sauce in a thin stream, beating constantly. Return mixture to saucepan. Put over medium heat and bring to a boil. Cook, stirring, for 1 minute. Strain through a fine sieve. Add seasonings and lemon juice to taste. Reheat if necessary. Makes about 2 cups.
NOTE: When serving the sauce on fish, 1 to 2 tablespoons soft butter may be added, bit by bit, to finished sauce.

BERCY SAUCE

For fish

- ¼ cup butter or margarine
- 2 tablespoons minced shallots
- ½ cup white wine
- ½ cup fish broth
- 1 cup Sauce Velouté
- 1 tablespoon soft butter
- 2 teaspoons minced parsley
  Salt and pepper

Melt butter and sauté shallots until transluscent. Add wine and fish broth. Cook until the volume is reduced by one half. Beat in Sauce Velouté, soft butter, and parsley. Season to taste with salt and pepper. Reheat. Makes about 2 cups.

Bercy Sauce for Meat

Substitute ½ cup beef or chicken bouillon for the fish broth.

CAPER SAUCE

For boiled lamb and fish

Add 3 to 4 tablespoons well-drained capers to 1 recipe Sauce Béchamel.

SAUCE CHAUD-FROID

For glazing slices of chicken or game, or whole boiled chicken or salmon; it must be used before completely set.

Heat 1 cup Sauce Velouté and add 1 envelope unflavored gelatin softened in ¼ cup cold White Stock or water, then dissolved over hot water. Add ¼ cup heavy cream. Makes about 1⅓ cups.

CHEESE SAUCE

For vegetables, fish, and some meat dishes

Add ½ cup grated Gruyére or Cheddar cheese to 1 recipe Sauce Béchamel.

CREAM SAUCE

For "creaming" any vegetable or seafood

To 1 cup Sauce Béchamel add from ¼ to 1 cup light cream. Heat; simmer until desired consistency is reached. Makes 1¼ to 2 cups.

SAUCE MORNAY

Use whenever a cheese sauce is desired

To 1 cup Sauce Béchamel add ⅓ cup heavy cream. Heat and add 2 tablespoons each grated Gruyère and grated Parmesan cheese. (This is the classic recipe; ¼ to ½ cup grated Cheddar cheese may be used instead.) Makes about 1⅔ cups.

SAUCE NORMANDE

For fish, oysters, and mussels

- 2 tablespoons butter
- 1 teaspoon all-purpose flour
- 1 cup liquid from cooking fish or shellfish, or bottled clam juice
- 2 egg yolks, slightly beaten
- ½ cup heavy cream
  Salt and pepper

Melt butter and blend in flour; brown lightly. Gradually add liquid and simmer about 10 minutes. Mix egg yolks and cream and stir into mixture. Bring to a boil and remove from heat. Season with salt and pepper to taste. Makes about 1½ cups.

SAUCE

HERB SAUCE
For any seafood or poultry

To 1 cup Sauce Béchamel or Sauce Velouté add 1 teaspoon each minced chives and parsley and ½ teaspoon minced fresh tarragon or marjoram. Heat, and serve. Makes 1 cup.

CREAMY EGG SAUCE
For fish

To 1 cup Sauce Béchamel add 2 chopped hard-cooked eggs and ¼ cup light cream. Heat before serving. Makes about 2 cups.

CURRY SAUCE, FRENCH STYLE
For chicken, veal, or lamb dishes

Add 1 to 3 teaspoons curry powder and 1 tablespoon fresh lemon juice to 1 cup hot Sauce Béchamel. Makes 1 cup.

SAUCE POULETTE
For chicken or frogs' legs

- 1 cup Sauce Béchamel
- 2 egg yolks
- 1 tablespoon light cream
- Juice of ½ lemon
- 1 teaspoon minced parsley

When Sauce Béchamel is hot, beat some of the sauce into egg yolks beaten with cream. Add egg-yolk mixture to remaining sauce and cook over low heat, stirring constantly, until smooth and thick. Just before serving add lemon juice and parsley. Makes about 1 cup.

SAUCE SOUBISE
For lamb and veal

- 1½ cups minced onions
- 2 tablespoons butter
- 2 tablespoons water
- ½ cup Sauce Béchamel
- Salt and pepper to taste
- Dash of ground nutmeg
- 2 tablespoons grated Parmesan cheese (optional)

Sauté onions in butter until they are translucent. Add water and stir well. Cook over low heat, covered, stirring occasionally, until onions are very tender but not brown. Onions must remain white or sauce will not be the right color. Press onions through a sieve or whirl in a blender. Beat in Sauce Béchamel, and heat. When hot add salt, pepper, nutmeg, and cheese, if desired. Makes about 1½ cups.

HOLLANDAISE AND MAYONNAISE SAUCES

HOLLANDAISE

- 3 egg yolks
- 1 tablespoon cold water
- 1 tablespoon lemon juice
- Dash of salt
- 2 tablespoons cold butter
- ¾ to 1 cup butter, melted
- Salt, white pepper, and lemon juice

Beat egg yolks in top part of double boiler about 1 minute. Beat in water, lemon juice, and salt. Place double boiler over simmering water, add 1 tablespoon cold butter, and continue to beat until mixture is smooth and creamy. Remove from heat and beat in remaining tablespoon cold butter. Continue beating and gradually add melted butter by quarter teaspoonfuls until mixture thickens. Season to taste with salt, white pepper, and lemon juice. Makes 1 to 1½ cups sauce.

NOTE: If Hollandaise Sauce separates, remove sauce from over the hot water at once, add 1 ice cube or 1 tablespoon boiling water, and beat it vigorously with a rotary beater or electric mixer. If this doesn't work, make half of the recipe again; be sure there's only 1 inch of simmering water in double boiler, and stir sauce constantly. Then carefully stir in beaten mess you were tempted to pour down the drain. Don't overcook.

BLENDER HOLLANDAISE SAUCE

- 3 egg yolks
- 2 tablespoons lemon juice
- ¼ teaspoon salt
- Dash of white pepper
- ½ cup melted hot butter

Place egg yolks, lemon juice, and salt and pepper into the blender. Whirl for 2 seconds. Uncover and gradually drip in the melted butter. Sauce will thicken immediately. Makes ¾ cup.

SAUCE BÉARNAISE

- 1 teaspoon chopped shallots
- ½ teaspoon each chopped fresh chervil and tarragon
- 12 peppercorns, crushed
- 2 tablespoons dry white wine
- 1 tablespoon cider vinegar
- 1½ cups butter or margarine
- 5 egg yolks
- 2 tablespoons light cream
- Salt and cayenne

Mix shallots, chervil, tarragon, peppercorns, wine, and vinegar. Simmer until volume is reduced to half. Melt butter, and pour off clear portion leaving whey behind; clear portion is clarified butter. Beat egg yolks with cream. Beat vinegar mixture into egg yolks and pour into top part of a double boiler. Cook over boiling water until creamy. While sauce is cooking beat constantly to avoid curdling. Gradually beat in clarified butter. Season to taste with salt and cayenne. Makes 1½ cups.

SAUCE

SAUCE AÏOLI

For fish, vegetables, and some meats

- 12 garlic cloves, peeled
- ½ teaspoon salt
- 3 egg yolks
- 1½ cups olive oil
- 3 tablespoons lemon juice, or more

In a mortar mash garlic with salt until garlic is puréed. In a deep bowl beat egg yolks with a whisk until well mixed. Add puréed garlic to egg yolks and continue to beat with the whisk until mixture is well blended. Now add oil, a drop at a time, whisking all the while. When several tablespoons have been added, add oil very slowly in a thin stream, still whisking constantly. When the mixture is like a mayonnaise, whisk in lemon juice. Add more salt if desired. If sauce is too thick, add additional lemon juice or water, ½ teaspoon at a time. Use more or less garlic and lemon juice, according to preference, but use only olive oil or the flavor will not be authentic.

To make this sauce in a blender, chop garlic into small pieces with a knife and purée in blender. Add salt, egg yolks, lemon juice, and ½ cup oil and blend at high speed until thickened, a few seconds only. Slowly add the remaining oil in a thin stream and whirl until well blended. Adjust seasonings if necessary. Makes about 2 cups.

CUCUMBER-MAYONNAISE DRESSING

For fish or vegetable salads

- ½ cup mayonnaise
- ½ cup diced cucumber
- Chopped green pepper to taste
- Dash of tarragon vinegar
- Salt and cayenne

Stir all together thoroughly. Makes 1 cup.

CURRY MAYONNAISE

For fruit or vegetable salad, potato or macaroni salad, seafood, poultry, or eggs

Add 1 to 3 teaspoons curry powder to 1 cup mayonnaise. Makes 1 cup.

GINGER MAYONNAISE DRESSING

For fruit salads

Mix ⅓ cup each mayonnaise and dairy sour cream. Add 2 tablespoons chopped candied gingerroot. Makes about ⅔ cup.

GREEN MOUSSELINE SAUCE

For fish, asparagus, or other vegetables

- ½ cup Sauce Béchamel
- ½ cup mayonnaise
- 2 tablespoons puréed cooked spinach
- Pinch of dried tarragon
- 2 hard-cooked egg yolks, mashed
- ¼ teaspoon anchovy paste

Combine all ingredients and blend well. Chill until ready to serve. Makes about 1¼ cups.

SAUCE MALTAISE

For chicken, broccoli, asparagus, or cauliflower

Follow the recipe for Blender Hollandaise Sauce substituting 1 tablespoon fresh lemon juice and 1 tablespoon fresh orange juice for 2 tablespoons lemon juice. After sauce is blended, stir in 3 tablespoons fresh orange juice and 1 tablespoon grated orange rind. Makes about 1 cup.

SAUCE MOUSSELINE

For soufflés, fillets of veal, chicken, asparagus, or artichokes.

- 4 egg yolks
- 1 cup milk
- 2 tablespoons butter
- Juice of ½ lemon
- Dash of ground nutmeg
- Salt
- ¼ cup whipped heavy cream

Combine egg yolks and milk in top part of a double boiler. Cook over boiling water until hot; add butter. Stir constantly until butter melts and sauce thickens. Add lemon juice, nutmeg, and salt to taste. Remove from water and fold in whipped cream. Makes about 1½ cups.

MUSTARD HOLLANDAISE

Follow recipe for Blender Hollandaise Sauce, adding ½ teaspoon prepared Dijon mustard to finished sauce. If desired, 1 minced anchovy may also be added.

MAYONNAISE

- 2 egg yolks or 1 whole egg
- 1 teaspoon sugar
- 1 teaspoon dry mustard
- 1 teaspoon salt
- 2 tablespoons cider vinegar
- 2 cups olive oil
- 2 tablespoons lemon juice

Put egg yolks and seasonings in small deep bowl. Beat with rotary beater or electric mixer until blended. Add vinegar very slowly, beating constantly. Add 1 cup oil, 1 tablespoon at a time, beating constantly. Add lemon juice and remaining 1 cup oil, 1 tablespoon at a time. Refrigerate. Makes 2 cups.

ANCHOVY MAYONNAISE

To 1 cup mayonnaise, add 6 anchovy fillets, minced. If desired, add 1 garlic clove, minced.

CREAM MAYONNAISE DRESSING

For fruit salads

Combine ½ cup heavy cream, whipped, 3 tablespoons mayonnaise, and 1 tablespoon grated fresh orange rind. Blend thoroughly. Makes about 1¼ cups.

SAUCE VERTE

For cold salmon, striped bass, other fish, or lobster

- 15 leaves each watercress and spinach
- 8 parsley sprigs
- 2 cups mayonnaise
- Salt and pepper

Wash watercress, spinach, and parsley and cover with boiling water. Let stand for 5 or 6 minutes. Drain, put in cold water, and drain again, pressing out all the surplus moisture. Rub wilted greens through a fine sieve. Mix thoroughly with mayonnaise; add salt and pepper to taste. Makes about 2 cups.

LOUIS DRESSING

For crabmeat, especially, but may be used on other seafood

- 1 cup mayonnaise
- ½ cup chili sauce
- ¼ cup French Dressing, preferably made with tarragon vinegar
- 2 tablespoons chopped green olives
- 1 teaspoon Worcestershire
- 1 teaspoon grated horseradish
- Salt and freshly ground pepper
- ¼ cup chopped scallions
- 2 tablespoons sweet pickle relish
- Juice of ½ lime

Mix all ingredients together. Makes about 2 cups.

RUSSIAN DRESSING

For greens, meat, poultry, or eggs

To ½ cup mayonnaise add ¼ cup chili sauce, 2 tablespoons pickle relish, and if desired, 2 tablespoons red caviar. Makes about ¾ cup.

THOUSAND ISLAND DRESSING

For seafood, greens, hard-cooked eggs, or vegetables

Mix 1 cup mayonnaise, ½ cup chili sauce, 2 tablespoons minced green pepper, 3 tablespoons chopped stuffed olives, 1 minced pimiento, 1 teaspoon grated onion or 2 teaspoons chopped chives. Makes about 2 cups.

VINAIGRETTE SAUCES

BASIC VINAIGRETTE SAUCE

- ½ cup olive oil
- 3 tablespoons cider vinegar
- Salt and pepper

Combine oil and vinegar and beat until well blended. Season to taste with salt and pepper. Makes about ⅔ cup.

FRENCH DRESSING

- ½ cup fresh lemon juice or vinegar
- 1½ cups olive or other salad oil
- 2 teaspoons salt
- ¼ teaspoon pepper
- 1 teaspoon dry mustard
- Dash of cayenne

Mix all ingredients in a 1-quart glass jar; cover tightly and shake until thoroughly blended. Store in the refrigerator. Makes 2 cups.

Garlic French Dressing—Follow recipe above, adding 1 or 2 peeled garlic cloves to other ingredients.

Sweetened French Dressing—Follow recipe above, adding 2 teaspoons sugar to other ingredients.

CERVELLE SAUCE

Double the recipe for Basic Vinaigrette Sauce and add 1 tablespoon each chopped capers, onion, parsley, and fresh tarragon. Add ½ cup chopped cooked calf's brains. Makes about 2 cups.

CHIFFONADE DRESSING

For mixed green or vegetable salads

- ¾ cup French dressing
- 1 tablespoon minced parsley
- 2 tablespoons chopped pimiento
- 2 tablespoons green pepper
- 1 teaspoon minced onion
- 1 hard-cooked egg, finely chopped
- 1 teaspoon chopped cooked beet (optional)

Combine all ingredients and mix well. Makes 1¾ cups.

COTTAGE-CHEESE FRENCH DRESSING

For fruit, greens, and vegetables

To ¾ cup French Dressing add 2 tablespoons cottage cheese, 1 tablespoon pickle relish, and 2 tablespoons chopped parsley. Makes about 1 cup.

GREEK GARLIC SAUCE
[Skordalia]

For fish and vegetables

- 6 raw medium potatoes
- 4 to 6 garlic cloves, minced
- 1 teaspoon salt
- ¾ to 1 cup olive oil
- ¼ cup lemon juice

Boil potatoes in their skins. In a mortar pound garlic and salt to a smooth paste; or whirl in a blender. Peel potatoes; while hot, add them to the garlic mixture, blending everything to a smooth paste. Gradually add olive oil, a few drops at a time, alternating with lemon juice. The sauce should be very smooth and have the consistency of thick cream. Makes about 3 cups.

NOTE: The olive oil may have to be adjusted, since different kinds of potatoes absorb olive oil differently. Mealy potatoes are best for this sauce.

SAUCE

SAUCE CRESSONIÈRE

To 1 recipe Basic Vinaigrette Sauce, add 1 chopped hard-cooked egg and 2 tablespoons chopped watercress. Makes about 1 cup.

DE LUXE FRENCH DRESSING

Use French Dressing recipe, adding several gashed garlic cloves, ⅓ cup chili sauce, 1 tablespoon prepared horseradish, and 1 teaspoon paprika. Makes about 2⅓ cups.

SAUCE GRIBICHE

*For cold boiled beef, chicken,
fish, and shellfish*

- 3 hard-cooked eggs, separated
- ½ teaspoon salt
- 1 teaspoon dry mustard
  Dash of pepper
- 1½ cups olive or salad oil
- ½ cup cider vinegar
- ½ cup chopped sour pickles
- 1 tablespoon capers
- 1 tablespoon mixed chopped parsley, chervil, tarragon, and chives

Put yolks in a bowl and crush until very smooth; add salt, mustard, and pepper. Beating vigorously, add oil a few drops at a time, until about 2 tablespoons have been added. Then add oil in a thin stream, beating vigorously. When mixture begins to thicken, add vinegar, a small amount at a time. Press out all the moisture from the pickles. Chop egg whites and add with pickles, capers, and herbs to the sauce. Makes about 3 cups.

HERB DRESSING

For greens, seafood, or meat

To ¾ cup French Dressing add 2 teaspoons chopped fresh dill, marjoram, rosemary, summer savory, or other herbs. Makes ¾ cup.

ROQUEFORT SAUCE

To 1 recipe Basic Vinaigrette Sauce, add 1 minced shallot or 2 tablespoons chopped scallions, and 2 tablespoons crumbled Roquefort cheese. Makes about 1 cup.

HONEY DRESSING

For fruit salads

- ⅔ cup sugar
- 1 teaspoon dry mustard
- 1 teaspoon paprika
- ¼ teaspoon salt
- 1 teaspoon celery seeds
- ⅓ cup strained honey
- 5 tablespoons cider vinegar
- 1 tablespoon lemon juice
- 1 teaspoon grated onion
- 1 cup salad oil

Mix dry ingredients; add honey, vinegar, lemon juice, and onion. Pour oil into mixture very slowly, beating constantly with rotary beater. Makes 2 cups.

MUSTARD DRESSING

For rice, potatoes, or other vegetables

Blend 2 tablespoons dry mustard with enough water to make a thick paste. Dilute slightly with wine vinegar; add salad oil, beating until creamy. While beating, add sugar and salt to taste.

TOMATO DRESSING

For raw vegetable salads

- 1 can (10½ ounces) condensed tomato soup
- ¼ cup water
- ¼ cup sugar
- 3 tablespoons grated onion
- 1 teaspoon dry mustard
- ½ cup cider vinegar
- ½ cup salad oil
- 1 tablespoon Worcestershire
- 1 teaspoon paprika
  Dash of salt

Combine all ingredients thoroughly. Store in quart jar in refrigerator and use as needed. Shake well. Makes 3 cups.

BARBECUE SAUCES

DEEP-SOUTH HOT BARBECUE SAUCE

*For beef, pork, veal, chicken,
turkey, duck, liver, kidneys,
bologna roll, frankfurters, potatoes,
green and Lima beans*

- 1 onion, chopped
- 1 garlic clove, minced
- 2 tablespoons cooking oil
- 1 can (10½ ounces) tomato purée
- 1 cup chili sauce
- 1 cup cider vinegar
- 1 bottle (7 ounces) ginger ale
- 1 teaspoon cracked black peppercorns
- 2 teaspoons seasoned pepper
- 1 tablespoon salt
- ¼ cup sugar
- 1 tablespoon ground allspice
- **1 teaspoon ground mace**
- ¼ teaspoon hot pepper sauce

Cook onion and garlic in oil for 10 minutes, stirring often. Add remaining ingredients and simmer at least 15 minutes. Makes about 3 cups.
NOTE: To use on pork chops, brown chops. Cover with sauce and simmer until tender. Or cook on grill, brushing several times with sauce.

SAUCE

BARBADOS BARBECUE SAUCE

For beef, pork, lamb, chicken, bologna roll, frankfurters, pears, peaches, and bananas

- ½ cup molasses
- ⅓ cup prepared mustard
- ½ cup cider vinegar
- 2 tablespoons Worcestershire
- ½ teaspoon hot pepper sauce
- 1 cup catsup

Combine all ingredients and mix well. Makes 2⅓ cups.
NOTE: To use on frankfurters, brown franks, brushing with sauce several times until well glazed.

CURRY BARBECUE SAUCE

For beef, pork, lamb, veal, fish, chicken, turkey, potatoes, onions, corn, Lima and green beans, apples, pears, peaches, and bananas

- 2 tablespoons curry powder
- 1½ teaspoons garlic salt
- 1 tablespoon dry mustard
- 2 tablespoons steak sauce
- ½ cup butter or margarine, melted
- ⅔ cup wine vinegar

Combine all ingredients and blend until smooth. Makes 1¼ cups.
NOTE: To use on fish, spread on fillets and cook on grill or in oven until done.

HERB BARBECUE SAUCE

For beef, pork, lamb, veal, chicken, duck, rabbit, liver, kidneys, bologna roll, frankfurters, meat loaf, hash, potatoes, corn, carrots, cabbage, peppers, Lima and green beans, and onions

- 1 cup catsup
- ½ cup water
- 3 tablespoons tarragon vinegar
- 1 tablespoon steak sauce
- ¼ teaspoon each dried marjoram, oregano, and thyme
  Dash of garlic salt

Combine all ingredients. Makes 1⅔ cups.
NOTE: To use on steak or hamburgers, brown meat on both sides. Brush with sauce several times, or until cooked to desired doneness.

PINEAPPLE-CHILI BARBECUE SAUCE

For ham or bologna slices while broiling; try on panbroiled meats, too.

Mix ⅓ cup chili sauce, 2 tablespoons Worcestershire, 1 cup firmly packed brown sugar, ¾ cup pineapple juice, and 1 tablespoon fresh lemon juice. Makes 1⅔ cups.

HONEY BARBECUE SAUCE

For ham, luncheon meat, or bologna

Mix ¼ cup each catsup, honey, and fresh lemon juice and a few dashes of hot pepper sauce. Makes ¾ cup.

RED-HOT SAUCE

For all kinds of barbecued meats

- 10 pounds ripe tomatoes
- 8 medium onions
- 2 hot red peppers
- 1 cup sugar
- 1 cup white vinegar
- 1 teaspoon ground cinnamon
- 4 teaspoons salt

Quarter tomatoes. Peel and quarter onions. Seed and core peppers and cut into pieces. Put vegetables in kettle and cook until soft. Put through food mill. Return to kettle and add remaining ingredients; cook until mixture begins to thicken. Reduce heat and simmer for about 45 minutes, stirring frequently. Makes about 2 quarts.

SHERRY BARBECUE SAUCE

For chicken

Mix 1 cup sherry; ½ cup cooking oil; 2 tablespoons steak sauce; 1 tablespoon each onion powder, dry mustard, and brown sugar; 1 teaspoon garlic salt; and ½ teaspoon each salt and pepper. Makes 1½ cups.

SMOKY BARBECUE SAUCE

For beef or other meat

In saucepan mix 1 cup tomato juice, grated rind and juice of 1 lemon, ¼ cup cider vinegar, ¼ cup liquid smoke, 2 tablespoons molasses, and 1 bay leaf; bring to boil. Makes about 1¾ cups.

BUTTER SAUCES

AMANDINE BUTTER

For fish or chicken

Melt ⅓ cup butter. Add 2 tablespoons shredded blanched almonds and sauté until nuts are lightly browned. Add 1½ teaspoons fresh lemon juice. Makes about ⅓ cup.

ANCHOVY BUTTER

For fish, eggs, or pasta

To ⅓ cup butter, add 4 minced anchovy fillets and ½ teaspoon fresh lemon juice. Makes about ⅓ cup.

SAUCE

BERCY BUTTER

For beef and lamb

- 2 teaspoons minced shallot
- ⅔ cup dry white wine
- 1 teaspoon lemon juice
- ¼ cup butter, melted
- 2 teaspoons chopped parsley
- Salt and pepper

Cook shallot, wine, and lemon juice until volume is reduced to one-fourth. Cool; add melted butter, parsley, and salt and pepper to taste. Makes about ½ cup.

BLACK BUTTER

For eggs

Heat ⅓ cup butter until quite brown. Add fresh lemon juice or wine vinegar to taste. Makes about ⅓ cup.

BEURRE BLANC
[White Butter]

For fish

- ¼ cup dry white wine
- ¼ cup white-wine vinegar
- 1 tablespoon minced shallot
- ¼ teaspoon salt
- ⅛ teaspoon white pepper
- 1½ cups chilled butter, cut into 24 pieces
- Lemon juice

Put wine, vinegar, shallot, and seasonings in saucepan and boil until reduced to about 1½ tablespoons. Remove from heat and at once beat in 2 pieces of chilled butter. As butter softens and blends into the mixture, beat in another piece. Then put over very low heat and, beating constantly, continue adding successive pieces of butter until all are added. When all is blended in, remove from heat and add lemon juice to taste. Put in a slightly warm bowl and serve at once. Makes about 1½ cups.

CHIVE BUTTER

For fish, meat, or eggs

To ½ cup melted butter, add 2 tablespoons finely chopped chives.

COLBERT BUTTER SAUCE

For fish

- 1 recipe Maître d'Hôtel Butter
- 1 teaspoon glace-de-viande or beef extract
- 1 teaspoon chopped tarragon

Mix all ingredients together. Makes 1 cup.

DRAWN BUTTER SAUCE

For vegetables

- ½ cup butter
- 2 tablespoons all-purpose flour
- 2 cups hot vegetable broth
- 2 tablespoons lemon juice
- Salt

Melt ¼ cup butter and stir in flour. Gradually stir in broth. Cook over low heat, stirring constantly, until smooth and thickened. Beat in remaining butter and lemon juice. Add salt to taste. Makes about 2½ cups.

LEMON BUTTER

For fish, veal, and egg dishes

Cut ½ cup butter into pieces and put in saucepan. When melted, skim off the foam and strain the clear yellow liquid into a bowl, leaving the milky residue in the bottom of the pan. Add 1 to 2 tablespoons of fresh lemon juice. Makes about ½ cup.

LOBSTER BUTTER

For fish dishes and sauces

- 1 cup cooked lobster meat, legs, eggs, tomalley (coral), and shells
- ½ cup hot melted butter
- Salt and pepper

Chop lobster meat, legs, etc., into small pieces or force through food chopper. Heat container or electric blender by filling with hot water. Drain and dry. Add lobster mixture. Pour in hot butter, cover, and blend at high speed. Pour into saucepan and heat until butter has warmed and melted. Blend again. Rub through a very fine sieve. As butter cools, beat with a spoon and season to taste with salt and pepper. Makes about ⅔ cup.

SHRIMP BUTTER

For an additive for sauces and a garniture for fish

Follow recipe for Lobster Butter, substituting 1 cup shrimp meat and shells for the lobster meat, legs, etc. Add a little ground mace, if desired.

MAÎTRE D'HÔTEL BUTTER

For meat and fish

- 1 cup butter
- 1 tablespoon chopped parsley
- Juice of 1 lemon
- Salt and pepper

Cream butter and add parsley, lemon juice, and salt and pepper to taste. Makes 1 cup.

MUSTARD BUTTER

*For beef, kidneys, liver, and lamb.
Also for use with sandwiches
as a condiment*

Melt ⅔ cup butter and, little by little, add 1 tablespoon prepared mustard. Makes ⅔ cup.

NOISETTE BUTTER

For fish

Heat ½ cup butter until lightly browned. Add ¼ cup toasted chopped hazelnuts (filberts). To toast, put chopped nuts in preheated moderate oven (350°F.) about 15 minutes. Makes ¾ cup.

NORMAN WHITE BUTTER SAUCE

For fish

- 1 cup strained fish Court Bouillon (See section on Salmon, To Poach)
- 2 tablespoons white vinegar
- 1 cup butter, cut into pieces
  Salt and pepper

Over very low heat simmer Court Bouillon and vinegar together for 10 minutes, or until liquid is reduced to ⅔ to ¾ cup. Add butter, 1 piece at a time, stirring constantly in the same direction. Add salt and pepper to taste. Pour into heated sauceboat as soon as butter is melted. Makes about 1¼ to 1½ cups.

POLONAISE SAUCE

*For noodles, creamed meat or fish,
or vegetables*

- 1 cup fine white-bread crumbs
- ⅓ cup butter, melted
- ½ teaspoons lemon juice
- 1 tablespoon minced parsley

Brown crumbs in butter. Add lemon juice and parsley. Makes about ⅔ cup.
NOTE: For green vegetables, add 1 chopped hard-cooked egg.

SHALLOT BUTTER

For meats

- ½ cup butter
- 1 shallot, minced
  Few parsley sprigs, chopped
  Few drops of vinegar (optional)

Mix well first 3 ingredients and add vinegar, if desired. Makes about ⅔ cup.

SAUCE

CONDIMENT SAUCES

COCKTAIL SAUCE

- ½ cup chili sauce
- ½ cup catsup
- 2 tablespoons lemon juice
- 2 tablespoons prepared horseradish
  Worcestershire, salt, and hot pepper sauce to taste

Combine all ingredients and blend well. Serve with shrimps, crabmeat, oysters, and clams. Makes about 1¼ cups.

HAWAIIAN TERIYAKI SAUCE

For marinating chicken or pork

Mix 1½ cups soy sauce, ¾ cup honey, 1½ teaspoons ground ginger, and ¼ teaspoon instant minced garlic.

SOY SAUCE DRESSING

For coleslaw

- 2 tablespoons soy sauce
- 1½ tablespoons water
- ½ cup salad oil
- 1 tablespoon catsup
- ½ teaspoon instant minced garlic
- ¼ cup wine vinegar
- 1 tablespoon firmly packed brown sugar
- ½ teaspoon paprika
- ¼ teaspoon pepper
- 2 dashes of hot pepper sauce

Mix all ingredients. Makes 1 cup.

HOT CONDIMENT SAUCE

- 2 quarts chopped ripe tomatoes (4 to 5 pounds)
- 2 carrots, chopped
- 3 onions, chopped
- 4 sweet red peppers
- 4 cups white vinegar
- 1 teaspoon pepper
- ¾ cup firmly packed brown sugar
- 2 tablespoons salt
- ½ teaspoon cayenne
- 2 teaspoons each ground cloves, allspice, nutmeg, cinnamon, and ginger

Combine all ingredients in kettle. Bring to boil and simmer, stirring occasionally. Force mixture through a fine sieve. Again bring to boil and cook for about 30 minutes, stirring often. Fill hot sterilized jars; seal. Makes 2½ pints.

SAUCE

MISCELLANEOUS SAUCES

CHAMPAGNE SAUCE

For ham, tongue, duck, and game

- 1¼ cups champagne
- ¼ cup minced lean raw ham
- ¼ cup golden raisins
- 2 teaspoons cornstarch
- 1 tablespoon water
- 1 tablespoon butter

Heat 1 cup champagne with ham and raisins. Simmer for 10 minutes. Mix cornstarch with water and add slowly to the hot mixture. Cook over low heat, stirring constantly, until smooth and thickened. Add butter and stir until butter is melted. Stir in remaining champagne, reheat slightly, and serve immediately. Makes about 1½ cups.

CHATEAUBRIAND SAUCE

For broiled steak

- ½ cup dry white wine
- 1 shallot, minced
- 2 tablespoons glace-de-viande or meat extract
- 1 tablespoon butter
- 1 teaspoon minced fresh tarragon
- Dash of cayenne
- ¼ teaspoon lemon juice

Cook wine with shallot until slightly reduced. Add remaining ingredients and reheat. Serve very hot. Makes about ½ cup.

HORSERADISH SAUCE

For cold cuts, braised, boiled, or roast beef, and fish

- ½ cup heavy cream
- Salt
- Freshly grated horseradish
- 1 teaspoon vinegar or prepared mustard

Whip cream until stiff. Add salt and horseradish to taste. Stir in vinegar. Makes about 1 cup.

SAUCE AMERICAINE

For broiled lobster

- 2 cups canned tomatoes
- 1 tablespoon olive oil
- 2 tablespoons butter or margarine
- 2 shallots, minced
- 1 garlic clove
- 1 tablespoon chopped parsley
- 1 tablespoon chopped chervil
- 3 tablespoons brandy

Cook tomatoes until they measure 1 cup. Strain. Heat olive oil with butter and sauté shallots until translucent. Add garlic, parsley, chervil, and tomato purée. Cook until shallots are tender. Add brandy and simmer for a few minutes longer. Remove garlic clove. Makes about 1½ cups.

ITALIAN TOMATO SAUCE

For meats, fish, and pasta

- ¼ cup olive oil
- 1 garlic clove, minced
- 1 medium onion, minced
- 1 can (32 ounces) Italian plum tomatoes, mashed
- 2 tablespoons tomato paste
- ½ teaspoon basil
- Salt and pepper
- Few parsley sprigs, chopped

Heat oil in saucepan. Add garlic and onion and cook for 2 or 3 minutes. Add tomatoes and tomato paste. Bring to boil and simmer for 15 minutes, or until of desired consistency. Add basil, and season with salt and pepper to taste. Add parsley. If desired, force sauce through a sieve before using. Makes about 3 cups.

SWEET BASIL SAUCE

For noodles

- 3 garlic cloves
- ¼ cup minced fresh basil
- 1 tablespoon butter
- ¼ cup olive oil
- 2 tablespoons grated Parmesan cheese
- ½ cup hot water

With mortar and pestle, or knife on chopping board, mash and blend garlic and basil into a creamy paste. Add butter, oil, and grated cheese. Mix thoroughly. Just before serving add boiling water. Stir well. Makes about ¾ cup.
NOTE: The sauce should be poured over cooked strained noodles, more grated cheese sprinkled on top of the dish, and it should be served immediately.

ENGLISH BREAD SAUCE

For roast chicken, other birds, and game

- 1 cup milk
- 1 small onion
- 1 whole clove
- Dash of ground mace
- ½ cup finely crumbled soft bread crumbs
- Salt and pepper
- 1 tablespoon butter
- 1 tablespoon light cream

Pour milk into top part of a double boiler. Add onion stuck with clove and cook over boiling water until milk is scalded; add mace. Sprinkle in crumbs and beat mixture with a whisk. Add salt and pepper to taste and ½ tablespoon butter. Cook, beating with the whisk, for 20 minutes. Beat in remaining ½ tablespoon butter and cream. Remove onion and clove and serve at once. Makes about 1 cup.

Bowknots with Anchovy Butter, peas, and sautéed mushrooms.

Cold spaghetti with French Dressing, tomatoes, and chopped mint.

Filled manicotti with Italian Tomato Sauce.

SAUCE

DESSERT SAUCES

BUTTERSCOTCH SAUCE

For puddings, cakes, and ice cream

- 1½ cups firmly packed dark brown sugar
- ¼ cup all-purpose flour
- 1 cup boiling water
- Dash of salt
- ¼ cup butter or margarine
- 3 tablespoons light cream or undiluted evaporated milk
- 1 teaspoon vanilla extract

Mix brown sugar with flour. Stir in boiling water and salt. Cook over low heat, stirring constantly, until smooth and thick, 6 to 8 minutes. Add more boiling water if sauce is too thick. Stir in remaining ingredients and blend well. Reheat and serve warm. Makes about 2 cups.

CARAMEL SAUCE

- 1 cup sugar
- 1 cup boiling water
- Dash of salt
- ½ teaspoon vanilla extract

In small heavy pan, heat sugar over low heat, stirring constantly, until sugar melts and is slightly browned. Very slowly add boiling water. Boil for 6 minutes. Add salt, and cool. Stir in vanilla. Makes about 1½ cups.

CHANTILLY SAUCE

- 1 cup preserved chestnuts, drained
- ½ cup milk
- ½ cup heavy cream, whipped

Cook chestnuts with milk until chestnuts are very soft. Press mixture through a sieve, and cool. Fold in whipped cream. Chill until ready to serve. Serve on pudding, ice cream, or fruit. Makes about 1½ cups.

CHOCOLATE SAUCE

- 2 squares (2 ounces) unsweetened chocolate
- ¾ cup milk
- ¼ teaspoon salt
- 1½ cups sugar
- 3 tablespoons light corn syrup
- 2 tablespoons butter
- 1 teaspoon vanilla extract

In saucepan over low heat melt chocolate in milk, stirring constantly. Beat until smooth. Add salt, sugar, and corn syrup. Cook, stirring occasionally, for 2 or 3 minutes. Add butter and vanilla. Makes 2 cups.

BITTERSWEET-CHOCOLATE SAUCE

- 8 squares (8 ounces) unsweetened chocolate
- 2 cups sugar
- 1 can (14½ ounces) undiluted evaporated milk
- 2 tablespoons strong black coffee
- Dash of salt
- 1 teaspoon vanilla extract

Melt chocolate in top part of a double boiler over boiling water; add sugar; mix well. Cover; cook over boiling water for 30 minutes. Add evaporated milk, coffee, salt, and vanilla; beat until smooth and thick. Serve hot. Make ahead, if desired; cool, and refrigerate. Will keep for several weeks. Reheat over boiling water. Makes about 3 cups.

CHOCOLATE CUSTARD SAUCE

- 4 egg yolks
- ¼ cup sugar
- ⅛ teaspoon salt
- 2 cups milk
- 2 squares (2 ounces) unsweetened chocolate
- ½ teaspoon vanilla extract

Beat egg yolks slightly. Add sugar and salt and mix well. Scald milk with chocolate. Beat to blend. Stir into egg mixture. Cook, stirring constantly, over hot water until mixture is thickened and coats a metal spoon. Add vanilla. Cool, and chill. Makes about 2½ cups.

CRÈME ANGLAISE
[Custard Sauce]

- 1½ cups milk
- ⅛ teaspoon salt
- 3 egg yolks
- 3 tablespoons sugar
- Vanilla or almond extract

Scald milk in top part of a double boiler over simmering water. Mix salt, egg yolks, and sugar. Stir in small amount of hot milk, return to top part of double boiler, and cook, stirring, until thickened. Cool. Flavor sauce with vanilla extract. Makes about 1¾ cups.

CRÈME PÂTISSIÈRE

- ¾ cups sugar
- 6 egg yolks
- ⅓ cup all-purpose flour
- ⅛ teaspoon salt
- 2 cups milk
- 1 piece (1 inch) vanilla bean

In heavy saucepan, combine sugar and egg yolks. Beat with wire whisk until thick and lemon-colored. Add flour and salt and mix only enough to blend. Scald milk with vanilla bean. Gradually stir into egg-yolk mixture. Cook over low heat, stirring vigorously, until mixture boils. Then

cook, stirring, for 2 minutes longer. Remove vanilla bean. Strain and cool, stirring occasionally, to prevent a skin from forming on top. Makes about 2 cups.
NOTE: If vanilla bean is not available, substitute 1 teaspoon vanilla extract; add to finished mixture.

WEINSCHAUM
[Wine Custard Sauce]

For cakes, puddings, and fruits

- 2 cups dry white wine
- ½ cup water
- 4 eggs
- ½ cup sugar

Beat all ingredients together in top part of a double boiler over boiling water. Be sure boiling water is not touching bottom of top pan. Beat with a whisk or an electric beater until mixture thickens. Beat constantly and serve hot or cold. Makes 6 servings.

FOAMY SAUCE

For puddings or plain cakes

- 1 cup sifted confectioners' sugar
- ½ cup soft butter or margarine
- 2 egg yolks, beaten
- 2 egg whites, stiffly beaten
- 1 tablespoon brandy or rum

In top part of a double boiler cream confectioners' sugar and butter. Add egg yolks. Cook over simmering water, stirring constantly, until thickened. Fold in egg whites and brandy. Serve warm. Makes 4 to 6 servings.

FRUIT SAUCE

- 2 cups (1 pound) peach jam
- ½ cup water
- Grated rind and juice of 1 lemon
- ¼ pound dates, cut up
- ¼ cup chopped cherries
- ¼ cup slivered blanched almonds
- 1 teaspoon rum flavoring

Heat first 4 ingredients. Add last 4 ingredients. Refrigerate. Makes about 2½ cups.

LEMON SAUCE

- ½ cup sugar
- ⅛ teaspoon salt
- 2 tablespoons cornstarch
- 1 cup boiling water
- 2 tablespoons butter
- 1 teaspoon grated lemon rind
- Juice of 1 lemon

In saucepan mix sugar, salt, and cornstarch. Gradually stir in boiling water. Cook, stirring constantly, until thickened. Remove from heat; stir in butter, grated lemon rind and lemon juice. Serve warm. Makes 1¾ cups.

ORANGE SAUCE

- 1 cup sugar
- 5 tablespoons all-purpose flour
- ⅛ teaspoon salt
- Grated rind of 1 orange
- ½ cup orange juice
- Juice of ½ lemon
- 3 egg yolks
- 1 teaspoon melted butter
- 1 cup heavy cream, whipped

In heavy saucepan mix together sugar, flour, and salt. Add orange rind, fruit juices, and egg yolks. Cook over low heat, stirring, until thickened and smooth; add butter, and cool; fold in whipped cream. Makes about 2½ cups.

HARD SAUCE

- ½ cup soft butter
- 1½ cups sifted confectioners' sugar
- 1 teaspoon vanilla extract or 2 tablespoons rum or brandy

Cream butter with confectioners' sugar until light and fluffy. Add vanilla. Chill. Makes 8 to 10 servings.

CALIFORNIA-WALNUT SAUCE

For ice cream, steamed pudding, or gingerbread, served hot or cold

In heavy saucepan mix 1 cup light corn syrup, ⅛ teaspoon salt, ¼ cup water, and, if desired, ¼ teaspoon maple flavoring. Add 1¼ cups coarsely chopped walnuts. Bring to boil, cover; simmer for about 25 minutes. Cool, and cover tightly. Refrigerate. Makes about 2 cups.

SABAYON

- 5 egg yolks
- 1 tablespoon cold water
- ¾ cup sugar
- ⅛ teaspoon salt
- ½ cup marsala, port, or sherry

In top part of a double boiler beat egg yolks with water until they are foamy and light. Whisk in sugar, salt, and wine. Beat over hot, not boiling, water until thickened and fluffy. This will take only a few minutes. Makes about 2 cups.
NOTE: To serve as dessert pile into sherbet glasses; serve hot. Makes 6 servings.

VANILLA SAUCE

- ½ cup sugar
- 1 tablespoon cornstarch
- 1 cup boiling water
- 2 tablespoons butter
- 1 teaspoon vanilla extract
- Dash of salt

In small saucepan mix sugar and cornstarch. Stir in boiling water. Simmer for 5 minutes. Stir in butter and **vanilla. Add salt. Serve warm. Makes 1¼ cups.**

Menus

50 Menus to help you plan more varied meals

BREAKFASTS AND BRUNCHES

Cranberry Applesauce
Salami Omelet
Corn Bread
Rose-Hip Jam
Coffee

Mixed Fruit Juices
Rice Pancakes with
Creamed Dried Beef
Café au Lait

Prune Juice
Cheese Ramekins
Fried Ham
Quick Corn Relish
Coffee

Honeydew Melon Wedges
Smoked Haddock with Butter
Whole Wheat Toast
Rhubarb and Strawberry Jam
Coffee

Whole Pears
Sautéed Calf's Liver
Broiled Tomatoes
Baked Rice and Cheese
Coffeecake
Coffee

Fresh Peaches
Steak Rolls
Green Tomato Relish
Coffee

Apricot and Yellow-Tomato Juice
Salmon Patties
Toasted English Muffins
Orange Marmalade
Coffee or Tea

Baked Rosy Rhubarb
Roast-Beef Hash
Spiced Crabapples
Sally Lunn Muffins
Coffee

LUNCHEONS OR SUPPERS

Stewed Apricots
Western Sandwiches
Dill Pickles
Raisin-Filled Cookies

Broiled Chicken Livers
New Orleans Rice Fritters
Yellow Tomato Salad
Coffee with Chicory

Ham Nuggets in Raisin Sauce
Noodles
October Salad
Tea

Greek Rice Soup
Chef's Club Sandwich
Fruit Cup
Herb Tea

Salami Skillet
Cucumber and Red-Pepper Salad
Hard Rolls   Butter
Peach Sherbet

Cold Cuts
Hot Cheese-Potato Salad
Garlic Italian Bread
Russian Cream

Green Pea and Potato Soup with Dill
Jugged Rabbit
Apple Relish
Pecan Ice Cream

Grapefruit Cup
Broiled Fresh Albacore
Lemon Wedges
Almond Coleslaw
Turkish Dreams
Turkish Coffee

Hot Clam Broth
Tuna Salad
Cherry Tomatoes
Poundcake with Butterscotch Sauce
Iced Tea

Mushroom Bisque
Fresh Grapefruit Shrimp Salad
Shredded Salad Greens
Rice à l'Impératrice
Café Filtré

Banana and Mandarin-Orange Cups
Broiled Split Lamb Kidneys
Herb Butter
Hashed Potatoes with Rosemary
Watercress
Cider

Cream of Sorrel Soup
Egg-Salad-Stuffed Tomatoes
Melba Toast
Fresh Rhubarb Betty
Coffee

Italian Sloppy Joes
Shredded Lettuce with Cottage Cheese French Dressing
Swedish Rye Cookies

Purée of Rice with Sorrel
Cucumber Aspic Ring filled with Crab and Water-Chestnut Salad
Crackers
Watermelon Sherbet

Tomato Soup
Baked Stuffed Eggplant
Fresh Mushroom and Parsley Salad
Lemon Sherbet
Jasmine Tea

Meat and Vegetable Salad
Onion and Parsley Finger Sandwiches
Custard Rice Pudding
Mocha Coffee

DINNERS

Roast Saddle of Veal
Cranberry Glaze
Mashed White and Sweet Potatoes
Cooked Vegetable Salad
Sour-Cream Dressing
Hot Rolls   Butter
Rhubarb-Apple Pie

Curried Salmon Triangles
Ham-Cheese Rice Bake
Chinese Cabbage Salad
Baked Winter Pears

Shrimp and Rice Jambalaya
Fresh Apple Coleslaw
Rye Crisp
Frozen Cheese and Raspberry
Dessert

Baked Red Snapper,
Florida Style
Surprise Rice Croquettes
Wax Beans with Pimiento
Tossed Salad with
Grapefruit Segments
Coconut Snowballs

Oysters in Aspic
Rockfish en Papillote
Vegetable-Avocado Salad with
Paprika Dressing
Bread Sticks   Butter
Orange Buttermilk Sherbet

Veal Rosemary
Pasta Bowknots with Zucchini
and Green Pea Sauce
Orange and Onion Salad
Crisp Seeded Rolls   Butter
Sabayon

Sweet and Pungent Pork
Baked Potatoes
Spinach
Shredded Chinese Cabbage
and Carrot Salad
Cooked Buttermilk Dressing
Angel Food Cake
Bittersweet Chocolate Sauce

Baked Turkey and Rice
Cauliflower and Tomato Salad
Hard Rolls   Butter
Sponge Cake with Apricot Sauce

Beef with Red Wine
Whipped Potatoes
Green Beans and Tiny Onions
Assorted Raw Relishes
Fresh Persimmons with Cream
Cheese and Lime Quarters

Zakuski (Appetizers)
Soldatskie Shchi
(Soldiers' Sauerkraut Soup)
Pumpernickel   Sweet Butter
Iablochnii Krem
(Cream of Apples)

Iablochnii Sup (Apple Soup)
Bread Sticks
Lamb, Cucumber and
Tomato Salad
Gingerbread
Butterscotch Sauce

Florentine Pork Roast Arista
Yellow Rice
Braised Fennel
Tossed Green Salad
East Indian Rose Pudding

Shashlik
Baked Kasha
(Mushrooms in Sour Cream)
Carrot and Sauerkraut Salad
Kissel

Russian Sturgeon Champagne
Soup
Salat iz Teliatini s Ogurtsamu
(Veal and Cucumber Salad)
Crisp Rye Wafers
Sweet Butter
Russkii Iablochnii Pirog
(Apple Pie)

Sesame-Baked Rosefish
Svezhiye Podzharenyye Ogurtzy
(Braised Cucumbers)
Romaine and Tomato Salad
with French Dressing
Fresh Raspberry Pastries

Glazed Roasted Stuffed
Rock Cornish Hens
Pecan Stuffing
Green Peas and Corn
Tomato-Apple Relish
Celery and Romaine Hearts
Ice Cream Cake

Mussel Soup with White Wine
Melba Toast
French Beef Salad
Basic Vinaigrette Sauce
Vienna Bread
Sweet Butter
Fresh Fruit
Assorted Cheeses

Shrimp and Artichoke Appetizer
Salmi of Duckling
Rutabaga au Gratin
Raisin Pie

Lamb Chops with Artichokes
Steamed Bulgur Wheat
Celery and Apple Salad
Lime Juice and Walnut-Oil
Dressing
Khvorost (Twigs)

Grill-Baked Stuffed Salmon
German Spinach Salad
Popovers   Butter
Sour-Cream Devonshire Pears

Shrimp Egg Rolls
Broiled Split Chickens
Caucasian Plum Sauce
Chinese Bamboo Shoots Salad
Kompot iz Apelsin i Chernosliv
(Prune-Apple Compote)

Tomato and Clam Juice
Cucumber Sticks
Japanese Shrimp and Egg Salad
Hot Buttered Rolls
Orange Gelatin with Weinschaum
(Wine Custard Sauce)

Rosemary Chicken in Cream
Buttered Green Peas and
Asparagus Tips
Carrot and Caper Salad
Toasted Cranberry-Nut Bread
Date Rice Pudding

Salt-Pork and Bean Chowder
Grilled Jumbo Shrimps
French Rice Salad
Whole-Wheat Italian Bread
Lime Sherbet with Raspberry
Sauce

Potato, Leek, and Tomato Soup
Sautéed Boneless Chicken Breasts
Spaghettini with
Mushrooms and Cream
Baked Spinach-Stuffed Zucchini
Italian Apple Tart with
Apricot Glaze

Ham Nuggets in Raisin Sauce
Noodles
Tossed Salad
Pound Cake with Foamy Sauce

Table of Equivalents

few grains = less than 1/8 teaspoon (tsp.)

3 tsp. = 1 Tablespoon (Tb.)

4 Tb. = ¼ cup

8 Tb. = ½ cup

5 Tb. plus 1 tsp. = ⅓ cup

16 Tb. = 1 cup

1 cup = ½ pint (pt.)

2 cups = 1 pt.

4 cups = 1 quart (qt.)

4 qts. = 1 gallon

16 ounces (oz.) = 1 pound (dry weight)

16 oz. = 1 pt. (liquid measure)